D1356036

Reading the
Sacred Text

Reading the Sacred Text

An Introduction to Biblical Studies

V. George Shillington

T & T CLARK
A Continuum imprint
LONDON • NEW YORK

T&T CLARK LTD
A Continuum imprint

The Continuum International
Publishing Group Ltd
The Tower Building
11 York Road, London, SE1 7NX
United Kingdom

370 Lexington Avenue
New York, NY 10017–6503
USA

Copyright © T&T Clark Ltd, 2002

All rights reserved. No part of this publication may be reproduced or transmitted in any form or by any means, electronic or mechanical, including photocopy, recording or any information retrieval system, without permission in writing from the publishers or their appointed agents.

British Library Cataloguing-in-Publication Data
A catalogue record for this book is available from the British Library

ISBN 0567 08824 3

Typeset by Fakenham Photosetting, Fakenham, Norfolk
Printed and bound in Great Britain by MPG Books Ltd, Bodmin, Cornwall

To my students . . .
Yesterday and today

Contents

Abbreviations

ABD	Anchor Bible Dictionary
BCBC	Believers Church Bible Commentary
BI	Biblical Interpretation
BJRL	The Bulletin of the John Rylands Library
CBQ	Catholic Biblical Quarterly
HTR	Harvard Theological Review
IDB	Interpreter's Dictionary of the Bible
Int.	Interpretation
JBL	Journal of Biblical Literature
JRE	Journal of Religion and Ethics
JSNT	Journal for the Study of the New Testament
JSOT	Journal for the Study of the Old Testament
LT	Literature and Theology
NLH	New Literary History
RS	Religious Studies
SJT	Scottish Journal of Theology
TDNT	Theological Dictionary of the New Testament

Preface

The vision for writing this book has been in the making for twenty years, since I was first asked to teach a course called 'Introduction to Biblical Studies'. As with all visions, this one came with a challenge: how to do justice to a subject as far reaching as this one. I had to content myself with 'approach', not 'survey'. While I elicit numerous biblical texts as case studies throughout, the book does not explore in detail all the literature of the Bible. That project is well beyond the aim and scope of this volume. The book focuses, rather, on ways of reading the biblical texts that could yield some fruitful results in understanding and living.

There seemed to me to be two vistas open for examination, balanced by long-standing traditions about the Bible. The first vista is the general, generative field of inquiry, and the second the specific functional approaches to reading the Scripture texts today. The traditions connected with the Scriptures could not be set aside nor taken for granted. They are present in our Church and culture, and affect how we proceed. Moreover, sandwiched between the 'generative field of inquiry' and the 'specific functional approaches' is a section focusing on the journey of the Bible from its beginnings to the present time.

The vision came to the first stage of fruition in the winter of 1998. That year Concord College (now part of the Canadian Mennonite University) granted me a half-year sabbatical leave to do additional research in some areas less familiar to me. I spent most of that winter of 1998 at the University of Toronto. The library facilities there are magnificent. By the end of the summer I had a basic outline in mind and some chapters written in first draft.

As the chapters will reveal quite readily, my special area of biblical studies is New Testament. I was, of course, glad for the opportunity to re-examine material related to the Old Testament. But I do acknowledge most of the examples are from the New Testament. (It is difficult to be *all things to all people*. I have never been able to figure out how Paul managed that (1 Cor. 9.22)).

I gladly offer much gratitude to many people for their resourcefulness and encouragement. I begin with a group of university students from the class of the Winter Semester 1999. Half of the book was written in first draft by that time. The students kindly agreed to read the chapters and offer their critique concerning the accessibility of the language. I offer them my sincere thanks, even if I did not always follow their direction.

I owe a great debt of gratitude to the late Professor Ben F. Meyer who introduced me to Bernard Lonergan in 1977. A small group of graduate students gathered around Professor Meyer in an effort to wrap our minds around Lonergan's deep thought and thickly textured language. Ben Meyer's patient coaching won the day, for me at least. I became thoroughly persuaded by Lonergan's *Method in Theology*, as is transparently evident in the chapters that follow. I was fortunate also to have a colleague here in Winnipeg in the person of Peter Monette, who is himself a thoroughgoing Lonergan scholar. Peter read several chapters, where Lonergan's theory was prominent, to make sure I had represented the great man adequately.

Above all, heartfelt thanks to my colleague and friend, Professor Waldemar Janzen, of the Canadian Mennonite University. Waldemar is a well-known Old Testament scholar. He agreed to read the manuscript before the final revision. His helpful comments in preparation for revision were invaluable, not that my work here has measured up to the high standards he has set for himself. I shall be forever in his debt.

Many more scholars and church people have contributed to the work, some through conversations and others through their writings listed in the Bibliography. I have tried to represent them responsibly, but certainly not exhaustively. I encourage readers to check out the bibliographic resources for themselves.

I wish the reader every success in the pursuit of competent study of the Bible and theology.

VGS
May 2002

I

Introduction

CBC Radio (Canada) carries a weekend program called 'Madly off in all Directions'. The program is taped in front of a live audience, and features a variety of performers, with plenty of spontaneous talk and laughter going on between them – some of it not too flattering. A handful of impromptu comments comes from the audience. People listen to the broadcast accordingly. They really are not concerned about who comes on next, or about what is said next. Their lives do not depend on catching every word, on hearing every nuance, on taking careful note of every performer and every song. After all, the program is called, 'Madly off in all Directions'. Why should listeners pay serious heed to the substance or structure (non-structure?) of the show?

Some studies of the Bible performed in our time are a bit like the CBC radio show. Since the Reformation people in the many Protestant denominations, not to mention the sectarian offshoots, are reading the Bible for themselves and by themselves. The same is happening also to some extent within the Roman Catholic Church since Vatican II. Many church leaders hail the practice as a virtue of some import: people reading the Bible for themselves must surely be a good move in the right direction. I know of one church that encourages its members to read the Bible through from cover to cover in the course of a year. At the end of the year the readers receive a new Bible as a reward.

Why the Present Book?

I am not here discouraging personal reading of the Bible, or the right of faith communities to interpret the texts in relation to their lives. But as history demonstrates, the Bible has been used to endorse immoral practices and oppressive ideologies.[1] The nature of the Bible itself, with

---

[1] Witness the biblically endorsed slave trade in the United States of the nineteenth century, and the South African apartheid of the twentieth century. Consider also 'scientific creationism' still evident in some quarters in the twenty-first century.

its multi-layered narratives, its richly textured poetry, and its complicated arguments, calls for interpretive competence.

Is it enough simply to say, 'read your Bible'? Can it be taken as a
matter of course that everyone who has learned the basic skill of recognizing letters, words and sentences (English or otherwise) is fully
competent thereby to read the ancient, sacred texts of Israel and the
early Christian Church? Answers to these questions are woven into
the tapestry of the chapters that follow.

The aim of the book is implicit in the title and sub-title: *Reading the
Sacred Text: An Introduction to Biblical Studies.* The emphasis is on the
act of reading, not reading in the general sense, but in the partialar
reading of the ancient text of the scriptures. Moreover, the book invites
participation in the life-giving adventure of reading the Bible with eyes
wide open to new possibilities, and hearts attuned to the voice of God
alongside (and inside) urging us on in our journey from here to
eternity.

The guiding principle in the book, in attempting to answer the
questions above, is that the more you know about reading the biblical
texts, and about yourself as a reader of the texts, the better equipped
you are to understand the significance of the texts and to perform their
'speech' in life. The reading of biblical texts calls for competence in the
reader, as much as the performing of a musical score calls for competence in the musician. Many people play music on one instrument or
another, but not everyone plays with competence. Not everyone is able
to exploit the full potential of the composition that the composer
intended. The more a performer knows about the theory of music,
about the life-situation of the composition, about the technique of
playing the particular instrument, the greater will be the enjoyment
of music for all concerned. Musicians have to practice the disciplined
technique of playing before they are able to engage the music at its
deepest level.

So it is with the reading of the Bible. The more we know about
the ancient, sacred texts, about their social, cultural and political
environment, about their literary-rhetorical texture, and not least
about our self-conscious reading of these great texts, the more likely
we are to enter into meaningful dialogue with the texts, and thus
also to grasp creatively and responsibly their intended sense and
significance.

The intent of this book is to invite the reader into the multi-faceted
discipline of biblical studies with a view to doing theology. Doing

theology is different from writing theology.[2] Theology written, whether in the form of church dogmatics or biblical theology, is secondary to the performance of theology. Theology has to do, on the one hand, with understanding God's acting out the creative word in the world, and on the other with believers joining God in the action. Like any other skill in performance, doing theology requires competence.

Reading through this book will not thereby bestow competence in biblical studies and theology. But reading it will, I hope, create (a) an awareness of the need to cultivate insight in all relevant areas, and (b) an encouragement to experiment with interpretive reading strategies for doing theology. It would help greatly if the book were studied in the company of others, and with the help of a facilitator who has traversed the field already.

Eliciting Bernard Lonergan

In 1977 I was introduced to the work of the late Bernard J. F. Lonergan for the first time. My first reading of his work left me numb. The texture of his language was dense and complex, and very much of it his own coinage. I stayed with his writings, especially *Method in Theology*,[3] long enough to appreciate his cognitional theory for doing theology. In many areas of my life, beyond those of my academic discipline, I have found my study of Lonergan urging me toward self-appropriation in the tasks I have undertaken.

What has impressed me most about Lonergan's general method is its flexibility and constancy, the two held together in dynamic dialectic.[4] Drawing fundamentally on the theological-philosophical synthesis in Thomas Aquinas, Lonergan's theory in practice accommodates both modern and post-modern sensibilities to a greater extent than some of his critics are willing to allow.

George A. Lindbeck, for example, in his book, *The Nature of Doctrine*,[5] finds (what he calls) Lonergan's experiential-expressionist approach to religions inadequate.[6] Lindbeck argues for a cultural-linguistic alternative

---

[2] On this theme see, for example, Stephen E. Fowl, *Engaging Scripture: A Model for Theological Interpretation* (Oxford: Blackwell, 1998), 56–96; 178–206.

[3] Bernard J. F. Lonergan, *Method in Theology* (New York: Herder & Herder, 1972).

[4] *Method in Theology*, 13, 'The basic pattern of conscious and intentional operations is dynamic. It is dynamic materially in as much as it is a pattern of operations, just as a dance is a pattern of bodily movements.'

[5] George A. Lindbeck, *The Nature of Doctrine: Religion and Theology in a Postbiblical Age* (Philadelphia: Westminster Press, 1984).

[6] *Nature of Doctrine*, 31–2.

as more amenable to the post-liberal climate in which we now live. The problem he finds with Lonergan's approach to religion, and by extension to Christian theology, is his insistence on an *a priori* human consciousness in which is found an awareness of the transcendent.[7] Lindbeck's cultural-linguistic approach compares religious thought to the way we learn language.[8] Religious awareness is not prior to experience, he argues, but develops out of human encounters in culture: it is shaped by ritual, myth, and symbol expressed in cultural context. There is no God-consciousness apart from the particularity of life, as in the learning of a particular language. People do not learn language, he insists; they learn *a* language. So also religion – people acquire religious understanding in cultural particularity.

What I find noteworthy in Lindbeck's comparison between experiential-expressionist and cultural-linguistic approaches to religion is his repeated reference to Lonergan's method, as though drawn to Lonergan's thought despite himself. In the opening chapter of his book Lindbeck admits that 'Lonergan in particular has proved influential on the following chapters'[9] in *The Nature of Doctrine*.

I grant that Lonergan's analysis of human consciousness, particularly in his *Method in Theology*, leaves language languishing in a sub-section under 'linguistic meaning'. Recognizing the need to exploit the nature of language in biblical studies, I have included a chapter on language intended to supplement Lonergan's limited treatment of the subject. As for Lonergan's view of religion, I think Lindbeck has short-changed him in favour of a post-liberal hypothesis oriented towards a narrative theology (not actually practised in Lindbeck's *The Nature of Doctrine!*).[10] Quite frankly, I find Lonergan's discussion of 'religion'[11] and 'doctrines'[12] more persuasive than Lindbeck's. Finally, Lonergan's analysis aims at accommodating any and all reasonable, aesthetic, ethical, responsible inquiry. His method is applied to theology, to be sure, but is not limited to theology.

I deploy Lonergan's general method explicitly and implicitly in the book as a way of welcoming all approaches to the negotiating table of

---

[7] *Nature of Doctrine*, 32. The problem for Lindbeck in Lonergan's idea of a common religious core is that it is not identifiable. If so, how can we postulate the existence of such a core?

[8] *Nature*, 32–41.

[9] *Nature*, 25.

[10] *Nature*, 112–35.

[11] Lonergan, *Method*, 101–24.

[12] *Method*, 295–333.

biblical studies and theology, and as a way of adjudicating between them in the interest of authentic interpretation of biblical literature for the purpose of human transformation toward the good and the beautiful and the holy.

Quoting Scripture

The Bible is quoted frequently in the book, and in two ways. First, short quotations appear in the context of the discussion. In that setting the direct citation will be in *regular italics* without quotation marks. Biblical texts also appear in illustrations and tables. In those instances the text will appear variously, depending on the function indicated for the table or illustration.

The translation selected for use throughout the book is the New Revised Standard Version (NRSV) published in 1989. I prefer the NRSV for several reasons. First, it tends to be more literal than most of the other recent translations. The committee of translators worked under the maxim, 'as literal as possible, as free as necessary'.[13] For purposes of study, a more literal translation is preferred. Second, it is recent. It uses a current critical text of the Hebrew Bible and the Greek New Testament, providing brief notes about other manuscript evidence. Third, the NRSV uses gender inclusive language. In the present cultural climate inclusive language in English is demanded. 'Many of the churches have become sensitive to the danger of linguistic sexism arising from the inherent bias of the English language towards the masculine gender, a bias that in the case of the Bible has often restricted or obscured the meaning of the original text.'[14]

Using the Book

The book lends itself well to a one-term course on biblical studies. With twelve principal chapters (apart from Introduction and Conclusion), corresponding more or less to a university or seminary term,[15] each week of the term could be devoted to a discussion of one chapter.

[13] Bruce M. Metzger, for the committee, 'To the reader', *The New Oxford Annotated Bible* (New York: Oxford University Press, 1991), xi.
[14] Metzger, 'To the reader', xi.
[15] The university/seminary 'term' reflects my understanding of North America. The length of term in the UK and Europe may be longer.

Footnote entries have been kept to a minimum, usually appearing only where direct quotation is documented. At points a comment appears in a footnote when it seems relevant to the subject, but not quite fitting into the flow of the discussion. If readers wish to explore subjects beyond these chapters, they are advised to consult the Bibliography, which is quite comprehensive.

The structure of the book is straightforward, with the chapters falling into one of three main categories: I: Venturing into Biblical Studies, II: Respecting the Traditions Reasonably, and III: Reading the Scriptures Responsibly.

The first part, consisting of four chapters, discusses the broad parameters related to the disciplined reading of Scripture texts. 'A Place to Start' deals with the person of the reader. Reading is interpreting, and as such belongs in the heart and mind of the person reading. How the heart and mind operate, and what is present already in heart and mind, comes into play in the act of reading.

'Method Making Methods' tackles the general notion of how particular reading strategies are found and appropriated. The particular 'methods', proper to the function of biblical studies and theology, need a generative matrix where they can be understood and judged as to their appropriateness. That matrix is in human consciousness, both individually and communally, and constitutes general 'method'.

'Aspects of Meaning' explores the various notions about human meaning, the difference between what is 'meant' in a text and what the text 'means' in the living 'text' of the interpreter and the community.

'Language, Speech and Text' investigates the role of language, not merely as a means of communication, but as the construction of human thought. Thought structured linguistically comes to intelligible expression in speech and text, to be appropriated by attentive minds.

The second part, Respecting the Traditions Reasonably, acknowledges the work of past architects of theology and literature, welded into traditions that have guided communities along the long road of Judeo-Christian history. 'Writing the Biblical Texts' considers the traditional view of the origin of the texts of the Bible, and encourages a review of the traditional understanding in light of recent research.

'These Books as a Rule' attempts to understand the idea of 'canon', the selection of certain books from a larger number that were in circulation in the faith communities. The selected documents became the 'rule of faith'.

'Behind the Printed Text' takes into account the fifteen-hundred-year trek of the biblical texts from their first appearance through many copies down to the printing press in the sixteenth century.

'In Other Words' investigates the problem and the promise of translation, focusing especially on English translations of the Bible.

Finally, the third part, Reading the Scriptures Responsibly, focuses on opening the Scriptures to new possibilities of reading for more authentic life and thought. 'The Inter-Act of Reading' discusses the complex, and mostly unconscious, activity of decoding text and bringing it forward into currency in life and community.

'Modern Ways of Reading the Ancient Scriptures' traces the development of reading strategies from pre-Reformation times to the second half of the twentieth century. Various aspects of the historical critical method come up for review and evaluation.

'Other Ways of Reading the Same Scriptures' outlines the major new methods of reading Scripture texts, appearing in the last thirty years, most of them showing the influence of the post-modern climate of thought and life.

Finally, 'Negotiated Reading' invokes the socio-rhetorical approach of Vernon Robbins and the theological method of Stephen Fowl as catalysts in the process of adjudicating between reading strategies, and between the academy and the Church.

As an aid to reading the chapters, I have included a guide at the head of each chapter called *On Course ...*, which sets out (1) the *objective* of the chapter and (2) a number of *lead questions*. An objective is an outcome, not a program. It is stated in such a way that the result of study is focused. A good idea would be to read *On Course ...* before reading the chapter, and then to return to it after completing the reading.

My earnest hope is that the book will facilitate a growing understanding of the 'world' of biblical studies, and that readers growing thus in understanding of the Scriptures will be *transformed into the same image from one degree of glory to another; for this comes from the Lord, the Spirit* (2 Cor. 3.18).

PART I

VENTURING INTO
BIBLICAL STUDIES

On Course . . .

Objective

To begin to appropriate the operations in conscious thinking and living, and to use the self-discovery for engaging the discipline of biblical studies and theology.

Lead Questions

1. *What would be an appropriate 'starting place' in biblical studies?*

2. *How does the 'image of God' relate to the 'starting place'?*

3. *In what sense is the operation of the Spirit congruent with self-understanding and the 'image of God'?*

4. *How does the interpreter keep subjectivity in check?*

5. *What is 'common sense'?*

6. *What does Bernard Lonergan mean by 'conversion' in the sphere of human consciousness?*

7. *What is meant by 'the principle of the empty head'? How valid is it?*

8. *How does one achieve objectivity? Illustrate with reference to Scripture texts.*

9. *What does it mean for an adult human being to 'mediate the world'?*

10. *What are the four levels of consciousness, according to Lonergan? How does this observation about human cognition help in biblical studies?*

11. *What is the place of 'insight' in interpretation? How does tradition help or hinder the process of coming to know an unknown?*

12. *Visualize the diagram of the 'Circuit of Knowing', and begin to self-appropriate the dynamic structure of consciousness.*

2

A Place to Start

If any authenticity we achieve is to radiate out into our troubled world, we need much more objective knowing than [people] commonly feel ready to absorb.

(Bernard J. F. Lonergan)

At the conclusion of a group discussion of a text of the Bible, one of the participants spoke laudably of the group leader: 'John knows the Bible!' The issue here is neither the extent of John's knowledge, nor of the kind of demonstration he gave that prompted the remark. What interests us here, first of all, is the grammar of the sentence. It is a simple sentence, having a subject (John), verb (knows) and object (the Bible). The critical element in the sentence is the subject, John. He is the one who carries out the action of knowing. John is the person who did something laudable to the object, in this case the Bible. Subject John performed the act of knowing, and demonstrated the result to his group.

Already we are edging away from the grammatical subject of the sentence to the living, thinking, feeling, willing, deliberating, learning, knowing subject: the human person, John. And that is the principal focus of this chapter, not John in particular, but any and every human subject interested in exploring the landscape of biblical studies and theology.

The starting place in any meaningful task in the world lies within the person performing the task: 'the reality, first, of the subject as subject',[1] not in the object of the task and not in the specific technique related to the task. Yet we tend to neglect, or at least take for granted, the dynamism of the human starting place in carrying out our intentional activities, including the activity of reading the Bible. The task and its object capture our imagination and drain our energies. We 'look out there' for something to happen as we work, study, read, write, excavate. We 'look out there' for a result of our expended energy. And looking out there we lose sight of the living, thinking, imagining,

---

[1] David Tracy, *The Achievement of Bernard Lonergan* (New York: Herder & Herder, 1970), 12.

intending, conscious, human self operating to achieve the desired result 'out there'. 'What counts is not the presence of what is looked at, but the presence of the subject that looks, even when he is looking at himself.'[2]

At least two anticipated objections to the focus on the human subject spring to mind right away. First, focusing on the subject can lead to subjectivity, someone might say. And we all know how disdainful subjectivity is in any field of endeavour, no less so in biblical interpretation and theology. The question is, how can we put a rein on the subjective element in our interpretive work? I submit that subjectivity is not curbed by ignoring the subject and focusing on the object, or on the specific technique involved in dealing with the object. Keeping subjectivity in check happens by coming to terms with the way the conscious subject operates, what Lonergan calls 'self-appropriation'.[3] Knowing one's active, conscious, human self, while it is not an easy matter, is necessary if we are to achieve an acceptable semblance of objectivity in biblical studies. Reading this chapter will mark only one small beginning in the process of heightening reader awareness of the dynamic operations in their own consciousness.

A second objection from readers might be that the emphasis on the human subject fails to give proper place to the Spirit of God in the activity of reading, studying, interpreting, theologizing. This is a serious and sober objection, and merits discussion before proceeding further with the notion of knowing the subject.

In the Image of God

The belief is generally accepted in Christianity and Judaism that all human beings bear the image of the invisible God. But there is no consensus on the description of the divine image in human form, and even less on the degree to which the image of God is freely operative in human subjects affected as they are by sin. Humans are mortal; God is not; humans are finite; God is infinite. Humans are bound by time and space; God is eternal. Yet within the mortal, finite, temporal, spatial

---

[2] Bernard J. F. Lonergan, *Collected Works of Bernard Lonergan: Understanding and Being* [The Halifax Lectures on *Insight*], ed: Elizabeth A. Morelli and Mark D. Morelli, with Frederick E. Crowe, Robert M. Doran, and Thomas V. Daly (Toronto: Toronto University Press, 1990), 15–16.

[3] *Collected Works*, 32, 'What we want is self-appropriation. This is what counts. Concepts are easy: we have them if we have words with meaning. But what counts is understanding, and this is what we must appropriate.'

existence of human beings there exists a consciousness of the Other, of God. 'We are never actually able to construct ourselves by ourselves,'[4] for self-consciousness is not self-construction. The consciousness of ourselves as bearing the divine image is not merely an insight or an idea about the supreme Other. Human consciousness carries in itself a reflection of what God is in God's being: thought-filled, active, responsible, loving, creating, protecting, redeeming God. 'Our native orientation [is] to the divine.'[5] There is no attempt here to equate human consciousness with the ultimate Other, God. '[T]he search for God through self-awareness equated with God-awareness is nothing other than idolatry of the worst kind.'[6]

My colleague, Waldemar Janzen, has argued persuasively that the *image* and *likeness* of God in Genesis 1.26f. is associated with relationship and task. Humankind, male and female, are in a relational partnership with God and are assigned the task of ruling creation, which does not include ruling other human beings in creation. In this view, 'humanity's creation in God's image indeed claims for humanity the status of God's royal regent over the rest of creation'.[7] I have no argument with this functional view of humanity in 'the image of God'. Where I do have a problem, however, is in pitting the ruling and relational image against the inherent quality of humankind to rule and relate. For humanity to act as God's partner and vice-regent in creation, there has to be some quality of being, some anthropological capacity, that enables humankind, collectively and individually, to operate in God's image. To deny the latter is to render the former incomprehensible. How can humankind rule creation as required by the divine command without the capacity to do so?[8] The question might be put: What does it take to rule in creation in relation to the divine command?

The subject is a complex one, deserving of more coverage than I can give it here. My contention, briefly put, is that human beings, in their thinking, creating, inquiring, knowing, formulating, loving, and

---

[4] Craig M. Gay, *The Way of the (Modern) World: Or, Why It's Tempting to Live As If God Doesn't Exist* (Grand Rapids: Eerdmans, 1998), 292.

[5] Lonergan, *Method in Theology* (New York: Herder & Herder, 1972), 103. See further about orientation to the divine in Waldemar Janzen, *Still in the Image: Essays in Biblical Theology and Anthropology* (Winnipeg: CMBC Publications, 1982), 3–8.

[6] Janzen, *Still*, 13.

[7] Janzen, *Still*, 55.

[8] I encourage readers to consult Janzen on this important subject, 'Created in God's Image', in *Still in the Image*, 51–60.

communicating, function as ruling representatives of their Creator-God in creation. Thus, to speak of the Spirit of God as somehow operative in the process of reading and studying and coming to know, is quite congruent with who we are as human beings created in the image of God.

Yet clearly some people are irrational, destructive, hateful, and chaotic. Do they also bear the image of God? They do, in so far as they have in their humanness the God-given dynamism to be intelligent, responsible, loving, creative people. And society and culture calls upon them to be so. Society as a whole recognizes the normative character of social responsibility and respectful relationship, and calls to account those who deviate from this norm.

The other day I heard a man on television confess publicly to the murder of a number of people in Northern Ireland. He had spent sixteen years in a tight-security prison for his crime. But then the man went on to say that he began reading and thinking while he was in his cell, and finally made a complete turn-around in his thinking about power and violence. Now out of prison, he lives at peace with his Northern Ireland neighbours, and is ashamed of his former acts of violence. This man went through a conversion that changed his mind, his heart, and his behaviour. The image and Spirit of God is now beginning to be represented in him.

Of course, the appeal to the Spirit of God can be an illusion, or a smokescreen to cover our own biases. It is an illusion to speak of the Spirit of God as a phenomenon out there that can be summoned at a whim to come to the aid of a person involved in a task, and then, when the job is done, the Spirit is free to leave, or at best be ignored. God the Sprit is not the hired servant of the human being, however respectfully addressed or summoned. Rather, God as Spirit is above all, and through all, and in you all, as the writer of Ephesians puts it (4.6).

In dealing with the matter of the self-conscious subject doing biblical studies and theology we come face to face with an age-old dilemma: subjectivity versus objectivity.

Subject–Object Dilemma

Some things in the world are said to be obvious, perceived by common sense without inquiry, without interpretation. The real is simply there to be had. Those who hold this (naïve realist) view cite the 'principle of the empty head'[9] in one form or another: the real simply enters the consciousness without process, without interference from the subject, without interpretation. Far from being a principle, this notion is a fallacy. Consider this example.

Two people looking at a tree do not debate whether or not it is a tree. They live in the same community, speak the same language, and share a common sense of the English word 'tree'. Yet one of the observers might note that it is an elm tree, and as the two move closer they note that Dutch elm disease has affected it. Now that they understand all the factors related to that particular tree, they have to decide what to do with it. One of the observers recommends cutting it down. But the other one owns the property on which the tree stands. His father planted the tree some sixty years before, so this particular observer is not so quick to decide to cut it down. He has vested interest in that tree, and his vested interest will affect his judgement about whether or not to cut it down.

The interactive relationship between the adult human subject and the objective world in which the subject lives is never a simple matter of the subject's inoperative presence in the world. By their being in the world, human beings act, react, hesitate, fail to decide, and so on. The world of objects is not immediate to a thinking, intending, human being, but is rather mediated by observing, thinking, reflecting, weighing the facts, and then acting on the result. 'Human beings are not logical thinking machines.'[10] The process of mediation, however one might describe it, is what gives the object reality: the tree is judged to be an elm; it is a diseased elm; diseased elms are usually cut down and destroyed; this tree is subject to being cut down.

Here is a somewhat different case where a human subject – the present writer – makes a judgement from insight without appropriate verification. My home is on Overwater Road. Shortly after our family moved to this new address in 1987 I walked along Overwater Road without giving much thought to the name of the road. Then I discovered that Overwater Road turned down a hill towards the Red River. Ah, now I see how the road got its name, I thought to myself. This road turns down this hill and ends at the water of the Red River. Hence the road, I deduced, is called 'Overwater'. When my friends

---

[9] The term Lonergan uses, with which he takes serious issue, in *Method*, 157.

[10] Quintin Quesnell, 'Beliefs and Authenticity' in *Creativity and Method: Essays in Honor of Bernard Lonergan, S.J.*, ed. Matthew L. Lamb (Milwaukee: Marquette University Press, 1981), 175.

asked for our address I told them about my insight, about how the road got its name.

Then after some weeks of living on Overwater Road a neighbour came over to visit, and asked if I had met George from the farm house down the road. 'What is George's last name?' I inquired. 'George Overwater,' my neighbour said. 'He owned all of this land at one time, and subdivided it. This road is called after him, Overwater Road.'

Imagine my embarrassment at having reached a decision from an insight of common sense, and then having told my 'finding' to my friends. Things like roads and trees are not simply out there. We observe them, think about them, have insights, form opinions. The objective world has reality for human beings only in so far as they mediate it by thinking about it meaningfully.

The same is true for the texts of the Bible, and other texts related to the discipline of biblical studies and theology. The texts are not merely out there to be apprehended by unverified insight arising out of common sense. 'Interpreters have *understanding*.'[11] A believing Christian interpreter, for example, will read the texts as a non-believer will not. A conservative lay person will read the texts differently from a liberal scholar. Each of the readers needs the others for self-correction, just as I needed my neighbour to help me correct my understanding about how Overwater Road got its name.

Some years ago, after a group discussion about the ordination of women to the ministry of the Church, a man made a very telling remark to me. With his Bible in hand and opened at I Timothy 2.11, he said: 'I cannot understand how it is that some people cannot read these words in this text. They are not very long words, and they are not unfamiliar words. What else can they possibly mean than their plain common sense? *Let a woman learn in silence with full submission.* The meaning is clear, women are to be silent and submissive. They are not to become leaders in church.'

Plainly the man had fastened onto two particular words of the text, 'silence' and 'submission'. He had not observed that the main verb of the text is 'to learn'. Women are *to learn*, and that was quite radical at the time of writing that text. When I asked the man what might happen when women come to know as much as the men through their learning, he was not sure how to respond. Something within his

---

[11] Robert Morgan with John Barton, *Biblical Interpretation* (Oxford: Oxford University Press, 1988), 1.

horizon of meaning kept his thought fixed on the words 'silence' and 'submission' in that text.

The biblical text as object, much more than trees or roads, is not just 'out there' to be 'looked at'. The text has to be read by a living subject, and all reading is interpretive. 'The reader's hold on the meaning of the text is mediated by the reader's own experience, intelligence and judgement.'[12] Even the texts that seem most clear, most obvious, are read and apprehended differently by different people. The subject–object dilemma is not easily resolved. Perhaps it would be better to say it is never resolved completely. But at least we can make a start at being more highly aware of our own consciousness in observing, reading, making sense, valuing, and deciding about truth in our finite lives. 'Contrary to a stubborn illusion born of naïve realism, *objectivity is not achieved by the flight from subjectivity nor by any and every cultivation of subjectivity, but by an intense and persevering effort to exercise subjectivity attentively, intelligently, reasonably, and responsibly.*'[13]

Authentic Personhood

I take for granted that readers of these words are awake and attentive. And I can probably further assume that these conscious readers are adults. They have grown out of the *immediate* world of an infant through the difficult stage of adolescence and into the adult world *mediated* by meaning.[14] The apostle Paul noted the difference between the two ways of being in the world: *When I was a child, I spoke like a child, I thought like a child, I reasoned like a child; when I became an adult, I put an end to childish ways* (1 Cor. 13.11). Of course, the apostle was not alluding to himself alone with his personal pronoun 'I'. His 'I' is that of every human person who develops from infancy through to adulthood, from whom also the community expects intelligent thinking and responsible behaviour.

The world in which adult human beings live is not merely *there* to be absorbed, as a sponge absorbs water. Adults experience the world with all its myriad forms, including texts of the Bible, through their senses. And no sooner do they experience the world than they seek to understand it. And no sooner do they understand the world than they

---

[12] Ben F. Meyer, *Reality and Illusion in New Testament Scholarship: A Primer in Critical Realist Hermeneutics* (Collegeville: Liturgical Press, 1994), 2.

[13] *Reality and Illusion*, 4.

[14] Lonergan, *Method*, 121.

seek to do something meaningful with it. They name its elements, shape its material parts, order its parts into design, represent its order, find shelter in it, secure sustenance from it, make boundaries through it. In short, adult human beings *attend* to the world and in doing so they *intend* something about it. So it is with the study of the Bible. An adult reader attends to the data of the texts under review and intends something about them. There is no escaping the dynamics of that operation. It is normal human consciousness. But what exactly is that inescapable state we call consciousness? And how is human consciousness a critical starting place for biblical studies and theology?

Before addressing these questions directly, a comment about the idea of a 'starting place' might be in order. 'Starting place' has the ring of a foundational idea, and in the current post-modern[15] climate it is not fashionable to speak of foundations, totalities, absolutes, transcendentals and the like.[16] Yet even thoroughgoing post-modern practitioners of deconstruction are obliged to admit their own consciousness, and likewise hope that their readers' consciousness lines up with their own. Else how can they teach their deconstructionist program? They expect their readers to give serious attention to their words. They hope the readers will be intelligent enough to figure out the pattern of the words in the sentence. They would want their readers to be reasonable persons in their assessment of the written text, and having done all of this, they would want responsible representation of their work. In a real sense, therefore, we all start from the same place: our *attentive, intending human consciousness*. But it is not enough merely to posit 'human consciousness' as the fundamental starting place for biblical studies (as for all human inquiry). There needs to be some sense of what 'human consciousness' is: how it operates in the various tasks that we humans perform in the world. It could be called self-authentication.

Although he was not the only one to explore the subject of human consciousness, Bernard Lonergan's writings exhibit a depth of analysis and a wealth of insight on the subject, immensely valuable to students in biblical and theological studies. He accounted for four levels of

---

[15] I hesitate to use the 'post-modern', now quite common, but am not able to find a suitable substitute. 'Neo-modern' may make more sense, but 'post-modern' now has currency and must suffice for the present time.

[16] See, for example, A. K. M. Adam, *What is Postmodern Biblical Criticism?* (Minneapolis: Fortress Press, 1995), 5: 'Postmodernism is antifoundational in that it resolutely refuses to posit any one premise as *the* privileged and unassailable starting point for establishing claims of truth.'

consciousness, structured dynamically within the human being, and operating in an observable pattern. The exercise of discerning the pattern of operation Lonergan calls 'self-appropriation'. Sounds simple enough, but only on the page before your eyes. The act itself is not an everyday occurrence. 'The transition from the neglected and truncated subject to self-appropriation is not a simple matter. It is not just a matter of finding out and assenting to a number of true propositions. More basically, it is a matter of conversion, of a personal philosophic experience, of moving out of a world of sense and of arriving, dazed and disoriented for a while, into a universe of being.'[17] In short, it is an exercise in 'knowing knowing'.[18]

The first level is the *empirical*. This is simply the level of sense without which human beings cannot apprehend the world. The ability to hear sounds, to see and touch things, to taste and smell elements belongs to the first level of consciousness, the empirical level. Deprived of one or more of these senses people have great difficulty mediating the world of meaning in which they live. Helen Keller managed to do so without sight or hearing, but with great difficulty, and not without the patient coaching of her mentor and friend.

On this first level of human consciousness a person *attends* to the multifaceted data of the world. In the case of biblical studies, one *attends* to the sense data of the texts. Nor can we afford to take this first level of consciousness for granted in biblical studies, or in any studies for that matter. We do well to catch ourselves in the act of our own attending to the data. But we cannot stop at level one of our conscious operations, because these levels of consciousness are not static but dynamic. Quick as a flash we detect a deliberate pattern in the arrangement of the ink on the page, and we have learned to speak of the pieces of the pattern: letters, words, sentences, paragraphs, punctuation. Upon seeing the pattern of the ink on the page we are urged from within ourselves to go without delay beyond the sheer data to the sense of the signs we detected so quickly. The detection of the pattern itself is a move out of the first level of consciousness onto the threshold of the second. The threshold between the two is dynamic, yet it can be observed and identified.

I recall a very adept student of the New Testament reading 1 Corinthians 2.6 incorrectly in a class. Five times his teacher asked him

---

[17] Bernard J. F. Lonergan, *A Second Collection: Papers by Bernard J. F. Lonergan*, ed. William F. J. Ryan and Bernard J. Tyrrell (London: Darton, Longman & Todd, 1974), 79.
[18] David Creamer, *Guides for the Journey* (New York: University Press of America, 1996), 75.

to read the text, and each time he read something that did not exist on the page before his eyes. How could that have happened? It happened that the student had already studied diligently Paul's argument in 1 Corinthians 1 in which Paul proclaims the folly of the cross as the saving word of God to both Jewish and Gentile people. The student had become convinced in his mind that Paul would never preach wisdom under any circumstances. Thus when he came to read another piece of Paul's argument in 1 Corinthians 2.6, instead of reading what was on the page, 'among the mature we do speak wisdom', he read 'among the mature we do not speak wisdom'. Five times he gave these words before he realized his mistake. Attending to the data is not a neutral matter. We bring with us decisions already made, biases already well established, feelings already very much alive.

It takes concerted effort to catch oneself operating on any one level of consciousness, but the gain to be had from this self-authentication is worth the effort.

The second level of consciousness is the *intellectual*. Whereas at level one of adult human consciousness one pays attention to the data, at level two one asks questions about what is perceived.[19] Asking questions leads to understanding. Asking questions lines up with insights, without which it is impossible to grasp what is going on. Insights help us sort out the myriad data we encounter every day. Without substantial insight our understanding is sadly impoverished. These insights arise out of the common fund of meaning already in store, and the richer the fund the greater the insights and the more comprehensive the understanding.

At issue here is the human quest for knowledge in any given field. The quest is to make an unknown known. 'Seeking knowledge is seeking an unknown. If we knew what we were looking for when we are seeking knowledge, we would not have to look for it, we would have it already.'[20] First we have to know that there is an unknown out there awaiting our human urge to make it known. Making an unknown known depends largely on what is already known. Take the text of 1 Corinthians 15.29 as an example. It is not enough to attend to the data of the text, level one, the empirical level. The two rhetorical questions

[19] Bernard J. F. Lonergan, *Insight: A Study of Human Understanding* (New York: Harper & Row, 1978, first published, 1958), 82–3.
[20] Bernard J. F. Lonergan, *Collected Works of Bernard Lonergan: Understanding and Being* [The Halifax Lectures on *Insight*], ed: Elizabeth A. Morelli and Mark D. Morelli, with Frederick E. Crowe, Robert M. Doran, and Thomas V. Daly (Toronto: Toronto University Press, 1990), 15–16.

in that text about baptism on behalf of the dead call for understanding, level two, the intellectual level. The two questions in the text call forth a further cluster of questions for understanding. Did the writer believe in proxy baptism of people of faith on behalf of people who died in unfaith? Do the two rhetorical questions suggest that the practice of proxy baptism was going on in the Corinthian church and was acceptable to the writer? How do baptism and resurrection relate to each other? Your insights about baptism already in store are your starting place, but are your insights up to the challenge of making the unknown of 1 Corinthians 15.29 fully known? Perhaps not. More questions are needed, more research, more consulting with other minds.

Similarly, the text-data of 1 Corinthians 5.5 signals a number of unknowns. What does it mean to hand an immoral man over to Satan for the destruction of the flesh? Does the destruction mean that the man will die physically? And whose spirit will be saved in the day of the Lord? The immoral man's spirit, or the spirit of life in the community? How can Satan be an instrument of salvation? Is there an echo of the atonement ritual of Israel playing into the texture of this text?[21] These kinds of questions operate on the second level of human consciousness where we try to find some pattern of meaning in the data of the text.

The third level of consciousness is the *rational*. Again, the threshold between the intellectual level and the rational is dynamic, yet discernible. When all the right questions have been asked, when all the insights are mustered in grasping the order of things, getting at the sense of the text, then comes the judging. Insights are useful, but they do not have the final say in the matter. Truth is at stake. What is real here in this set of data? What solid evidence is here to help determine the reality of what is present to my consciousness? The answers are often not final or certain. Results of inquiry can be stated in three realms: possibility, probability, or certainty. What remains in possibility today may move into probability tomorrow and into certainty the next day. Yet even when certainty is reached in any given issue other questions arise for further investigation. Judging between right and wrong, good and bad, likely and less likely continues. Good judgement rests on carefully cultured insights and firm evidence. The insights and the evidence by themselves are not judgement. Judgement happens

---

[21] I explore this text in some detail in Chapter 13 to illustrate 'negotiated reading'. See also my article, 'Atonement Texture in 1 Corinthians 5:5' in *JSNT* 71 (1998), 29–50.

within the dynamic structure of human consciousness after understanding what is present.

Some years ago one of my students in a Greek exegesis class asked a question after translating the text of Matthew 5.13: *You are the salt of the earth, but if salt has lost its taste, how can its saltiness be restored? It is no longer good for anything, but is thrown out and trampled under foot.* The student asked simply: 'When does salt lose its taste?'[22] His one question led to a whole battery of further questions to the text. When the evidence was marshalled and further insights added to the discussion the result was that the salt in this text is not sodium chloride – table salt – as traditionally stated in commentaries, but a rock fertiliser for the earth, as in soil. Suddenly all the traditional interpretation of that text was up for re-examination. A new judgement was made, a judgement that met much better the demands of the text of Matthew 5.13–14 (par. Luke 14.34–35), and one that took the relevant evidence into account. Sodium chloride is never good for the land nor for the manure pile (Luke 14.35). Potassium, phosphate and nitrate are good, and were available in abundance around the Dead Sea. Thus, the metaphor of 'salt' in Matthew 5.13 is not about adding flavour to the society or about preserving the good that is already there, but about transforming an otherwise sterile situation into a productive one.[23]

Moreover, while the second level of consciousness, the intellectual, is where one asks questions for understanding, the third level, the rational, is where one weighs the evidence, assesses the value, judges the worthiness, all in preparation for the next level of human consciousness.

The fourth level of consciousness is the *responsible*. This is where decision is made, where action ensues. The real purpose for operating as we do as human beings is to know how to behave in relation to the multifaceted world in which we live and move. The question is: Do we move forward responsibly and morally? The decision can be right or wrong. The discovery of atomic energy, and the harnessing of its power, can be directed towards the human good, or it can be used for weapons of destruction of human life. The rain forests can be stripped away or they can be maintained for the good of the planet. Relationship in marriage can be strained by the self-serving of one or both partners, or the relationship can be loving and therapeutic. 'And this choice, like

---

[22] Credit goes to Tom Koop.
[23] See my article, 'Salt of the Earth?', in *Expository Times*, 112, 4 (Jan. 2001), 120–1.

any other, is just as good – no more, no less – as the understanding and judgment from which it proceeds and on which it depends.'[24]

Similarly, a reader can reach a judgement about the meaning of a text of Scripture, but the person still has to act one way or another on the outcome of experience, understanding and judgement related to the text. To illustrate, recall the text of 1 Timothy 2.11–15. The traditional reading of that text bars women from ministry in the Church. What if other insights are brought to bear on that text, and other evidence marshalled to prove that the intended sense is not to restrict women universally and permanently from ministry, but rather to encourage women of the Church *to learn* so that they will be properly equipped to teach and to lead? When that judgement is made reasonably and well, the person thus judging is then responsible to call for a new appropriation of that text. A decision not to follow through on the good judgement, is still to act, but to do so irresponsibly without moral conscience.

Conclusion

In summary, we have within ourselves the starting place for biblical studies: the dynamic structure of consciousness. Biblical studies are like an adventure. When we move into new terrain, we carry with us a bundle of ideas that guides us on our way. But before long the guiding store of insights encounters new data and undergoes change as the adventure unfolds in our experience. So also with biblical studies. We start out with a bundle of ideas and insights already formed, perhaps formed for us out of tradition and enculturation. Then gradually new vistas open up before our eyes. We want to understand and judge what we see and feel without abandoning what we have learned already from home and church and culture. Yet what we have received must pass down through judgement, understanding and into experience, only to be turned upward again through new experiencing, understanding, judging and deciding.

The challenge in starting out in biblical studies is to acknowledge the operations of consciousness, to observe yourself operating, to draw on insights from your received fund, and to hold in check the biases

---

[24] Walter Conn, 'Moral Development: Is Conversion Necessary?' in *Creativity and Method*, ed. Matthew L. Lamb (Milwaukee: Marquette University Press, 1981), 320.

that would short-circuit the operations that lead to truth and goodness and love in action.

The massive and masterful work of the late Bernard Lonergan is boldly reflected in this chapter, and that without apology. I consider his cognitional theory invaluable in coming to grips with the texts and traditions of the Jewish and Christian heritage of faith. It may be helpful at this point to set out in diagram form the key terms of reference that Lonergan used to set forth his theory of human knowing. Notice that his overarching frame of human consciousness is *love*. Lonergan was a devout Christian thinker who believed that God's encounter with the human race has the character of love, epitomized in the self-sacrificial love of Jesus Christ. To know God is to fall in love with God out of the experience of God's love for humankind. Lonergan often quoted Romans 5.5 in this regard: *God's love has been poured into our hearts through the Holy Spirit that has been given to us.* But this love poured in human hearts is not a private sentimental emotion. It is the drawing power for moral judgement and authentic living in the created world.

Ponder the diagram[25] below not only as a summary of the cognitional theory outlined in this chapter, but also as a guide to self-authentication. Throughout the chapters of Part I this schema will recur in various contexts, so it would be wise to study it well at this time. The point is not merely to commit the terms of the diagram to memory, but to understand them sufficiently to constitute your self authentically. To attain this state of self-awareness is nothing short of intellectual, emotional, and moral transformation.

[25] I am indebted to David G. Creamer's several diagrams, from which this table is adapted, *Guides for the Journey: John MacMurray, Bernard Lonergan, James Fowler* (Lanham: University Press of America, 1996), Table 5.2, p. 91.

Table 2.1   A diagram of Lonergan's 'dynamic structure of consciousness'

The Circuit of Knowing

Loving		
Decisions, and values constituted/received	Deciding	Acting authentically based on judgement: **Being responsible**
Reflection on decisions and values	Judging	Reflecting and weighing evidence: **Being reasonable**
Inquiry into decisions and values	Understanding	Inquiring, raising questions, applying insights and ideas: **Being intelligent**
Decisions and values active in experience	Experiencing	Taking account of the data: **Being attentive**
Pre-conscious		

On Course . . .

Objective

To be able to distinguish between specifically 'functional methods' and approaches to biblical studies and the 'general method' that gives rise to them, as to other functional methods.

Lead Questions

1. What problems arise between groups when a specific approach is viewed as universal method?

2. Name two generally accepted conceptions of method in biblical studies and theology.

3. How would you define 'ideology'? Give some examples.

4. To what degree does ideology become 'method' in biblical studies?

5. How easy might it be to assume that 'tools' and 'rules' constitute all there is to 'method'?

6. Name seven useful 'tools' used in the discipline of biblical studies?

7. What might be the limitation of relying on the 'tools' and 'rules'?

8. What is Longergan's definition of 'method' that gives rise to specific approaches to a given task?

9. What is the 'rock' of which Longergan speaks?

10. In what respects is 'general method' cross cultural?

11. In what sense is 'general method' not subject to revision?

12. Offer your own critique of method as Longergan defines it.

3

Method Making Methods

In any act of cognition it is not only the object known but also the subject knowing that is involved.

(Karl Rahner)

Method in biblical studies is a subject of sizeable proportion in our time, so many and varied are the 'methods' that call for recognition. Through the centuries divisions of various kinds have torn the Church apart, not least because of diversity of method in the interpretation of Scripture, with a resulting diversity of theology. In some sense diversity is healthy for the Church, as for any organization. But when diversity turns into factious hostility between groups, each faction claiming to worship the one God more properly, to honour the one Christ more highly, then the life and witness of the Church suffers serious disaffection.

A problem occurs when a group hails their particular way of reading and interpreting the texts of Scripture as universally applicable, the right way to read the text. In such a case, method becomes for them a principle on par with the tenets of historic faith. This confusion of method with doctrine is a delusion. Equally problematic is the notion that fabricated method for biblical studies and theology, however well construed, is somehow superior to other fabricated methods used by other groups. Method, properly understood, can no more be the prized invention and possession of any one group than the sunrise and sunset can be deemed a cultural phenomenon. Method must operate across the board, across groups, across cultures.[1] A working definition of such a method I will hold in abeyance for the moment, to allow for discussion of 'methods', which regularly pass for 'method'.

Some Conceptions of 'Method'

To be sure, one culture will read and construe differently from another culture. But the particular reading and construal in a given culture is

[1] See the discussion in H.-G. Gadamer, *Truth and Method* (London: Sheed & Ward, 1979, from *Wahrheit und Methode* 1965), 460–91.

not because of a different method used. Method cannot be bound to a culture. A culture is constituted by a bundle of ideas and habits of the heart, including language, shared by a group.[2] Method is not bound by culture, for if it were then we would be forever lost in a global sea of cultural confusion. The fact is, people from one culture can cross over into another culture. They can experience the customs, ideas, habits, codes and language, and understand them, and even live them out after a while. Method is not bound by culture. It transcends culture.

At the same time, method does not enter culture from some alien planet. It comes, rather, from within culture, in that it resides within human consciousness. For that reason people from one culture can enter another and learn its ways. Yet method from within is not quickly and immediately discerned, as one observes a house or a car or a tree. Method – in the general sense that I hope to elucidate in this chapter – lies buried under a large fund of collected experience: loves and hates, rules and regulations, political bents, theological convictions, educational achievements, science and technology.[3] The list is long.

Before advancing further into the discussion of method from within it might be well to identify two contending modes that often pass as 'methods' (consciously or unconsciously) in biblical studies: (1) controlling ideologies, and (2) tools and rules. While a full discussion of the influence of these two modes on biblical studies would take us well beyond the scope of this chapter, a brief survey of both will help set the stage for the imminent treatment of method in the present chapter, as well as for discussions in the ensuing chapters.

Controlling ideologies

The phrase, 'controlling ideologies', is somewhat redundant. Ideology, by definition, controls. We live our lives by the configuration of ideas we cherish, ideas we inherited or learned, and now use to get through our daily lives in any given location on the cultural map. David Brion Davis' definition of ideology is about as useful as any I have seen: 'ideology is an integrated system of beliefs, assumptions, and values that reflects the needs and interests of a group or class at a particular

---

[2] See, for example, the discussion in Philip K. Bock, *Modern Cultural Anthropology: An Introduction* (New York: Alfred A. Knopf, 1974), 51–86.

[3] Frederick Lawrence offers a helpful discussion on method as hermeneutical in 'Method and Theology as Hermeneutical', *Creativity and Method* (Milwaukee: Marquette University Press, 1981), 96–104.

time in history.'[4] A person thinks, feels, and acts in life out of an ordered collection of ideas shared by the group in which the individual resides.

The ideas, of course, are not collected as one collects pebbles on a beach. They are culturally transmitted, picked up in conversation, in observation, in reading, and in joining the group activities under the conventional labels. 'A "culture" includes all of the expectations, under-standings, beliefs, or agreements which *influence the behaviour* of members of some human group.'[5] The system of ideas by which we live is usually not learned by rote, or even by skilled argument. The system is learned in much the same way that we learn a particular language in childhood. A language is a specific pattern of expression of thought that a child imitates in an adult and soon comes to use to fulfil desires. As Bock puts it, 'each growing child learns the language(s) of his/[her] community by *imitation* and *instruction*, and by *inference* from the verbal behaviour of others.'[6] The language then carries ideas about the way life unfolds, how the universe runs, what makes a good society, why one should work for a living or not.[7]

At the same time, the system of ideas is also consciously learned. In Euro-American society today children must attend school. The formal education of children is believed to be a great good in our society. Without a formal education, so the ideology has it, a young person does not have good prospects for a respectable job. That ideology is learned from parents, schoolteachers, and peer groups, and is then passed on to the next generation in the same social group. It becomes an ideology, a controlling influence in how we think about life and world. Ideology is powerful, as indeed it must be for a culture to survive. Of course, ideological power can become oppressive to some groups in society who, for one reason or another, do not measure up to the standard the brokers of the system set for all the members.

---

[4] David Brion Davis, *The Problem of Slavery in the Age of Revolution 1770–1823* (Ithica, NY: Cornell University Press, 1975), 14, quoted in Vernon K. Robbins, *Exploring the Texture of Texts: A Guide to Socio-Rhetorical Interpretation* (Valley Forge: Trinity Press International, 1996), 96.

[5] Bock, *Modern*, 14.

[6] *Modern*, 51.

[7] Lindbeck views language and culture as the determining factors in knowing and believing. They are input, one might say, to the fund of insights, but they are not determinative to the extent that Lindbeck implies. The human mind is the determining source. Ideologies can be revised, or rejected, not by the input of language and cultural mores, but by understanding, judging, and deciding. These abilities do not derive from language and culture; they are inherent to human beings. Lindbeck stresses the degree to which 'human experience is shaped, molded, and in a sense constituted by cultural and linguistic norms', *Nature*, 34.

Does ideology have bearing on the reading of the biblical texts? Indeed it does. In its own way, ideology becomes the method by which the meaning of texts is extrapolated and appropriated. To illustrate how this works let me lay out some controlling ideologies in our society.[8]

From the socio-political side consider first 'democracy'. The democratic model that so controls our social and political lives is no less evident in how we tend to work in biblical studies. In a democracy the vote of the majority is taken as the true and the right. The minority is obliged to fall in line with the rule of the majority. Granted, checks and balances are usually set up in most of the democratic societies to forestall oppressive treatment of the minority by the majority. But the ideology still stands: the rule of the majority is to be considered fair and right. Does the ideology of democracy play a part in the reading of the Bible? Without a doubt it does.

In many modern commentaries and monographs on the biblical texts it is quite common to run across such phrases as 'majority opinion', 'a growing consensus', or 'as yet no consensus'. Catchphrases like these are clear markers of an ideology of democracy at work in the process of reading the text. If there is a 'majority opinion' on a point of interpretation then that view should be adopted, according to the ideology of democracy. An example of the democratic methodology comes up in the commentaries on Romans 7.7–25. Paul uses the first personal pronoun 'I' repeatedly in this text about the struggle between good and evil: *For I know that nothing good dwells within me, that is, in my flesh. I can will what is right, but I cannot do it. For I do not do the good I want, but the evil I do not want is what I do* (Rom. 7.18–19). For many years the 'majority opinion' was that Paul was writing Christian autobiography here. He was describing his own inner struggle as a believer in Christ in trying to do right. Some years ago someone decided to break the hold the democratic 'method' had on that text. Maybe the repeated 'I' is not Christian autobiography at all, but a personal identification in solidarity with humanity caught in the plight of sin apart from the grace of God in Christ. It took years before that minority reading of the text gained a respectable hearing. As this example demonstrates, the ideology of democracy acts as a powerful control over the reading of texts.

---

[8] For another angle on large-scale ideologies in modern society see, Craig M. Gay, *The Way of the (Modern) World. Or, Why It's Tempting to Live As If God Doesn't Exist* (Grand Rapids: Eerdmans, 1998), 56–62.

Staying with the socio-political for a moment, persons committed to a socialist ideology will read the biblical texts according to the socio-political thinking that raises an egalitarian standard as the ideal for all. It would not be surprising to find persons, committed to socialist ideology, drawn to such texts as Acts 4.32: *Now the whole group of those who believed were of one heart and soul, and no one claimed private ownership of any possessions, but everything they owned was held in common.* A socialist ideology might consider this text central to the whole New Testament, or even to the whole Bible. In that case, their ideology would be the controlling influence in the reading of biblical texts. Other texts that do not contain the same egalitarian texture would have to fit the ideological meaning of the 'central' text.

A conservative capitalist ideology would move differently in the thought-world of the biblical texts. A successful capitalist Christian living in a free enterprise ideology would understandably be attracted to the parable of the talents, for example (Matt. 25.14–30; par. Luke 19.12–27). A conservative capitalist ideology would see in the parable of the talents a biblical warrant for the industrious investment of money, and the corresponding judgement on those who cautiously withhold their entrusted money from the profit-making moneylenders. The last of the three is 'the scrupulous servant who takes no risks'.[9] The text seems crystal clear to a person of such an ideology: *For to all those who have, more will be given, and they will have an abundance; but from those who have nothing, even what they have will be taken away* (Matt. 25.29). A free enterprise, capitalist ideology has no trouble seeing the rich man who entrusted the money to his servants as a God-figure,[10] even though the text does not say so. In reading thus, they consider their ideology endorsed and their practice of increasing capital divinely sanctioned. Without further inquiry, people controlled by a free enterprise ideology can claim, 'the Bible says' their system is well founded, ordained of God. In this case, the ideology constitutes (perhaps unconsciously) the 'method' of reading.

Readers with a socialist ideology would be puzzled by the same text about the entrusted money. They would wonder how to fit it into their system. They might even see in the person who saved the talent a worthy servant who refused to do the bidding of the ruthless rich man not satisfied with less than a hundred per cent profit earned on the

---

[9] C. H. Dodd, *The Parables of the Kingdom* (New York: Charles Scribner's Sons, 1961), 118.
[10] Dodd, *Parables*, 119.

backs of his less fortunate countrymen. They might say the man who gave back the talent was the real hero of the parable, a 'whistle-blower' if you will.[11] He will have to pay the price for standing up to the powerful rich man. Again, ideology controls the reading and is in this sense the 'method' of locating the meaning in the text.

Take another example from socio-cultural ideology. In the last quarter of a century the feminist revolution has led to a feminist ideology now current throughout most of the industrial world. For centuries women were denied equal social status with men. They were barred from certain jobs in society, and when they did land a job that a man beside them had occupied they were not given an equal wage with the man in the same job. The feminist revolution was long overdue, and still has some distance to go in our industrial and religious world.

With the coming of the feminist movement comes also a feminist ideology that plays itself out in such matters as gender inclusive language in publications and in Bible translations,[12] in advertisements that do not discriminate against women, and in affirmative action in employment that grants a woman a position over a man who has the same qualifications. The Bible now has its feminist interpreters (after ages of male-dominant interpretation). Does the feminist ideology enter the reading of the biblical texts? Indeed it does, as might be expected. Texts that have for ages been virtually overlooked by male readers have now come into the light and are treated as highly important to the reading of the rest of the Bible. For example, the text in Mark 14.3–9, recounting a woman's anointing of Jesus, is no longer a minimal text about devotion to Jesus. In the hands of the well-known feminist interpreter, Elisabeth Schüssler Fiorenza, that text takes a title role in her large and influential book, *In Memory of Her*.[13]

A feminist reading is an ideological reading, just as a male-dominant reading is an ideological reading. The point of the example again is that ideology becomes method in biblical studies. No one is exempt from this method. But all of us can at least become aware of its presence in our own reading and also of its potential pitfalls.

---

[11] So William R. Herzog II, *Parables as Subversive Speech: Jesus as Pedagogue of the Oppressed* (Louisville: Westminster/John Knox Press, 1994), 150–68.

[12] Witness the NRSV Bible published in 1989.

[13] Elisabeth Schüssler Fiorenza, *In Memory of Her: A Feminist Theological Reconstruction of Christian Origins* (New York: Crossroad, 1983).

Religion is no less susceptible to an ideological reading of Scripture. Religious ideology is at least as strong as the socio-political and socio-cultural ideologies. The other day I picked a book off my library shelf entitled, *Protestant Biblical Interpretation*.[14] Here is an explicit example of interpretation of Scripture in keeping with a religious ideology. According to the book there is a Protestant 'method' by which the Bible can (and should) be read. The book outlines various 'principles of interpretation' characteristic of the Reformers (as interpreted by the modernist Protestant author!). Do these so-called principles not work for Catholic readers or Jewish readers?

An ideological 'method' such as this is fine, as long as it allows for the presence of others in the hermeneutical spiral. When an ideological method sets itself up as foundational then the potential of pluralism of insight is stifled. Method, in the final analysis, should not be located exclusively within a religious ideology of any kind. If minds are to meet around biblical studies and theology, as meet they surely must these days, they must meet on the issue of method that transcends religious and cultural particularity. As long as ideological 'method' continues to be viewed as foundational, so will interpretation of biblical texts be truncated and groups of believing readers divided from each other.

It should not be surprising that religious ideology exercises an exceedingly powerful control over the reading strategy of biblical texts. When believers are committed to a particular religious movement, when they wholeheartedly adopt the thinking of the movement, when they believe the thinking to be sealed by the Spirit and unchangeably true, the pattern of thinking then becomes the 'method' of reading the Scripture texts. A charismatic, evangelical Christian will read the texts of Scripture in accordance with that ideology. A non-charismatic, liberal Christian will interpret through the corresponding ideology. Ideological reading is part and parcel of who we are and how we operate as cultural, religious people. All reading is interested reading. When people open the Bible to read they do so because they are interested in what it has to say to them. The interest comes not from the act of reading itself, but from the pre-reading experience in life, from the interlocking ideas presently in mind.

If the Bible is to act as a catalyst for positive change in human thinking and behaviour, if the texts are to speak loudly into our

---

[14] Bernard Ramm, *Protestant Biblical Interpretation: A Textbook of Hermeneutics for Conservative Protestants* (Boston: W. A. Wilde Company, 1956).

human consciousness, if they are to initiate us into the ever unfolding mystery of salvation,[15] if they are to contribute to the unity of the Spirit in the bond of peace, then the ideology that controls our reading must become transparent to allow the sense of the texts to enter our minds and hearts with newness of life at every reading.

Finally, ideology cannot be considered 'method' in the general sense. Ideology becomes 'method' in general when it (consciously or unconsciously) exercises absolute control over the reading process. 'The value of critical realism [discussed below] is its inbuilt antibodies against ideology'[16] that becomes foundational.

The challenge for the student entering biblical studies is to objectify the ideological stronghold and then allow the reading experience to speak to the claims of ideology. Success in this endeavour comes not instantly or aimlessly but intentionally and honestly.

Tools and rules

Method in biblical studies is also often associated with 'tools' and 'rules'. If you have the right tools and follow the right rules you can be assured of a successful outcome of your reading of the biblical texts. Experience has taught us otherwise. The tools-and-rules method, however necessary for the reading task at hand, is no guarantee of a competent reading. That is not to say that 'tools' are unimportant to the enterprise of biblical studies, or that their proper use can be ignored. On the contrary, knowing the so-called 'tools', and how to use them effectively, goes a long way in opening up the texts to investigation. A list of the standard 'tools' might be in order at this point, with a brief comment on each of them.

A *lexicon* helps determine the nuance that a word may carry in a given context. A word in any language does not represent a single, fixed meaning. Take the English word 'earth' for example. It can mean the planet by that name, or the world where people live in society, or soil in a garden. A lexicon assists the reader with the nuance a word may have in a particular context. In biblical studies it helps to know the original languages of the Bible to be able to use the best biblical lexicons. Most good biblical lexicons work with

---

[15] 'The text is an initiation into mystery', Ben F. Meyer, *Critical Realism and the New Testament* (Allison Park, PA: Pickwick Publications, 1989), 46.
[16] Meyer, *Critical Realism*, 142.

the words of the original languages of the Bible (Hebrew and Greek).[17]

A *concordance* lays out all the places where a word occurs in the biblical documents. With this aid the student can trace the ways in which a word functions from one place to another in a document, and from one document to another throughout the whole biblical tradition. A good concordance can be particularly useful in tracing the development of a theme.[18]

A *Bible dictionary* performs a valuable service in opening a window onto a biblical subject/topic. The articles are usually brief, but often carry bibliographic information for further research. While dictionary articles contain some valuable information they should not be used exclusively or uncritically.[19]

Journal articles on texts and themes provide insight and analysis that can facilitate an understanding of texts. Numerous journals related to biblical studies are on the market, and on the shelves of theological libraries in universities and seminaries. Wise use of these resources can yield some worthwhile results. But how does one find the appropriate article from among the array of theological journals? One of the principal tools for locating articles on a text or topic of the Bible is the *Religion Index*. Many university/college libraries now have the *Religion Index* online for quick and easy access. Some libraries provide both the digital and bound versions. Another useful tool for locating journal articles is *Old Testament Abstracts* and *New Testament Abstracts*. The advantage of this device over the *Religion Index* is its précis of the argument and conclusion of the article.

Commentaries on the books of the Bible illustrate how some readers understand the text. Commentaries vary in their purpose and usefulness. Some are strongly exegetical, while others are homiletical and/or devotional. Whatever their style and purpose, commentaries do

---

[17] William F. Arndt and F. Wilbur Gingrich, *A Greek-English Lexicon of the New Testament and Other Early Christian Literature* (Chicago: University Press, 1957); Johannes P. Louw and Eugene A. Nida, *Greek-English Lexicon of the New Testament Based on Semantic Domains*, second edition, Vols. I and II (New York: United Bible Societies, 1989); *A Hebrew-English Lexicon of the Old Testament*, ed. F. Brown, S. R. Driver and C. A. Briggs (Oxford: Clarendon Press, 1907/1957).

[18] James Strong, *Strong's Exhaustive Concordance* (Nashville: Crusade Bible Publishing Inc., n.d.); W. F. Moulton and A. J. Geden, *A Concordance to the Greek New Testament* (Edinburgh: T&T Clark, 1978).

[19] David Noel Freedman, ed., *The Anchor Bible Dictionary*, Vols. 1–6. (New York: Doubleday, 1992); G. E. Buttrick, ed., *The Interpreter's Dictionary of the Bible*, Vols. 1–4 (New York: Abingdon Press, 1962–1976).

not give the final word on the meaning of a text. They are conversation partners in the challenging and worthy endeavour of capturing the sense and significance of biblical texts.

Maps of the Ancient Near East give some idea of distance between place names, the kind of terrain, bodies of water and courses. Maps can help the student of the Bible visualize in some measure the location of the events of deliverance, holy war, settlement, etc.

Biblical Archaeology has supplied a wealth of information about the culture implicit in biblical literature. The stratigraphic excavations of key sites in the Ancient Near East have yielded a body of important data that helps locate many of the events and people recorded in the Bible within a historic and social context. Of course, the context and function of the excavated artefacts are themselves subject to interpretation before they can serve any useful purpose in the reading of the biblical texts. One useful tool for keeping up with the ongoing excavations of sites in biblical geography is the journal, *The Biblical Archaeologist.* There are, in addition, numerous recent books that recount the past achievements in recovering the cultural context of biblical documents.[20]

With these and other tangible tools available one would think that an interested reader of biblical texts could readily retrieve the full extent of the meaning from biblical narratives, songs, oracles, poems, parables, and arguments. That seems not to be the case. Tools assist; they do not interpret. Tools require alert, intelligent, responsible minds to put them into competent operation. Specific tools for biblical studies, important as they are within the discipline, do not qualify as general method. General method provides the framework for the disciplined use of the tools.

The same is true for the rules, or principles, in biblical studies. Principles, so-called, are derived from the reading experience itself, and also from the ideology that informs the reading process. I return again to the example of *Protestant Biblical Interpretation*. In this book Bernard Ramm devotes two long chapters to 'Principles of Interpretation', one

---

[20] E.g. La Moine F. DeVries, *Cities of the Biblical World* (Peabody: Hendrickson, 1997); James H. Charlesworth and Walter P. Weaver, eds., *What Has Archaeology to Do With Faith?* (Philadelphia: Trinity Press International, 1992); Amihai Mayor, *Archaeology of the Land of the Bible: Anchor Bible Reference Library* (New York: Doubleday, 1990); Jack P. Lewis, *Archaeological Backgrounds to the Bible People* (Grand Rapids: Baker, 1971); Kathleen M. Kenyon, *Archaeology in the Holy Land* (London: Ernest Benn, 1970); G. Ernest Wright, *Biblical Archaeology* (Philadelphia: Westminster Press, 1962).

to general principles and the second to specific principles. The general principles are said to 'act as a general guide for all interpretation'.[21] Upon examination though, even these general principles are derived from a previous understanding of the text and from an explicit predisposition about the text. For example, three of Ramm's general principles are (1) the principle of the priority of the original languages, (2) the principle of progressive revelation, and (3) the principle of the unity of the sense of Scripture. The point here is not to discuss the merits of the principles as such, but rather to demonstrate that these 'general principles' arise out of the specific study of Scripture from within a particular reading tradition. As such they do not measure up to the demand for method that guides the process of deriving the 'principles' themselves. As one examines these 'principles', a prior question cries out for an answer: What method is at work in the construal and construction of the principles into the form of rules for interpreting biblical texts? When an answer to that question is reached satisfactorily we have come face to face with method in the general sense.

Since Ramm's analysis of 1956 concerning the issues surrounding biblical interpretation many more rules have come to the fore.[22] Some of them have led to a revision of Ramm's rules. Others have all but sabotaged them. The point is, all rules are subject to revision, correction, modification, or even dismissal. How is one to determine whether the rules are sufficient for their intended task? What operation is at work in revising the rules when necessary? Method that unites us all in the transforming exercise of reading and interpreting biblical texts, and in construing theology, must transcend the rules and tools. Method in this general sense does not admit revision in the same way that the rules do. Nor can it be part of one or another cultural ideology that guides the thought and life of a particular community or society.

---

[21] Ramm, *Protestant*, 107.

[22] As recently as 1991, Grant Osborne devoted 128 pages to what he calls 'General Hermeneutics'. Strangely, in that large section he concentrates on the functional speciality of interpreting the texts of the Bible – hardly general hermeneutics. His project fails to grapple theoretically with such fundamental hermeneutical issues as method, meaning, language, and cognition; see, *The Hermeneutical Spiral: A Comprehensive Introduction to Biblical Interpretation* (Downers Grove: InterVarsity Press, 1991), 19–147.

Method

We come now to the matter of discovering method that generates the rules, that calls for a revision of rules, that imagines the tools, that envisions approaches to the various genres of biblical literature, history and theology. At heart, the job of discovering 'method' is nothing less or more than a *self-discovery*, in so far as method in the first place resides within the our human self. Understood in this way, method gives rise to the variety of specific functional 'methods' in biblical studies.[23]

For a honed definition of first-order method (as I choose to call it) we return to the work of Bernard Lonergan. He defined method as '*a normative pattern of recurrent and related operations yielding cumulative and progressive results*'.[24] What we have expressed in this carefully sculpted statement is a theory of cognition, the means by which we acquire knowledge of the world with its myriad forms and hidden treasures and governing laws. Method, thus defined, is the non-negotiable, non-revisable, non-restrictive operation for exploring the wonder-filled world of biblical literature, history, culture, and theology.[25] In saying it is non-negotiable and non-revisable does not mean that new words could not be found to describe this notion of method. Whatever words are used the method operates in the process of revising. In that sense it is non-revisable. Even the act of discrediting this notion of method altogether will use the method to do so.[26] That is what the non-negotiable and non-revisable character of 'method' signifies.

Method viewed in this way is the heart of the critical realist approach to life and world, as compared to a naïve realist approach that believes the real is 'out there' to be observed without the intelligent, reasonable, judgement of the observer. Critical realist method differs also from rules-and-tools approaches that tend towards predictable outcomes. By

[23] The alternative, argued by Lindbeck (among others), is a 'cultural-linguistic model', in which the individual internalizes the skills etc. resident in the external culture. No one would deny that, but acknowledging that process only begs the question of how the internalizing happens. And what happens once the external skills, theories, beliefs, and behaviours are internalized? Are they simply lodged in mind? Hardly. The human mind makes something of them. In that 'making' is found method. See Lindbeck's quite sophisticated discussion in *Nature,* 32–42.

[24] Lonergan, *Method,* 5.

[25] The same method applies to the investigation of all aspects of creation.

[26] Careful scrutiny of Lindbeck's critique of Lonergan will detect the method operating in the process. The operation does not come from culture or language. It is prior to both in Lindbeck's critique.

definition, first-order method may call for amendment to the rules at any moment, and point to a restructuring of the tools in keeping with new understanding.

Each phrase of the above definition of method merits focused attention and reflection. The method is said to follow *a normative pattern*. The pattern is normative in so far as it is not subject to change in the presence of new insights, new inventions or new situations, cultural or otherwise. It is not one method today and another tomorrow. To elucidate the normative character of the method let me draw on a down-to-earth illustration from my childhood and teenage years on our family farm in Northern Ireland.

One of the important tasks on the farm was the saving and storing of hay in the summer to provide fodder for the animals in the winter. My earliest childhood memories of making and storing hay are of gathering the hay with rakes and hayforks into a location in the field, and then building it into stacks. When the time came in the fall to store the hay in the shed my father would hitch a horse to the tipping hay float. Once in the field, he would back the float to the haystack, unwind a long rope from the winch on the float, wrap the rope around the base of the stack, and then turn a handle on the winch to pull the stack up onto the float. The horse would then draw the float-load of hay home to the shed for storage. The hay had to be pitched with a two-pronged fork high up into the shed. The whole operation was heavy, tiresome work. That was a 'method' of making hay in Northern Ireland when I was a boy.

Then the tractor came on the scene, followed shortly thereafter by a stationary baler. This new baler required someone to fork the hay into its mouth, at which point several prongs grabbed the hay, pulled it forward, and squeezed it into neat square bales for easy stacking – quite an improvement over pitching the loose hay high into the shed. The stationary baler was the first baler 'method' for storing hay. Within five or six years of the appearance of the stationery baler another type came on the scene. This new baler marked a major advance over the first one. Tractor-pulled, the new baler picked up the hay from the ground, pulled it into the rectangular squeeze box, and pushed out the tightly-packed, convenient, rectangular bales. That was the new pick-up baler 'method'.

Could any one of these so-called 'methods' of harvesting hay be called normative? Not at all. Each method gave way to another and another. The mechanical movement of the parts in each instance might be called recurrent and related, but it was mechanical, not normative. With each model the outcome was guaranteed (provided the machine did not break down). One could expect rectangular bales, tied with twine, in exactly the same way as all bales before were rectangular and tied with twine. Like all mechanical inventions, each 'method' in the sequence was subject to revision and improvement. Moreover, the pattern of operations for harvesting hay was not normative. The 'method' changed from fork-stack-and-float to stationary baler, to pick-up baler.[27]

The same has happened in biblical studies, especially in the twentieth century. The 'methods' have not been in short supply in our time. For each new method there develops also a school around the 'method' to protect it from the ineptitude of unskilled users. Recognized practitioners of a given 'method' adept at using it, admit to the guild only those who can prove that they too have learned how to apply the 'method' as efficiently as all other members. In such a scenario, the result is usually predictable, in line with the limits of the method. Take the social-science method in biblical studies, for example. When experts in this method apply their skill to a given text you can count on a social-science result of the reading activity.[28] Other aspects of the texture of the text lie veiled beneath the socio-cultural reading. When an interpreter is convinced of the currency of one 'method' for reading the biblical texts the result can be somewhat monotonous – a bit like the assured bales produced by the baler.

First-order method in biblical studies – as in all disciplines – is that which lies behind the specific front-end procedures, such as a social-science approach. The method in view here is the method that comes up with the idea of a hayfork and the float, the same method that produces the stationary baler, and the same method that imagines and invents the pick-up baler. The pattern of operations that does so is dynamically normative: the same pattern will be there for every new invention for saving and storing hay.

Unlike any one of the mechanical operations in compacting the hay, the method in view yields *cumulative and progressive results*. Each new approach to biblical studies builds on former ones, and every new

---

[27] Today in Northern Ireland hay has been largely replaced by grass silage, the old style balers having become antiquated.

[28] An apt illustration of social-scientific method of commentary on biblical texts is that of Bruce J. Malina and Richard L. Rohrbaugh, *Social-Science Commentary on the Synoptic Gospels* (Minneapolis: Fortress Press, 1992).

discovery derives from earlier ones. The pattern of operations that yields such cumulative and progressive results is not 'out there', as a baler is out there, nor is it in the skilled hands-on operating of a machine. Method operates within the human subject that invents a new baler, the same method that envisions the benefit of applying the socio-cultural approach to biblical studies.

With this discussion of Method making methods, we hear a rather loud echo of the discussion of the last chapter. Method fundamentally is rooted in the normative pattern of operations in a conscious human subject: *experiencing, understanding, judging, and deciding.* Out of this normative pattern comes the new baler, the new method of reading the texts of Scripture, to the end of producing cumulative, progressive and morally good results. Culture did not prescribe the baler through language, as Lindbeck seems to argue.[29] In that case, there never could be a truly new idea and a truly new product, such as a baler. But there are new ideas and new approaches and inventions. Both the idea, the term of expression, and the product of both are produced first in the operations of the human mind. To be sure, there is interaction with the data of sense in a cultural context. But the method that creates new ways of doing things, new social realities, does not come from outside the human person, but from inside, in the normative pattern of operations.

Furthermore, the method is self-correcting. A decision to act in a certain way may be wrong. A judgement may have been made prematurely, perhaps for lack of evidence. Understanding may not have been thorough and complete for reasonable judgement to be made. But the operation is self-correcting. Additional information and further insights lead to better understanding; better understanding induces more reasonable judgement; more reasonable judgement opens the way to more responsible action, and the God of love and justice is honoured more and more.

Method, understood in this way, can unite us all in the ever-widening horizon of biblical studies and theology. Conscious of this method from within ourselves, aware of method that makes all specific 'methods', we can cross cultural boundaries and join ranks in the enriching discovery of truth and meaning. Method in this preliminary

---

[29] He uses the example of Luther's doctrine of justification by faith. Luther did not invent it, says Lindbeck. He found it in the Bible and his discovery and experience 'generated a variety of fresh expressive symbolisms', *Nature*, 39.

sense is not relative; it is not cultural. It is normative and fruitful in creating human community, once it is grasped self-consciously under God. Genuine self-appropriation becomes method, and puts our reading and interpreting of Scripture on a firm footing. As Lonergan claims:

> There is then a rock on which we can build . . . The conscious and intentional operations themselves . . . as given in consciousness are the rock; they confirm every exact account; they refute every inexact or incomplete account. The rock, then, is the subject in his/[her] conscious, unobjectified attentiveness, intelligence, reasonableness, and responsibility. The point to the labour of objectifying the subject and his/[her] conscious operations is that thereby one begins to learn what these are and that they are.[30]

From this methodological starting place new approaches can be developed as appropriate, and with every new approach will come also new insights into the meaning of the texts. The result should be a wholesome, loving, lively theology enriching personal faith and life, as well as the life of the faith community.

[30] Lonergan, *Method*, 19–20.

Objective

To clarify the interaction between 'meaning' encoded in a text of Scripture and 'meaning' as it is lived out in the situations of life.

Lead Questions

1. What do some people see as a 'problem of meaning'?

2. How do you understand the notion of 'original meaning'? Is it possible to recover the original meaning?

3. Why is the separation of meaning from significance in the reading of texts a false dichotomy?

4. In what way is intersubjective meaning different from meaning derived from reading a text? Is intersubjective meaning carried in the texts of Scripture?

5. Describe three other 'carriers' of meaning in the act of communication.

6. How is language the most effective means of communicating meaning from subject to subject?

7. How do you understand the notions of 'common sense' and 'horizon'?

8. What does Gadamer mean by the 'fusion of horizons'?

9. What do people usually mean when they use the term 'real world'? What is the problem with the common use of that term?

10. What is the difference between 'intention' and 'meaningful act'?

11. What claim do texts have on the reader, according to Ben Meyer?

12. How does the claim that texts have on the reader correspond with the notion that texts have polyvalence? Explain polyvalence.

4

Aspects of Meaning

'Right' and 'wrong' are said to have once meant 'straight' and 'sour'.
(Owen Barfield)

One can hardly entertain the thought of engaging in biblical studies without giving due consideration to the notion of *meaning*. Meaning is first and foremost an integral factor in human living, not merely ideas in texts. It does not exist outside human thought and life. Meaning is more verb than noun, more active than passive, more dynamic than static. 'Meaning enters the very fabric of human living'[1] and governs the way we work, play, read, build, plant, harvest, create, destroy, communicate or not. Meaning is at the heart of human knowing and doing.

The decision to enter into biblical studies is itself a meaningful act. When a person opens the Bible to read there is already active meaning (i.e. intending) involved even before the investigation of the text occurs.

Is There a Problem with Meaning?

Some scholars have identified a problem with meaning in biblical studies. Grant Osborne, for example, devotes two long appendices in his book to 'The Problem of Meaning'.[2] In his first Appendix he traces the development of various reading strategies in this century in an attempt to identify the problem of meaning in biblical studies. Without doubt, the many new modes of interpreting the texts of Scripture present a problem, but not a problem of meaning. If there is a problem involved at all in the multifaceted approaches to the Scripture texts, it is a problem with method, not a problem with meaning.[3] Osborne argues for an idealist, enlightenment model of recovering objectively the author's original meaning in a text. 'The original meaning of a text', says Osborne, 'is a possible and positive and

[1] Lonergan, *Method*, 81.
[2] Osborne, *Spiral*, 366–415.
[3] See the discussion in Chapter 3.

necessary' goal of interpretation.[4] Laudable as the goal seems to be, it does not thereby eliminate the so-called problem of meaning.

The recovery of original meaning, assuming that such is possible, is itself a meaningful act on the part of the interpreter. When the recovery is made it now means something to the one who retrieved it. Is the retrieved meaning in the mind of the retriever completely identical to the meaning in the mind of the writer as he[5] wrote the text in question? Surely not. When we think we have grasped the author's mind as he inscribed *these* words and not other words with his quill, we have only proximated his active, living, thinking, feeling meaning. Our own grasp of the sense of the text is itself a meaningful act, distinct from the original author's production of the text. Once *our* grasp is firmly in mind we then state it in *our* words, not those of the original author. If we could grasp the original author's meaning completely then we would use his words without comment, without elaboration or explanation. The fact that we have to explain the author's words with our words means that we do not have a complete grasp of the author's meaning as he or she had it in the first instance of writing the text.

In their effort to retrieve the exact and complete meaning the biblical authors had in mind, some interpreters distinguish between meaning and significance. The text has meaning contained within it somehow. The meaning can be unlocked from its text-container and stated as 'original' in words other than the original words. At the same time these interpreters admit that the 'original' meaning is not always applicable to contemporary life situations, so they search for a separate significance. The separation of significance from the 'original' meaning is artificial, regardless of attempts to make analogous connections with the stated 'original' meaning.

Text is meaningful *sign*, nothing more. Its sign-effect, or significance, is triggered in the process of reading. The text signified something to the minds of the first readers, as it has done to various reading communities that followed down to the present day. Let us say for the sake of argument we could reconstruct exactly what the author meant by the words of the text, and exactly what the first readers felt and thought as they heard the text read (or read it for themselves). If the reconstructed meaning is the meaning the author had in mind as

---

[4] Osborne, *Spiral,* 415.
[5] I use the masculine pronoun ('he', 'him') to identify biblical authors, because I assume they were all men.

he wrote then why not appropriate that meaning for ourselves? We do not, because we cannot. Attempts to do so would be inauthentic, without meaning. What an author *meant* (history) is not, and cannot be, what a text *means* (conscious living). Meaning happens in the act of engagement with the words, sentences, paragraphs, documents. The act is specific and socially conditioned. The text as sign points the way to meaning. But meaning as conscious, active, dynamic, thinking and living happens within the subject investigating the text.[6]

Finally, there is no basic problem with meaning *per se,* any more than there is a problem with experiencing the world, thinking about it, reflecting on it, and acting responsibly within it. Meaning is woven into the tapestry of human intentionality, guiding thought, feeling, mood, intention, action, and movement. Meaning is more than a collection of ideas. Ideas have to coalesce into a useful pattern in the conscious mind of the individual. Yet the ideas that hold meaning for an individual do not stand in isolation from the same (or similar) ideas in the minds of others. Meaning has a way of bringing people together into community. But meaning also separates one community from another in the course of self-definition. It builds structures, forms denominations, creates industries, forms governments, shapes character, and sets a course for life. Meaning always stands in need of communication.

Communication

Meaning is not closed up within human subjects any more than it is contained within signs on the page. It is carried from subject to subject on various vehicles. When a group of people gather together in an arena to watch a hockey game they communicate with each other, not in words, but by their living, corporate presence at the game. They share a value that appears in their being together in the seats, by their waving arms when play is good or bad.

Imagine the feeling if only one fan arrived for the game on a Saturday night to find no one else present in the arena. Numerous questions would arise in the mind of this single soul. Did I miss something about these teams? Is this merely a practice? Is it Saturday night, hockey night in Canada? The meaning of a hockey game in an arena exists not merely between the teams playing on the ice, but also

---

[6] The 'subject', as I use the term here, could be a community of readers, not merely an individual reader.

among the people gathered together watching, participating in their imagination, screaming when the 'right' team scores a goal. This way of communicating meaning is *intersubjective*. It does not depend on words but on personal, contagious presence of subject with subject.

Body gestures, especially facial expressions, communicate meaning between subjects present to each other. Lonergan draws on the phenomenon of a smile to illustrate intersubjective meaning. A smile is more than a combination of facial muscles moving in a particular way to create a specific shape in the face. His words are worth quoting at length:

> Because that meaning [of a smile] is different from the meaning of a frown, a scowl, a stare, a glare, a snicker, a laugh, it is named a smile. Because we all know that that meaning exists, we do not go about the streets smiling at everyone we meet ... Smiles occur in an enormous range of variations of facial movements, of lighting, of angle of vision. But even an incipient, suppressed smile is not missed, for the smile is a *Gestalt*, a patterned set of variable movements, and it is recognised as a whole ... The meaning of the smile is a discovery we make on our own, and that meaning does not seem to vary from culture to culture, as does the meaning of gestures.[7]

Such intersubjective meaning is missing in the reading of biblical texts, missing because it cannot be communicated in the absence of person with person. Even where the texts describe intersubjective meaning, the meaning itself is not in the text but in the intersubjective act of meaning.

For example, John 11 records a scene of mourning at the tomb of a man named Lazarus. His sister Mary and the Jewish mourners come to meet Jesus near the grave. The text describes the scene of mourning. *When Jesus saw her weeping and the Jews that came with her also weeping ... he was deeply moved ... Jesus began to weep* (John 11.33–5). That is a description of intersubjective meaning, but as description it is not intersubjective meaning. I have yet to see a person cry upon reading that text from a pulpit. It could happen, of course, that the reading of a well-written text could move a person to tears. Even so, the feeling that the reading stirs is not the feeling that comes from the sheer presence of person with person in the absence of text. To experience the intersubjective meaning between the mourners you had to be there. We can say 'yes' to the description to be sure. We understand. We have been

7 Lonergan, *Method*, 59–60.

to the funerals of friends ourselves. When we have stood beside the close relatives of the deceased and have watched the loved ones cry we cannot hold back the tears ourselves.

There exists a fellow feeling between the members in the group. That communication of meaning as such does not exist in the reading of the texts. We are not inclined to weep when we read of Mary and the mourners and Jesus weeping; we are not subjectively involved in the intersubjective communication. Mind you, the writer of John 11 may well have felt a trace of the intersubjective meaning of the moment as he wrote. He was closer to the event than we are. His recollection in tranquillity may have summoned a memory of the feeling, especially if he was a participant in the group of mourners.

In the course of writing a book about my father many years after his death I found myself at points unable to hold back the tears as I wrote. I was closely and subjectively involved with his life. When I tried to write a narrative about his grief at the death of his mother and two brothers I found myself having to leave the computer to gain my composure. The stranger or casual acquaintance reading the final text-description of those events would carry on without a tear. Did they pick up the 'meaning'? They would doubtless say 'yes'. The sentences in the description consist of short, common-sense language. The loss of a loved one would be familiar to them. Yet they would not weep as I did when I wrote, or as my father did at the time of his loss. What is missing in the text-description is intersubjective meaning.

Meaning is also conveyed in *art forms*. A musical score is more than a series of random sounds. The composer, moved in heart and mind, brings together a particular pattern of sounds, a certain cadence and rhythm and phrasing of the sound. When the pattern in the composer's mind is produced on instruments and voices, the result is aesthetic, meaningful pleasure to the minds of listeners. The meaning will not be exactly the same between all listeners. But all of them will be able to talk about their experience of the performance. They all heard the same pattern of sounds, but the meaning will be mediated in terms of the particular social location of the listeners.

An artist paints a picture of a previous emotion recollected in tranquillity. The artist does not know who will look at the blending and patterning of colours on the canvas. Nor does the artist expect to produce the same feeling in the observers of the painting. The observers will look this way and that at the painting on the wall, and will glean from the work of art a meaning they did not have before. It will not be identical to the meaning in the mind and heart of the painter, but the art form will communicate meaning in connection with itself, yet beyond itself. The painting as object does not contain meaning. It requires interested, attentive, intelligent, reasonable and responsible observers. In the subjective act of observing the art object, meaning is produced in the minds and hearts of the observers, each of them experiencing differently the same work of art.

Persons, places and things also communicate meaning. We may call this *symbolic* meaning. A professor may make such an impression on a student that the student thinks of the *person* of the professor as the embodiment of wisdom, insight, humour, or the like. In short, the person evokes a feeling in the student, and the feeling is meaningful. Conversely, the feeling of wisdom-insight-humour may come over the student at some point, and at once the image of the professor comes to mind. The same is true of places and things.

I own an old Ford-Ferguson tractor. It was manufactured in 1941. People ask me why I have such an old tractor. I do not need it where I live, but I have it. That old tractor is exactly the same kind as the one I drove in my teenage years on the old family farm in Northern Ireland. It reminds me of the experiences I had in those years. When I drive it now it evokes a whole nest of feelings I treasure. The tractor carries symbolic meaning for me.

The Bible is itself symbolic for many people, not as text to be read, but as a holy book to be owned and revered. Its presence in a home or on a communion table in a church represents something good and religious. But the *texts* of the Bible do not carry symbolic meaning in the same way that the holy book, or tractor or the person of the professor do. Texts describe, explain, inspire; they do not carry symbolic meaning in and of themselves. 1 Corinthians 11 describes the eucharistic celebration in the Christ-community at Corinth. The symbols for the celebration are described as bread and wine; both elements are to be ingested by the gathered community. All of this we learn from reading the text. But the words 'bread' and 'wine' are not themselves the symbolic elements. If the words were the symbols of meaning then the Christian Church could simply satisfy itself with the reading of those words that describe and enjoin the symbols. But reading the text does not convey symbolic meaning. The act of eating the blessed bread and drinking the blessed wine conveys the symbolic meaning. Even in the eating and drinking, the meaning of the symbol comes through only to those whose minds and hearts have already been touched by the love of God in Jesus Christ, who have committed themselves to a life of faith in Jesus and membership in the community of faith.

By far the most complex system for communicating meaning is *language*. As the discussion of language in the next chapter demonstrates, the capacity of language to communicate ideas is infinite. Its complexity and universality serves as a powerful, liberating vehicle for carrying meaning between persons and groups. A child learns a language early in life, and as the child develops vocabulary and linguistic skill it has the means at hand for mediating the world to itself. Language is open to numerous possibilities. Language is the outlet for human intentionality, for calling for change, for creating institutions, for gaining support for a project. Language has within it all the facility necessary to convey ideas, feelings, actions, events, about every subject imaginable. Verbs with their tense, voice and mood can tell the kind and time of action, whether actual or potential, whether the action is performed by the subject or by an agent. Adverbs assist in the task. Bring in the nouns, adjectives, participles, infinitives, prepositions, conjunctions, articles, and particles, put them in their proper form and place in the sentence and the meaning soars from mind to mind creating laughter or tears, revolution or submission, peace or war, joy or sorrow. The possibilities for the communication of meaning in language are endless.

To this point, however, we have not distinguished between the oral and written forms of expression, nor between common-sense language – as in everyday conversation – and technical/classical language. The language that two people of the same town use between them is not the same as the language in a text of classical literature. A person who enjoys chatting with a friend does not necessarily enjoy Shakespeare's *King Lear*, much less a textbook on calculus. Similarly, an avid reader of newspapers, journals and novels is not necessarily drawn to an ancient language such as that of the Bible. The meaning in modern newspapers, journals and novels is easy enough to mediate. It does not require competence beyond common sense.

Reading ancient literature, by contrast, does require an acquired competence beyond the everyday conversational language. The meaning scripted in the signs comes out of another social location, and since all knowledge is socially located the reader has difficulty grasping the meaning at a glance.

Common Sense and Horizons of Meaning

I have heard people appeal to 'common sense' when they speak of the untrammelled clarity of their point: 'common sense should tell you!' Everyone in the world should get it. Common-sense language, however, is not common to people everywhere, but to a group of people located within the same social and linguistic structure in the same time frame.

The sense of any sentence is not at all common to everybody in the world, perhaps not even to everyone in a given culture. Common-sense meaning is that which is carried in the repertoire of a whole group. It could be a culture or a subculture. Members of the group understand the sense, because they have lived in the group and have grown accustomed to the way of thinking and speaking. They share the same cultural metaphors and idioms. The language they use is that of trade, family, sport, politics, dress, etc. People living in the same common sense of the language share the same bundle of insights about life and world. By that common fund of insights, which feeds into the language, they are able to carry out their intentions within the limits of their horizon of meaning.

Their common sense, however, does not equip them for grasping meaning outside their range of meaningful speech or text. A church person may pick up a book on a familiar subject from the Bible: parables of Jesus, the Exodus, Paul's opponents at Corinth. When they open the book to read they discover it well nigh impossible to grasp. What they did not know from the title was that the book was intended primarily for scholars or university and seminary students. The language and style of the book assumes considerable research in advance of reading the book. Words and ideas are unfamiliar. There is, in short, too much *uncommon* sense in that book, too much academic jargon.

The question might be put: Is the language of the Bible any more common sense than the textbook for scholars and students? Even the Psalms have unfamiliar terms, strange place names, people we do not know, a temple in which we do not worship, a monarch we do not honour in our political lives. Assuming that the Bible was written in common-sense language for people of that time and that place, the sense would be common only to those people. In the first place the languages of the Bible (Hebrew and Greek) are foreign to readers who do not know them first hand. These later readers need a translation. Right away the common sense in the original form of address recedes, regardless of the effort of the translators to retain the literal sense of the text. Let me illustrate the point from the salutation in James 1.1.

The readers are addressed thus: *tais dôdeka phulais tais en tê diasporâ.* The NIV translators rendered these words, *to the twelve tribes scattered among the nations.* The last phrase, *scattered among the nations,* is supposed to capture the meaning of *en tê diasporâ.* This Greek phrase was a common-sense phrase to the author and first readers, but not to modern readers. So the NIV translators transform it into a more common sense for contemporary English readers. But does the Greek phrase, *en tê diasporâ,* carry exactly the same sense as *scattered among the nations?* The *diasporâ* was not individual Jewish people scattered individually among the nations. The 'scattered' people lived in tightly knit Jewish communities located here and there throughout the Roman Empire. The NRSV translation, recognizing this common-sense meaning of *diasporâ,* decided to give a single, close equivalent and capitalize it: *to the twelve tribes in the Dispersion.* Is 'Dispersion' a common-sense term for English readers? Will they have precisely the same reading experience as the first writer and first readers when they used their term *diasporâ?* Probably not. Modern readers have to do some research before they can appropriate the meaning the term might have had for first readers.

The solution is not to abandon the effort to understand the common sense of the language of the text in favour of a contemporary, common-sense rendering of the original language. The more common sense is made of the text for contemporary readers – that is, the less the engaging research and discovery – the further removed readers are from the common-sense meaning of the text.

Related to common sense, yet not identical to it, is the notion of horizon. 'Horizon, literally, is the limit of what can be seen from any given vantage point. Metaphorically, it is the limit of what one knows and cares about.'[8] H.-G. Gadamer (following Husserl) made much of the metaphor of horizon for interpretation. 'A horizon is not a rigid frontier, but something that moves with one and invites one to advance further.'[9] Of course, a person may live without a horizon, or at least without paying any attention to the horizon, and thus not see the possibilities beyond the immediate experiences.

---

[8] Meyer, *Critical Realism,* 69.
[9] Gadamer, *Truth and Method,* 217.

A person who has no horizon is one who does not see far enough and hence overvalues what is nearest. Contrariwise, to have a horizon means not to be limited to what is nearest, but to be able to see beyond it . . . Similarly, the working out of the hermeneutical situation means the achievement of the right horizon of inquiry for the questions evoked by the encounter with tradition.[10]

Like common sense, a person's horizon of meaning is limited by the extent of inquiry and discovery. And no matter how much research a person carries out, the horizon is still limited to the social location of thought and life in which the person lives. In that case we may ask: Is it possible at all to enter the horizon of the biblical texts? Can we place ourselves within the horizon of the biblical texts? And if so, how is that accomplished?

The situation implicit in biblical texts is different from our own, and the difference must first be acknowledged if we are to understand the text. The horizon of the text becomes evident when we find the text prompting questions in our mind as we read. Without the question from the horizon of the text there cannot be an answer regarding the meaning of the text. With the raising of one question that leads to another and another we find ourselves encountering the horizon of the text from within our own horizon. In the sensing of the questions that the text-horizon evokes we begin to understand the sense of the text. Such understanding does not mean that we acquire the precise life-meaning the author and first readers experienced and understood at the moment of writing and reading.

The encounter between the two horizons, that of the inquiring reader and that of the text, in an attempt to understand the sense of the text leads to 'a real fusion of horizons'.[11] That means that the difference between the two horizons becomes less visible, less two and more one. The reader's horizon is widened to include within it something of the text horizon in the act of inquiry-in-reading. When we can finally say, 'I understand', what does that mean except that we have fused the horizon of the text meaning with our own meaning in living. How can it be otherwise? 'Understanding is always more than the mere recreation of someone else's meaning'.[12] The process of understanding is a meaning-filled operation. Meaning, in the active verbal sense, is a way of 'ordering one's world and orienting oneself within it'.[13] In this

[10] *Truth and Method*, 269.
[11] *Truth and Method*, 273.
[12] *Truth and Method*, 338.
[13] Lonergan, *Method*, 70.

sense, the words, sentences, paragraphs of a text are always a 'meant' that becomes meaning in the act of interpretive reading. This is what Gadamer seizes upon in his discussion of the fusion of the two horizons.

The fusion of horizons in the mode of question-answer reading eliminates the artificial separation of 'original meaning' from 'significance'. Making this distinction and separation merely highlights the reality of the two horizons, but it also stymies the project of fusing the contemporary reader's horizon with the horizon of questions that the text poses in the reading encounter.

The 'Real World' and Meaning

Once in a while, as theory abounds in a class lecture and discussion, a student will pluck up enough courage to ask, 'What does this have to do with the real world?' What the student apparently is experiencing at that point is a sense of disconnection, a feeling of boredom, an absence of meaning. The 'real world' in the student's question, as far as I can tell, is the familiar, the near, and common-sense world of eating and drinking, of driving a car, of going out on a date, of withdrawing money from the bank to buy groceries, of finding a job, of planning a vacation, of having coffee with a friend. It is the world of common sense. In that world two people can meet and talk without first preparing the terms of the conversation, as one would prepare the text of a lecture. The words come easily. Conversation flows from one to the other without hesitation or embarrassment. In this 'real world' a person does not have to think much about what they are doing. They just do it because common sense tells them they should. It is a world of television, radio, newspapers and stereos; a world of family, friends, work mates and bosses. The 'real world' understood in this way is one in which the person looks at things, and by merely looking knows what to do with them.

Even in that 'real world' scenario a person might go beyond looking at things, and may stop to think about things. If such persons happen to be assigned a job they have not done before, such as nailing drywall to a wall, they might stop and ponder the procedure before they begin. They would look for the tools and materials and probably measure the wall to make sure the piece of drywall fits. In all of this operation in the 'real world' everything is out there to be seen, handled, constructed. It is real because it is out there. Ideas, on the other hand, are not out there. Motives are not out there. Intentions are not out there. Theories are not out there. And because they are not, the 'real-world' person is inclined to consign them to some unreal domain and refuse to deal with them deeply.

When the same people are encouraged to think, not about things in the world out there, but about the interior world of their own perceiving, wondering, theorizing, judging and deciding they consider themselves to have left the 'real world'. The problem in this case is one of a limited horizon of meaning. Nothing short of an intellectual revolution will change the 'real-world' mentality. Theories are real. Ideas are real. Theories and ideas shape the world 'out there', form communities, build structures, create institutions. Persons who try to make sense of the world, who theorize about a cure for disease, who imagine a way of reaching planets other than Earth, who construe ways of bringing wholeness to society, these are engaging truly in real entities in the world.

What does this have to do with biblical studies? Much in every way. There is a 'real-world' way of reading the Bible. For many committed believers the Bible resides in the 'real world' where they live. They have been instructed by their church leaders to read the Bible every day to find help and comfort and direction for their lives. Its texts should yield their meaning by the sheer act of reading from where they live. The meaning should be in line with the common sense of the 'real-world' experience, since the Bible resides in the 'real world' of church and personal family life. In this horizon, the Bible is treated as though it were written today, as a daily newspaper is written. Or it is treated, perhaps, as always there, not written by any human minds and hands in time and place and circumstance.

Treated in this way, the horizon of questions that the biblical texts would otherwise put to an inquiring reader is veiled by the 'real-world' mentality. The 'real-world' reader of the Bible ends up caught in an illusion in which meaning from the 'real world' is unconsciously super-imposed onto the horizon of the biblical text: readers come away thinking they have latched onto the real meaning of the text because it matches the meaning of their 'real world'. Nothing short of a radical transformation in the mind of the reader will change the pattern from 'real-world' thinking to critical realist thinking. As long as the 'real-world' thinking persists the meaning of the texts has less chance to come alive in the mind and life of the reader. When the radical trans-formation of mind occurs, the reader begins to inquire of the text, and gives the text ample, open opportunity to put its questions to the mind of the inquiring reader. In this critical realist way of reading, the reader and the reading community experience transformation *from one degree of glory to another* (2 Cor. 3.18).

Intention

Meaning and intention are kindred subjects. Whereas we perform acts of meaning, including speech-acts, that fulfil our hopes and dreams, that orient us in our world, that mend broken relationships and create new ones, we also intend acts of meaning in advance. These latter may be called potential acts of meaning constituted in intention. Intention sees with the mind's eye, sizes up a situation, aims at some outcome, and decides to act out the plan. As I write this chapter, for example, I have in mind also the intention of going on a holiday with my brother to our home country of Northern Ireland in the spring. Now I have written the intention on this page, but the writing of the intention is still not the act of meaning itself. The meaning in the intention – conceived, spoken or written – has yet to be realized. To be sure, the intention is itself meaningful but not in the same way that the act of being in Northern Ireland with my brother will be meaningful. The two connect, the intention and the act of meaning; they must connect. There cannot be a meaningful act without the potential act of meaning, intention.

Intention is meaningful in so far as it lines up with the act of meaning to follow. Of course, the potential act of meaning may not come to fruition exactly as intended. There may be surprises when the intention is enacted; there could be avenues we did not anticipate. Yet the intention and the action in experience do correspond in large measure. The human mind is capable of conceiving meaningful, responsible action in advance of the act itself, and capable also of achieving the goal within the limits of time, skill, and circumstances.

Biblical texts (as all texts) have intention built into them, intrinsic to them. The act of writing a text is not the meaningful act in completion. The writing of the text is still part of the intentional act of the writer, a potential act of meaning. The text achieves its potential in the act of appropriation, in being read by some living soul. This issue of whether intention is in texts or in reader has been hotly debated in the last quarter of the twentieth century, and is not about to subside very soon.

At one extreme is the notion, proposed by E. D. Hirsch,[14] that the meaning in the text is the object of interpretation, and that the intention, or will, of the *author* of the text can be deduced from the text. Hirsch believed it was incumbent on the interpreter to construct a history of the author from his text. This endeavour should be the aim and focus of reading an author's text, according to Hirsch. At the opposite end of the debate are reader-response theorists, such as Stanley Fish, who see meaning produced in the mind of the reader in response to reading the text. If meaning were contained in the text exclusively, then the text would exercise a tyrannical hold over the reader. But that is not the case, says Fish. The reader's job is not the recovery of meaning embedded in a text, but the production of meaning in the act of reading. 'Meaning ... develops in a dynamic relationship with the reader's expectations, projections, conclusions, judgements, and assumptions.'[15] In this model, the reader is 'freed from the tyranny of the text and given the central role in the production of meaning'.[16]

Every text has an implied author, just as it has implied readers. But one cannot jump immediately, as Osborne seems to do, from an implied author to the real author and then argue for 'the true intended meaning', by which he seems to suggest the single intention of the original author.[17] A text is a creation out of the author's intention to be sure, but the world of meaning referenced in the text is not identical with the world of the author, nor does the intention in a text capture everything in the mind of the author as he wrote. The idea that the original intention of the *author* can be retrieved is what is called the 'intentional fallacy'.[18] The fallacy involves the attempt to reconstruct the real author out of a literary creation by an author. The two – real author and literary creation – are not the same. I refer again to Romans 7 to illustrate.

When the text of Romans 7 presents the narrative character ('I') as unable to do the things he wants, but does the things he does not want, is the narrative character describing the author? Should we construct a picture of the author tortured in his believing soul by the conflict

---

[14] E. D. Hirsch, *Validity in Interpretation* (New Haven: Yale University Press, 1967), 8–12.

[15] Stanley Fish, *Is There a Text in This Class? The Authority of Interpretive Communities* (Cambridge: Harvard University Press, 1980), 2–3.

[16] *Is There a Text?*, 7.

[17] Osborne, *Spiral*, 414–15. 'The original author had a certain audience in mind,' and thus the goal of interpretation is that 'original meaning of a text.'

[18] W. K. Wimsatt and Monroe D. Beardsley, 'The Intentional Fallacy' [1954], *The Verbal Icon* (New York: Noonday, 1958), 3–18, cited in Meyer, *Critical Realism*, 49.

between good and evil? Or should we construct, instead, a picture of the real author from the next chapter (Rom. 8) where the text announces complete victory over the works of the flesh through the law of the Spirit of life in Christ Jesus? Neither of these is to the point. The two texts are part of a literary text created in the mind of the author to generate an effect in the minds of the readers. It is simply not true that 'if one removes the author, the text floats in a historical sea of relativity, open to multiple meanings'.[19] How does an appeal to the author of these two chapters of Romans anchor the two texts in history and make interpretation of their original meaning possible?[20] There is no real author to remove from the text, since the real author is not there. Even if the real author were alive to tell us his intention as he wrote, his presence and his voice are not required to make his text effective. His classic, literary text of Scripture stands on its own without its real author's help. On its own terms the text stands (or falls), with its *implied* author/narrator and its referential world, all wrapped up in its words, sentences, syntax, rhetoric, and general verbal texture. The text is the only anchor required for intelligent, reasonable and responsible interpretation of its intended sense.

Reading communities along the road of history will not read the text in exactly the same way. They are in different situations. But the text calls them back to itself again and again to test their insights and prompt them to explore further. That is how it should be. Yet the meaningful interpretations, whether they are produced in Alexandria or Antioch in the third century, in Rome or Winnipeg in the twenty-first century, in a Catholic monastery or a Mennonite congregation, they find their reference point in the text of Scripture. The readers return to the text to read again, and with each reading new questions arise, new insights accrue, and meaning is enhanced. The process is cumulative and progressive, not to the end that one common meaning will be found, but that meaning as lived out in the encounters with the texts will be enlarged.

It would appear from this variety of meanings in different reading communities that a text carries multiple meanings, called polyvalence. Indeed that is so by the very nature of the *text-and-reader* phenomenon. A text carries meaning in code. The encoded meaning has to be decoded, not by the author – who is not around in any case – but by

---

[19] Osborne, *Spiral*, 394.
[20] As Osborne posits, *Spiral*, 394.

the reader. Some texts are more polyvalent than others. For example, the intended sense of the narrative of 2 Samuel 23.20 is straightforward: 'Benaiah ... went down and killed a lion in a pit on a day when snow had fallen.' It hardly needs explanation in words other than those of the text. We may want to know more about the man called Benaiah, and we can do so from the context surrounding this small narrative. We will find that this Benaiah was a brave warrior in Israel. One could extrapolate plenty about bravery and valour implicit this little text.[21] But the sense is plain. A reader is not free to change the snow to rain or sunshine, nor the lion to a sheep. The code words are quickly deciphered and their structure readily discerned. Our imagination quickly moves down into a pit with a man named Benaiah to kill a lion on a snowy day. The interpretive questions raised by that little text are few and far between.

The same is not true of the narrative parables of Jesus. Is the parable of the Good Samaritan of Luke 10 about doing good to one's neighbour? Yes it is. Does it deal with the problem of racism? Indeed it does that too. Is this parable signalling a dysfunctional temple system? It is about that also. Does it carry a certain critique of a religious system? Yes. Does it tease the mind into active thought?[22] Yes it does. No wonder the church fathers found it necessary to allegorise this parable among others.[23] Meaning in the narrative parables of Jesus in the Gospels is not singular and fixed; the parables tease and shock the mind into thinking about alternative possibilities. Polyvalence is part of the narrative fabric of the parables of Jesus: a new meaning emerges in the light of a new angle of vision.

Giving proper place to the reader's interest in and response to the texts of Scripture in the reading experience does not at the same time give warrant to reckless abandonment of the form of the text. The form has to be taken seriously into account for the encounter to be authentic. Ben Meyer's point has some merit: 'the text has a primary claim on the reader, namely, to be construed in accord with its intended sense.'[24] This does not make the reader a slave to the text, as Fish implies. Nor does it contradict the polyvalent meaning in parables. If it

---

[21] I heard a sermon on this text many years ago from a man who had preached it three hundred and ten times already in the United States and Canada.

[22] C. H. Dodd's term, *Parables*, 5.

[23] See J. Ian H. Macdonald's treatment of this subject, 'Alien Grace' in V. George Shillington, ed., *Jesus and His Parables* (Edinburgh: T&T Clark, 1998), 35–51.

[24] Meyer, *Critical*, 17.

can be shown that the nature of the parables of Jesus is to tease the mind, to challenge conventional ways of thinking about the issues raised in a given parable, then that factor is part of the form of Jesus' parables and has to be taken into account. The intended sense of an argument in Romans, however will be quite different; that of the Decalogue in the Pentateuch different yet again. The particular form of the text presents its own cluster of questions to the mind of the reader in construing what Meyer calls the intended sense.

At heart, the meaning of biblical texts is not merely about the history of persons, places, things, events, but about mystery, the mystery of salvation. The text, as Meyer says, initiates the reader into the mystery of salvation.[25] Beyond all other aspects of meaning, the most profound meaning for human beings finally is in coming to know God through a redemptive relationship with the Christ of God in the Church of God. Biblical studies can facilitate that kind of meaningful fulfilment. '[Human beings] can reach fulfilment, peace, joy, only by moving beyond the realms of common sense, theory, and interiority and into the realm in which God is known and loved.'[26]

---

[25] Meyer, *Critical*, 46.
[26] Lonergan, *Method*, 84.

Objective

To understand the relationship between language as the structuring of thought and language as expression of thought in a pattern of sounds (speech) and a pattern of signs (text), and to be able to apply the insight to the reading of Scripture.

Lead Questions

1. *Give a basic definition of 'language'.*

2. *In what sense is language operating prior to expression? Can you demonstrate this phenomenon for your self?*

3. *What is meant by 'semantic universality'? Is semantic universality present in some languages but not others, or is it inherent in all language systems?*

4. *How is human language akin to the ancient Hebrew and Greek notions of Word and word?*

5. *Which came first, speech or writing?*

6. *What is the advantage of language as speech over language as text?*

7. *Why is language as expressed in conversation more productive of meaning than language expressed in monologue or in text?*

8. *How (according to Gadamer) is it possible to engage a text in 'conversation'?*

9. *Name three related cultural innovations that had massive influence on human culture.*

10. *What is the relationship of writing to history?*

11. *Trace the development of writing up to the invention of alphabet.*

12. *How does alphabetic writing simplify text and at the same time accommodate semantic universality?*

13. *Define the following: cuneiform, pictogram, ideogram, hieroglyphic.*

14. *How does your understanding of language, speech and text (after reading the chapter) affect your approach to reading the text of Scripture?*

5

Language, Speech and Text

Words, words, words.
(Shakespeare, *Hamlet*, II, 2, 193.)

A major part of the adventure in biblical studies involves an exploration of the nature of language. How could it be otherwise?
Language is at the heart of everything we do, not least in studies related
to the Bible. The term 'bible' itself comes from the Greek root *biblos*,[1]
which came to mean a papyrus sheet or roll containing meaningful
script, a written expression of language. Language theory is thus
inescapable in biblical and theological studies. Schleiermacher declared
that 'everything presupposed in hermeneutics is but language,'[2] and
Heidegger that 'language is the ... arrival of being itself'.[3]

It should come as no surprise, therefore, that the Church, from its
earliest self-understanding to the present time, believed the revelation
of the will of God to have come not only through the incarnate Christ
but also through language, spoken and written. Members of the newly
formed communities of faith in God, whether the first commonwealth
of Israel or the first-century Christ-community, heard the word of God
spoken through the prophets and apostles out of their experience of
divine activity. As they advanced their mission and began to define
their communal life in the world, the leaders committed the message of
salvation and life to *writing* for their communities and for generations
of communities to follow. Hence the three-pronged topic of this final
chapter of Part One: language, speech and text.

---

[1] *Biblos* is a loan word from Egyptian, used first to refer to the pithy core of the papyrus reed
that grew abundantly by the Nile. This *biblos* from the papyrus was then processed into a writing
material (sixth century BCE), to become the successor to wooden tablets in Greece. Later the
diminutive, *biblion*, came to mean a papyrus scroll-manuscript (e.g. John 21.25; 2 Tim. 4.13; Rev.
20:12). By about 400 CE the plural *biblia* was applied to the collection of sacred Scriptures. See
H. W. Beyer, βιβλιό, *TDNT* I, 615–20, and notes.
[2] F. Schleiermacher, quoted in Gadamer, *Truth and Method*, 343.
[3] M. Heidegger, quoted in Kenneth Hamilton, *Words and the Word* (Grand Rapids: Eerdmans,
1971), 29.

Language

The subject of language is highly complex, deserving much more discussion than this space allows. I offer this much merely to point up the relationship between three aspects, or levels, of language: language as an *inherent capacity* in human beings for structuring thought for communication, language coming to *expression in speech*, and language coming to *expression in text*. The first of these three is fundamental.

In the planning stage of writing this chapter I asked a friend over coffee for a definition of language. My friend is not a linguist, but uses language with the rest of us. Her user-definition might be just as helpful for our purposes as the highly sophisticated definition of a linguist. Here it is: 'Language is a way of making myself understood.' The three key terms in that sentence struck me right away: 'a way', 'myself', and 'understood'. I shall weave some reflection on each of these ideas into the ensuing parts of the chapter. For the moment, though, let me suggest that language is our built-in capacity for knowing the world and for generating communication of our acquired knowledge with our comrades.

A human 'self' is not satisfied to live alone and speechless, alienated from all other humans beings. The inner capacity for making intricate and intimate connection between persons in community I am calling 'language'. Human understanding, or thinking, (discussed earlier), is part and parcel of language, and language part and parcel of under-standing. 'There is this close correspondence between language and thinking.'[4] Language, so I would argue, is first and foremost a charac-teristic of human make-up for making my understanding connect authentically with the understanding of other human selves. Language finds 'a way' to make that connection, 'a way of making myself under-stood'. 'The way' is nothing more nor less than making use of a convention of sounds (speech) and a convention of signs (text) resident in the community.

Someone might object, as Lindbeck does, that the community already provides 'the way', which the individual then adopts. We simply learn the conventions, make them our own and use them to make ourselves understood. According to Lindbeck, 'there are numberless thoughts we cannot think, sentiments we cannot have, and realities we cannot perceive unless we learn to use the appropriate symbol systems'

---

[4] Ernest R. Hilgard and Richard C. Atkinson, *Introduction to Psychology*, fourth edition (New York: Harcourt, Brace and World, Inc., 1967), 375.

resident in language and culture.[5] I agree that *a* language of a particular culture has to be learned before communication can take place. But I am arguing here for the complexity of the inner capacity, not only to learn an external linguistic pattern, but also to adapt it and reconfigure it in such a way that the new expression can be understood. Language is first of all the *inner ability* in our human minds to construct reality, or to deconstruct it, and then to communicate the result to other minds using linguistic conventions agreed upon in the given culture.

To elucidate the notion of language as an inner capacity, prior to the learning of a cultural linguistic convention, I elicit the work of anthropologist Marvin Harris. His insights on language provide a worthwhile framework for biblical hermeneutics. His point about the 'semantic universality' of human languages, as compared to the communication systems of other primates, is particularly striking. Cultural take-off, he says, is linked with 'the uniquely human capacity for language and for language-assisted systems of thought'. The uniqueness is summed up in the term 'semantic universality'.

> A communication system that has semantic universality can convey information about all aspects, domains, properties, places or events in the past, present, or future, whether actual or possible, real or imaginary, near or far.[6]

This capability of human languages is not possible in any species other than human beings. As compared to the various calls and gestures observed among gibbons, for example, human language has the capacity for unlimited communication of detailed information. The number of semantic domains is infinite.

Language, as I am trying to describe it here, is the moulding of thought. The particular patterns of a language (English for example) are the ways of moulding thought. One language pattern will produce a thought world somewhat different from the thought world produced by another language system. Benjamin Whorf studied this phenomenon and concluded thus:

> The forms of a person's thoughts are controlled by inexorable laws of pattern of which he[/she] is unconscious. These patterns are the unperceived intricate systematisations of his[/her] own language – shown readily enough by a candid comparison and contrast with other

---

[5] Lindbeck, *Nature*, 34.
[6] Marvin Harris, *Culture, People, Nature: An Introduction to General Anthropology* (New York: Thomas Y. Crowell, 1988), 138.

languages, especially those of a different linguistic family ... And every language is a vast pattern-system, different from others, in which are culturally ordained the forms and categories by which the personality not only communicates, but also analyses nature ..., channels his[/her] reasoning, and builds the house of his[/her] consciousness.[7]

Whorf's point granted – that a language system controls a person's thought pattern – I would argue that a person, having learned the Persian language, and the world-view moulded by that language, can also learn English and the world-view associated with that language. Whatever way thought is construed in one language the human mind has the capacity for construing the world in other ways, and for communicating the new construal in any language system. The single point I wish to make from this discussion is captured in one word, repeated several times in this section, *capacity*. Language is first and foremost an inner capacity for (1) learning a communication system, (2) employing the dynamics of the system to structure thought, and (3) communicating the structured thought to other minds.

In this sense, language is innate. One source suggests that 'children come into the world genetically programmed to look at language in certain ways, that operating principles may be part of our biological heritage'.[8] The particular language system – Spanish, French, German, Chinese, English, Greek ... – is secondary to the human capacity for semantic universality.[9]

All particular language systems manifest the same human capacity for communicating an infinity of details about all aspects of life. In short, every human language system consists of *phonemes* (units of sound), *morphemes* (units of meaning), and *grammar* (rules of sentence structure).[10] A child does not simply learn the conventional sounds of a home language. He/she discovers how to structure the phonemes and morphemes into appropriate word patterns, and the words into a meaningful sequence according to the conventional rules of grammar. The result is not merely a rote repetition of observed sounds, but a

---

[7] Benjamin Whorf, *Language, Thought, and Reality* (New York: Wiley, 1956), quoted in Harris, *Culture*, 151.

[8] Ernest R. Hilgard, Rita L. Atkinson and Richard C. Atkinson, *Introduction to Psychology*, seventh edition (New York: Harcourt Brace Jovanovich, 1979), 266.

[9] Compare this with the instrumental notion of language: 'Language ... is essentially an instrument for the communication of fact or for the establishment of verbal conventions', F. Ferré, *Language, Logic and God* (New York: Harper & Row, 1961), 8.

[10] Hilgard, Atkinson and Atkinson, *Psychology*, 260–4. See further discussion below under 'Speech'.

dynamic expression of a mental structuring of the child's world. 'Thus the child not only *learns* sentences but he/[she] *produces* (generates) them.'[11] This is what psychologists call a generative theory of language.

To put this discussion into the frame of the opening definition of language, the phonemes, morphemes and grammar are 'the way' of making oneself understood. We do not merely pick and choose sounds and signs from a cultural repertoire to send bits and pieces of information. Instead, we have in our human make-up the potential (1) for creating a complete image of a world of meaning, and (2) for communicating the image to other human minds. In turn the receiving mind grasps the image and generates another world of meaning out of the one received in a never-ending operation of forming world from world. This is the broadest notion of language, but seems like a worthwhile starting place for thinking about the language of biblical texts and the language of theology.

In the area of philosophical and theological discussion of language, Gadamer, in my view, has done his most commendable work. He makes the point that 'human language must be thought of as a special and unique living process in that, in linguistic communication, "world" is disclosed'.[12] 'World' is not the planet Earth with all of its material components. 'World' is what human beings formulate and create from within the universe in which they live and move and have their being, and they do so by *structuring*.

The structuring occurs not in the forming and fixing of material with hands and instruments merely, but in mental activity mainly. Mental structuring thus may be called communication in potential. Take the sculpting of a marble statue, for example. Before the activity of hammering and chiselling begins, language is actively preparing the way for the sculpting of the marble. The same holds for the presentation of an acceptance speech, or the writing of a poem. Language, I submit, is at work shaping and designing the product of thought. What emerges is *the expression* of the structure of thought.[13] 'Whoever has language "has" the world.'[14]

The work of art – visual, auditory or literary – is not nor can it be the full expression of the language that gave it birth. The literary

[11] Hilgard and Atkinson, *Introduction to Psychology*, fourth edition (New York: Harcourt, Brace & World, 1967), 373.

[12] Gadamer, *Truth and Method*, 404.

[13] Robert Funk, *Language, Hermeneutic and Word of God: The Problem of Language in the New Testament and Contemporary Theology* (New York: Harper & Row, 1966), 4.

[14] Funk, *Language*, 411.

expression, sure enough, is more complete and more circumscribed than a sculpture or a painting. Yet even the literary expression of the mind is finite, whereas the potential of language is infinite. The poem or the sculpture will generate further expression, and that expression yet another and another.

So it is that interpretation, whether of a sculpture or a biblical text, will generate further insight from which other interpretive language will ensue. The observer-interpreter must be allowed to probe the finite expression for an infinity of meaning that the particular object represents and prompts. Involved in this notion of language is the idea of play. That is, the expression offers hints and clues and pointers to meaning lodged within itself and beyond itself, but never totally separated from itself. An interpreter is not free to play outside the claim that the linguistic form lays on the person.[15] Truth is at stake, the truth represented in the linguistic expression. A way must be found to lay claim to the truth encoded in the expression. That 'way' is not in some method external to our human personalities. It lies within us (as outlined in Chapter 3), in the dynamic operation of consciousness, in the language of understanding that shapes and fills the world of meaning.

Generation after generation of scholars have grappled with the issue of finding the connection between *language as expression* and *language prior to expression*. On one hand, distinguishing linguistic expression from that which gives rise to it is convenient for discussion purposes. On the other hand, it invites confusion by separating the sentence from its source, the conversation from its centre. The source of human expression of meaning is often called simply 'thought', in distinction from speech or text, thereby separating each of them from its respective home in the human mind. Whether the term 'language' is appropriate for that which is as yet unspoken or unwritten is debatable, I admit, especially so since the English term commonly means audio/visual expression of thought. Still, I want to argue for using 'language' to indicate *the interior way we order our thought-world*, the way we mean something before we say it or write it, but also *the way we make our meaning understood in our communal lives*.

One can find warrant for using a single term, 'language', for both the linguistic expression of thought as well as thought itself, not only from

[15] Meyer, *Critical Realism*, 17. '[T]he text has a primary claim on the reader, namely, to be construed in accord with its intended sense.'

the great thinkers of the past but also from a careful self-analysis. Here is a challenge. Go for a walk alone and become conscious of yourself thinking. Look for evidence of the way you think without speaking or writing. Find out if your thoughts take shape in language. I believe you might be surprised how your language and thought co-mingle in your mind as you walk in silence. I have found myself looking at a man painting his house, and asking myself why he chose that brilliant red paint; why he uses a roller rather than a brush; how he stabilizes the ladder, etc. I do not speak those words, nor do I write them. I simply structure the thought using the learned linguistic patterns I have at my disposal.

This is how we are. We structure our thought by language without uttering a word, without writing a single syllable. All of this is *language*, both the structuring of a thought-world, and the expression of thought. Construed in this twofold way language is not far removed from the ancient Greek notion of *logos*, usually translated 'word'. It could just as well be translated 'language'.

For Plato *logos* could designate the world of Ideas or the active expression of an idea. The two could not be separated completely, even though the world of Ideas is the 'real' world beyond the temporal, changing world, and the expression of an idea a shadow of the real. Plato's doctrine of *logos* came into its own in the Neoplatonists, such as Philo, a Jewish philosopher of Alexandria at the time of Jesus. *Logos* is the principle of creation in Philo, of reason and design, of life and thought, of all that exists in concert with justice and goodness. *Logos* is the language of the divine mind. And the *logos* also lives in the human soul as well, paving the way to salvation. *Logos* is the invisible activity of intelligence that leads to the right and the real. Philo also uses *logos* to mean a verbal expression with meaning, as in individual words (*logoi*) or in a discourse (*logos*).

The prologue to the Gospel of John (John 1.1–18) likewise uses the term *logos* as the active, creative mind of God that enlightens every human being that comes into the world, and then identifies the *logos* in the world with the person of Jesus (1.14f.). The rest of the Fourth Gospel uses the term to signal the verbal expressions of Jesus' thought, especially in the signs that he performs. With every manifest sign comes also a word that gives life: *Stand up, take up your mat and walk* (5.8); *Lazarus, come out* (11.43).

No doubt, the idea of *logos* (translated Word) in the prologue of John has roots in the Greek world, but no less so in the Hebrew tradition. F. F. Bruce suggests that, 'the true background to John's thought and language is found ... in Hebrew revelation'.[16] In the creation narrative of Genesis 1, for example, *God* said ... *and it was so.* Similar phrasing occurs in other parts of the Old Testament, especially in the book of Psalms. By *the word* of the Lord the heavens were made, the mountains formed, the seas bounded, and life ordered. It is as though 'the word' were somehow the acting agent of God's prior Word. In this sense, it seems, the writer of the Fourth Gospel had this Hebrew idea of 'word' (*dabar*, translated *logos* in John 1.1ff.) in mind for the opening of his Gospel.

How does this ancient notion of *logos* relate to our discussion of language as the structuring of thought, and language as the expression of thought? The connection between *logos* (singular) as invisible power that comes to expression in *logoi* (plural) is analogous to 'language' as the power of the human mind to structure the thought-world and then to put the structured image into some form of expression.

And what does this notion of language have to do with biblical studies? I am suggesting that a grasp of the inherent place and power of language within the human family provides a framework for the activity of reading and interpreting the biblical texts. When thought comes to expression, as in the texts of Scripture, the reader is not immediately confronted with the 'language' in the mind of the author, but with the written linguistic expression. As the bounded world of the text enters the mind of the reader, another world of meaning emerges in another language system in another mind, the mind of the reader(s). More will be said on this topic in due course. We turn now to speech as a form of expression.

Speech

'Speech is linked with the abundance of the heart', says Robert Funk. Linked yes, but speech is not identical with the abundance. Has this ever happened to you? You are sitting with a good friend chatting about various aspects of your common life and suddenly your friend says something you cannot quite understand. It happens to all of us. Here is part of an actual conversation that happened in a coffee shop in a small city in Manitoba, Canada.

---

[16] F. F. Bruce, *The Gospel of John: Introduction, Exposition and Notes* (Grand Rapids: Eerdmans, 1983), 29.

'Gordon will have to find another place to have coffee with his friends.'

'Gordon who?'

'Gordon Frazer . . .'

'O yes of course, that Gordon. With the closing of his favourite restaurant he will need to find another meeting place.'

And so the conversation continued. The pieces had to be cleared up, sorted out, for the conversation to serve its purpose. The two conversation partners knew three people named Gordon quite well. The first speaker had one of them clearly in mind before making the verbal comment about Gordon having to find another place to have coffee with his friends. What happened in this case was that the first speaker had an inner conversation with herself before speaking verbally to her friend. In the inner conversation the identity of Gordon was perfectly clear. But when the inner language moved into the audible, verbal sentence the other partner missed part of the inner conversation. In the speaker's mind the sentence was meaning-full, but not so in her spoken words.

Conversation is like that. It requires at least two people to make it work well. When one makes a statement from which inferences can be drawn, the person listening to the statement must have opportunity to question the speaker before making the inferences. Again, truth is at stake. The question – 'Gordon who?' – is needed in conversation in order to make appropriate inferences. This give and take is the essence of authentic conversation, which in turn provides the context for arriving at truth. Perhaps this is why Papias, a second-century Christian writer of Hierapolis, derived not 'so much benefit from books as from the living voice of those that are still surviving'[17] after the death of the apostles. There is something dynamically authentic about spoken conversation between partners present to each other, which does not happen in written statements in the absence of each other.

Radio and television are another matter. To be sure, the word is spoken in these media but it is one-way speech for the most part. Even talk shows and call-in programs are a notch below the uninhibited person-to-person conversation. Conversation is interactive and dialectical.

---

[17] From Eusebius Pamphilus, *Eccleastical History,* popular edition, trans. C. F. Cruse, ch. XXXIX, 'The Writings of Papias' (Grand Rapids: Baker Book House, first printing, 1955), 125.

We shall have occasion to relate the topic of conversation to biblical studies in a moment. Before doing so we should consider the origin and significance of *speech*.

Speech, as a convention of audible verbal communication with semantic universality, pre-dates written communication by an indeterminate number of years. We can locate the beginning of writing within cultural and temporal parameters, but speech seems always to have been the practice of human beings in communities from their first appearance.[18] We draw that inference by analogy with the later literate communities. The problem with the cultural remains of human habitation prior to writing is the lack of evidence for the particular speech-convention used. The inference is reasonably secure, however, that as long as human beings have inhabited the earth they have found a linguistic way of making themselves understood with semantic universality. They have found the way simply because they have had the capacity to do so.

Speech consists of a complex series of sounds that reproduces thought in such a way that the ear can pick up the pattern of sounds and decipher it intelligently. The deciphering process amounts to interpretation; that is, the reconstituting of images and ideas transmitted from the other mind through the medium of speech. One might say the act of speaking intelligently creates an event of greater moment than the demolition of a building or the crashing of a plane. Speech sends an audio-picture into the air for perception (hearing) and integration into the thinking of the hearer (interpretation). And thus cultures are created and destroyed, relationships fused and fractured, and nations formed and re-formed. In short, speech-language generates 'world' by the interaction of thought with thought.

Take some of the notable speechmakers of this century, for example. Adolph Hitler welded the nation of Germany together under his Nazi regime largely by his public speeches. So also Winston Churchill in calling the British nation to war against the Nazi advance. Martin Luther King Jr likewise by speech called the United States to account for its oppression of African Americans. Speech has the power of good and evil; power to create 'world' or to destroy it.

The ancients were no less conscious of the power of speech to create or destroy. Saint Paul knew the power of speech in bringing Gentiles to

---

[18] Cf. Owen Barfield, 'The Origin of Language', in *Saving the Appearances: A Study in Idolatry* (New York: Harcourt Brace Jovanovich, n.d.), 122–5.

faith in Jesus Christ. To the Galatians he is able to say, *It was before your eyes that Jesus Christ was publicly exhibited (proegraphe) as crucified!* (3.1) On the surface, this is a strange statement. The Galatians were not eyewitnesses to the crucifixion of Jesus. Yet Paul writes to them as though they were. In so far as Paul had reproduced the event in his *proclamation* of Jesus crucified they had witnessed the event of Jesus' crucifixion – Paul spoke the event. In this sense, therefore, Paul's speech itself became an event in the minds of his audience at Galatia. By the speech-event they witnessed the historic event as if they had been physically present in Jerusalem some twenty years earlier.[19]

We return now, as promised, to the question of conversation in relation to biblical studies. On my library shelf is a book entitled *The Old Testament Speaks.*[20] But the Old Testament does not speak, not literally. It is text, not speech as we have been working with the idea to this point. When someone suggests that a text 'speaks' they are using figurative language to describe the effect of a text. The fact that people use this figure of 'speech' about texts suggests (to me at least) that they wish the text would speak literally. Speech implies a living presence, personality, life, especially so in conversation-speech. Text speaks only in so far as it can 'be transformed back into language'.[21] In this we find a crucial aspect of biblical studies and theology.

So far we have used the term 'conversation' to illustrate speech as primal linguistic expression. Conversation involves partners sharing a topic of interest. They focus on an object of thought together. The speakers interact with each other. Conversation is never one-way. It seeks the truth by asking moot questions that lead to further information and further questions and ultimately (one hopes) to the certainty of the matter.

To return to our illustration of conversation about Gordon's need for another coffee shop to meet with his friends. One of the partners in the conversation was able to ask, 'Gordon who?' The question is key to understanding the object of the conversation. The sense became clear very quickly since the speaker who had the language in mind was present in the conversation. The answer came right away. Can we apply the structure of conversation to the reading and understanding of texts? Gadamer claims we can.

---

[19] See further on speech as event in Funk, *Language*, 20–71.
[20] Samuel J. Shultz, *The Old Testament Speaks* (Harper & Row, 1960).
[21] Gadamer, *Truth and Method*, 352.

He applies the question-and-answer factor of real conversation to the reading and understanding of texts, especially the ancient texts of the Bible. But there is quite a difference between asking a question within a real conversation and asking a question of a text. The text does not answer promptly as in the living conversation – 'Gordon Frazer ...'. Yet there is a question to be asked in any reading of the text of Scripture. As Gadamer rightly points out, the historic text 'asks a question of the interpreter'.[22] This question that the text puts to the interpreter sets the stage for the understanding of the meaning of the text. While the question will be specific to the text, at heart it will ask what Philip the Evangelist asked the Ethiopian treasurer in Acts 8.30: *Do you understand what you are reading?* And if the interpreter is open and honest in the 'conversation' he/she will answer as the Ethiopian answered: *How can I, unless someone guides me?* It is not enough to read the words on the line without asking what lies behind the line. When readers see terms like 'Pharisee', 'Samaritan', 'Sadducee', 'High Priest', 'temple', 'expiation', 'resurrection' etc. within the complexities of geography, politics, religion, social structures, and economic values, do they quickly understand what they are reading? The text puts questions to the honest reader. What is a High Priest? Who appoints him? What are his duties? What was the political situation in which he ruled? Out of this horizon of questions come answers and more questions, but always a greater grasp of the truth conveyed in the text.

In this metaphorical sense, then, we may justly apply the term 'conversation' to the interpretation of texts. Having admitted that much, the view remains that real conversation is the encounter of living mind with living mind, personality with personality, which is not possible in the question-and-answer reading of a text. The text is not equal to the living experience of the writer of the text, nor are the signs on the page the full weight of the language behind the signs in the mind of the author. The signs 'need to be transformed back into speech and meaning'[23] in the mind and life of the reading partner. We are already broaching the subject of the text.

---

[22] Gadamer, *Truth and Method*, 333.
[23] Gadamer, *Truth and Method*, 354.

Text

'Writing is the graphic counterpart of speech',[24] the end product of which is a text. A text is a set of signs on a surface that represents human thought. The signs can be manuscript (hand-written) or typescript (as on the pages of this book) or digital (as on a computer screen). Whichever way, text is a *visual* object exclusively. All of the other senses (hearing, touch, smell, taste) take their leave from the operation of reading a text. Of course, a text can be read aloud to an audience. In the audible reading, though, the text has already moved into interpretation by the inflection in the reader's voice, by the reader accenting one word and not another, and by the personal presence of the reader.

One wonders, for example, why leaders of churches that provide pew Bibles do not set aside a few minutes in the worship service for silent, individual reading of the Scripture text. The reason, I suspect, may be several-fold. Reading (especially the reading of the Bible) is more like work to many people than worship. Listening to a human voice reading the Scripture inspires the soul more so than silent reading. The public reader, by the effective use of voice and reading skill, provides an interpretation for the audience.

In short, text is not speech. A text can come to speech, as in public reading, and thence be transformed into thought-language. Or a text can be read silently with essentially the same effect: it is transformed into thought-language and takes on meaning.

The writing of signs to represent language was a major invention within human history, matched in massive influence by the inventions of agriculture and the printing press. Agriculture, which seems to have had its beginnings at the site of Jericho,[25] provided a surplus of goods for settled life. Settled life in turn provided the situation for the development of writing, among other things. The printing press provided the means for literacy.

But it was the invention of writing that marked the beginning of history. Without a record of human intention, activity, and achievement, there could be no human story. Artefacts cannot

---

[24] David Diringer, *The Alphabet: A Key to the History of Mankind*, third edition (New York: Funk & Wagnalls, 1968), 4. Hereafter referred to as Third Edition to distinguish it from the original publication of 1948, referred to as *Alphabet*.

[25] According to Kenyon (*Archaeology*, 45), 'at a stage when the expanding population [at the site of Jericho] required a large area of fields, irrigation channels must have been constructed to carry the waters of the spring farther afield.'

communicate personality, to the extent that written records can. Of course, the invention of writing did not suddenly bring with it widespread reading ability throughout the given culture. Only a privileged few in a settlement could read the linguistic signs in the ancient world. Reading was a learned skill, and not everyone in the ancient world had the interest, the time or the resources to acquire the skill.

The advance of more widespread literacy lagged until the invention of movable type in Europe in the fifteenth century. Johann Gutenberg is credited with printing the first book in Europe (c. 1456 at Mainz), the Mazarin Bible. With the success of the printing press the stage was set for the full flower of the Renaissance and Reformation, and the ensuing literacy campaigns in Europe and beyond. Looking back from the present vantage point in history it is fairly safe to say that writing, whether in manuscript or in mechanical type, 'has become the vehicle of civilization, and so of learning and education'.[26]

With these few broad strokes about text before us we return now to the story of the development of writing, a practice we take so much for granted in literate cultures of the world today.

Long before the appearance of the first alphabet human beings found ways to transmit their thoughts by signs of various sorts. Objects carved in stone or wood, or made with clay, are symbols of thought. Objects drawn on walls likewise convey ideas. When an object gains currency in a culture the same object appears in many places in a given period. The people in that place and time understand the sense of the object. This is true not only for pre-alphabetic cultures, but also for modern multiculturalism, so evident in a country like Canada. For example, in public buildings a stylised picture of a man or a woman on the door or wall signals the toilets for men and women. Roads leading to the airport have drawings of an aeroplane posted. McDonald's restaurants are known the world over by the image of a large yellow, double arch. In modern societies these 'picture-words' are convenient but very limited in their ability to transmit complete and complex ideas. They are not capable of semantic universality, but they are moving in that direction.

The earliest picture writing (Upper Palaeolithic period, 20,000–10,000 BCE) probably functioned as sympathetic magic, not the communication of ideas or the recording of events. Sympathetic magic involves, for example, the drawing of a crude picture of the hunt

---

[26] Diringer, Third Edition, 1.

on the wall for the purpose of performing a kind of ritual dance in front of the picture in an attempt to assure the success of the actual hunt to follow. Such a picture was found on the wall of the Tabun cave in the area of Mount Carmel in Israel. Old Stone Age paintings of various shapes and sizes were discovered in caves in northern Europe, North Africa, Spain, Italy and elsewhere. All of these pictures seem to have been the earliest stage of representing human thought, or action, on a surface.

That may be overstating the case. It may be more accurate to call these drawings devices for carrying out activities of life and culture. They can scarcely be called primitive writing, if by writing we mean the complex communication of structured thought by visual representation.

The pictogram is the first stage of writing, as we know it. A circle might represent the sun, a square might represent a house, and the shape of an animal might represent the particular animal shown. A sequence of such drawings forms a kind of story that can be read by anyone in the culture, and even beyond the culture. For example, a pictogram of a man facing a square followed by an animal facing the opposite direction and a circle above all three, could be read as follows: 'The man who lives in this house hunts an animal on a sunny day.' Obviously, the scope of such pictographic objects is limited. Such drawings do not represent speech fully, in that the pictographic sequence lacks the semantic universality present in the complex sounds of a spoken language. But 'picture-writings are found everywhere. They are the work of ancient peoples in their primitive stage of culture, or of modern tribes.'[27]

Pictograms represent something concrete. When a pictogram represents something other than its form it is called an *ideograph*, a related thought. A smile on a face indicates happiness; a heavy burden on a person's back may represent oppression. Again, as in pictographic drawings, the ideograph does not connect directly with the sounds in the spoken word. That invention came in the next stage: phonetic writing.

Phonetic writing seeks to represent the *sounds* of a spoken language in *signs*. The signs are no longer pictures, but marks that stand for *syllables*. This syllabic signing is still one step away from alphabetic writing, in that the syllabic signs capture the vowel sounds primarily,

---

[27] Diringer, Third Edition, 10–11.

but not with semantic universality. The system, while culturally advanced, did not represent the full complexity of stops and inflections (consonants) present in the flow of sounds in a spoken language.

Syllabic writing, such as Akkadian and Sumerian, was able to capture grammatical structure and thus communicate quite well the thought of the writer. The famous code of Hammurabi, for example, was written in phonetic syllables. Readers then (as now) familiar with the agreed syllabic signs could decipher the code and understand the laws of their Babylonian king.

The syllabic system of writing was widespread in the Ancient Near East. Cuneiform writing of Assyria, for example, uses a syllabic system.[28] The term 'cuneiform' comes from the Latin *cuneus*, 'wedge' and *forma* 'shape'. As the term implies the letters were wedge-shaped. The instrument would have been shaped like a nail, or a chisel, having a tapered end. With the tapered stylus the letters were formed in soft, yet firm, clay. The clay blocks were then set out in the sun to bake into hard tablets. Numerous cuneiform tablets were found in sites in ancient Assyria. Exactly when this kind of writing came into being is hard to say. The existing tablets can be dated somewhere in the fourth millennium BCE, which means that the invention of cuneiform script pre-dates these tablets by a number of years, perhaps 500–1000 years. The law code of Hammurabi, mentioned above, is a classic example of cuneiform writing.

Hieroglyphic writing may have developed in Egypt at the same time as the cuneiform script in the area of Babylonia-Assyria.[29] The word 'hieroglyphic' comes from two Greek words, *hieros*, 'sacred', and *glyphein*, 'to carve'. Thus hieroglyphic writing was associated with the inscriptions carved on temple walls, royal tombs, and the like. But hieroglyphic writing was also painted on stone, wood, and earthenware. Hieroglyphic script dates back to about 3000 BCE, and reached its high point in the first dynasty of Egypt in the thirteenth century BCE. The sequence of hieroglyphic signs ran horizontally from right to left, although not consistently.

Hieroglyphic script was made up of hundreds of pictograms with about twenty consonantal signs to transcribe foreign names. But the system had different signs for the same sound. Thus the Egyptian hieroglyphic system, while moving towards a consonantal alphabet, was

---

[28] For a fuller description of cuneiform script see Diringer, Third Edition, ch. 1.
[29] For a fuller description of hieroglyphic script see Diringer, Third Edition, ch. 2.

not quite there. A true alphabet has one sign for each consonant. There can be little doubt that both the Egyptian hieroglyphics and the Babylonian cuneiform script together influenced the invention of the final stage of representing all the consonants of speech, namely the *alphabet*.

Alphabetic writing proper, according to Diringer, was invented and used first by 'the Semitic-speaking inhabitants of Syria and Palestine ... in the Hyksos period, which is now commonly dated 1730–1580. ... However, the exact birthplace of the alphabet [in Syria or Palestine] is unknown.'[30]

The invention of alphabet created a single sign for each kind of stop, or inflection, in speech. The alphabet thus achieved in sign what speech had achieved already in sound, semantic universality. Out of the first invention of the alphabet in Syria-Palestine came four branches: (1) the Canaanite branch, subdivided into the early Hebrew and Phoenician; (2) the North Semitic branch, or Aramaic; (3) the South Semitic branch; and (4) the Greek branch, from which came the Western alphabets. The alphabet simplified writing by reducing the number of representative signs to between twenty-two and twenty-six, rather than thousands of signs in the earlier forms of writing.

> Thanks to the simplicity of the alphabet, writing has become very common; it is no longer a more or less exclusive domain of the priestly or other privileged classes, as it was in Egypt, or Mesopotamia, or China. Education has become largely a matter of reading and writing, and is possible for all.[31]

The intention in the foregoing discussion of the development of 'text' was twofold: (1) to demonstrate the immense contribution writing has made to the advance of humankind socially and culturally, and (2) to alert the reader to the interpretive challenge of decoding (reading/interpreting) the linguistic signs, and so to transform them into thought-language. Reading, like writing, is a learned skill that cannot be taken for granted. The skill needs to be developed, honed into an art, particularly in the reading and understanding of the ancient texts of the Jewish/Christian Scriptures. The deep tradition attached to these texts of Scripture demands respect and insight.

---

[30] David Diringer, *The Alphabet: A Key to the History of Mankind* (New York: Philosophical Library, 1948), 214, 218.

[31] Diringer, *Alphabet*, 37.

PART II

RESPECTING THE TRADITIONS REASONABLY

On Course . . .

Objective

To witness to the complex character of the literatures in the books of Scripture as pointing to their origin and development in the believing communities.

Lead Questions

1. *In what sense can the 'Bible as literature' also be viewed as 'the Word of God'?*

2. *How are the traditions about the Bible in tension with a present-day critical reading of the texts of the Bible?*

3. *When is it appropriate to speak of the Bible as one book?*

4. *When is it appropriate to speak of the Bible as a collection of many books written at different times in various situations by different people?*

5. *What is the difference between codex and scroll?*

6. *How expensive was writing material 2000 years ago?*

7. *What importance should be attached to social, political and religious circumstances for understanding the biblical texts?*

8. *Why was it important for the early faith communities to attach a personal name to a document of Scripture?*

9. *What are the four letters designating four sources textured into the Pentateuch? What is the explanation of these four letters?*

10. *Write a brief description of each of the four strands of tradition textured into the Pentateuch.*

11. *How do you explain one Jesus and four Gospels?*

12. *What is meant by 'Synoptic tradition', and 'Johannine tradition'?*

13. *How do the Synoptic Gospels compare with each other, and together with the Gospel of John?*

6

Writing the Biblical Texts

We write you nothing other than what you can read and also understand.
(St Paul, 2 Cor. 1.13)

For people of faith the Bible is nothing less than the Word of God. Not all of them agree on the precise meaning of the Bible as the Word of God. At one end of the discussion are those who say that God speaks to the human condition *through the texts* of the Bible written at different times by various human writers in communities of faith. At the other end are those who believe that *God wrote the words* in the Bible quite apart from any human agency. In the thinking of this latter group, to suggest that there is a human side to the Bible robs the Scripture of its authority, invalidates the idea of divine inspiration, and reduces the Word of God to the level of fallible, human intentionality. Implicit in this view is the belief that any thoughtful investigation of the texts of Scripture flies in the face of divine revelation. And sometimes the implicit becomes painfully explicit, as in the following example.

A number of years ago I was teaching a course called, 'Survey of Biblical Literature'. When I tried to lead the class into a responsible reading of the different types of literature incorporated in the Bible one student raised a hand in vehement opposition. 'The Bible is the Word of God,' she said, 'not literature.' Her objection was understandable. She had come from a church tradition that taught, without equivocation or qualification, that God is the real author of the Bible, which makes the Bible the Word of God, not literature. She had been instructed in her church to read the Bible regularly and prayerfully, because the words of the Bible are God's words, not the words of human writers. That meant, for her, that she could choose to read any part of the Bible and she would encounter the Word of God directly for the nurture of her soul. She, like many others from the same branch of Christian tradition, believed it quite in order to pick and choose a verse from here and a phrase from there without any attempt to understand the literary context from which the words came, or the communal-social setting of the words, or the kind of book in which the words were found, or the agrarian cultural context in which the words were anchored. That is one extreme. There is a middle ground, of course, a 'more excellent way'[1] of treating the Bible as the Word of God in written form.

Faith traditions have a good and proper place in our lives, especially traditions associated with the Bible as the Word of God. In the words of the lead character in *Fiddler on the Roof*, 'Without our traditions our lives would be as shaky as a fiddler on the roof.' Granting that they would, I would add that our lives are equally shaky if we allow our traditions to stand unquestioned in our lives from one generation to another, from one community to another, from one stage of faith to another.[2] However precious the traditions, when they stifle thought and cramp the imagination that gives lustrous meaning to our human life then our traditions have failed us.

The challenge for us is to respect the traditions about the Bible within a healthy spirit of reverent inquiry that lights the path to truth. That is how I intend to proceed in this chapter about the writing of the biblical texts, which have become for us in the Jewish and Christian traditions[3] the authoritative Word of God.

Many Books in One

Christians speak of 'the Bible' as though it were one book. And so it is in a way: to the Jewish Scriptures were added early Christian documents to form a single collection of inspired writings to guide the Church's life and thought. (See further on this topic in the next chapter). Yet when someone opens the Bible to read, they soon discover sections marked off from each other. Christians see at a glance, for example, that their Bible has two large (yet unequal) parts called the Old Testament and the New Testament. What Christians now call the Old Testament the Jewish people simply call 'the Bible'. The early Christians, most of whom were Jewish, as Jesus was, witnessed the dawning of a new day in the life-death-and-resurrection of Jesus as

---

[1] An allusion to 1 Cor. 12.31.

[2] See James W. Fowler, 'Stages of Faith: Reflections on a Decade of Dialogue', *Christian Education Journal* 13.1 (1992), 1323; and David G. Creamer, *Guides for the Journey*, 125–60.

[3] The Jewish Bible was the Bible of the early Christian community, and remained so even after the composition, collection and canonization of the twenty-seven documents of the New Testament. It was only after the acceptance of the twenty-seven books of the Christian community (the New Testament) that the thirty-nine books of the Jewish Hebrew Bible were called 'The Old Testament'. See further on this subject in Chapter 7.

the Messiah (Christ), and with the new day they discovered in themselves a new understanding of life in the world. Out of this new understanding in the Spirit of Jesus Messiah they wrote about the vision they found in him, a vision of the rule of God in the present world coupled with a blessed hope of new life in the world to come. Their writings about the new age of Jesus Messiah were eventually called collectively 'The New Testament', while the Scriptures they had inherited from the Jewish community were rendered 'The Old Testament' in the presence of the new collection of writings about Jesus Messiah. Yet Christians, for the most part,[4] saw the two testaments (or covenants) as one, the first leading into the second.

Besides the large twofold division of the Christian Bible, readers find also sections marked off under titles (e.g. Genesis = origins, Exodus = a way out, the Acts of the Apostles) or the names of people (e.g. Jeremiah, Ezekiel, Matthew, John, Galatians, Romans). These sections under titles and proper names are generally called 'books' for want of a better word. When we think of a book, though, we think of pages bound together under a cover, like this book you are reading. This book form, called *codex*, was not invented until the second century CE. The 'books' of the Bible, prior to the invention of the codex form, were individual documents written on parchment (made from skins) or papyrus (made from a reed that grew largely in the area of the Nile in Egypt). Depending on the size of the document the parchment/papyrus would be a sheet or a roll. A small sheet would serve a document like 3 John or Jude or Philemon, whereas a larger document, such as Isaiah or The Acts, would require a long *roll* of papyrus or parchment, perhaps thirty feet long. 2 Timothy 4.13 refers to documents made from both types of material (*biblia*, papyrus sheets/rolls, and *membranai*, parchment sheets/rolls). These materials were expensive.[5] Only a privileged few could afford them in any quantity. Those who could write, and who had something important to write about, but lacked the funds to buy the material, might find a patron to provide the funds.[6] Still, the parchment and papyrus opened the way to much more prolific writing than was possible in earlier times

---

[4] A second-century confessing Christian, Marcion, and his followers rejected the books of the Jewish Scriptures (Old Testament) as the divine word, now that Christ has come to fulfil all the hopes and dreams of Israel past. See further comment in Chapter 7.

[5] See William Barclay, *Introducing the Bible* (Nashville: Abingdon Press, 1972), 20–1.

[6] It is possible that Theophilos of Luke 1.3 and Acts 1.1 was such a patron of the writer of Luke–Acts.

when writing was limited to chiselling the letters in stone or imprinting them in clay with a stylus.[7]

Time and Place

When the inspired writers of the documents of the Bible took stylus or reed-pen[8] in hand, they did not all write together at the same time in the same place under the same political and social circumstances. The writing of the Bible took at least a thousand years to complete.[9] As one generation of writers died off another came along to carry forward the story of God's revelation and redemption. As we might expect, composition that stretches over such a long period shows signs of political, cultural and social change within its contents. The early documents of the Bible read very differently from the later ones. To use a cliché, we can see that times have changed from one document to another, from an earlier to a later. This piece of information about the time-frame of the writing of the biblical texts affects how we read the different documents: with the change of time comes also a change of circumstances and change of culture that produced the parts of the Bible.

Permit me to draw an analogy from the last one thousand years to make the point. Suppose someone were to bring together into one volume in one language (English) a number of written works from well-known writers of the last eight hundred years or so. At the beginning of the book we have a treatise from Thomas Aquinas (1225–74), followed by other works from Martin Luther (1483–1546), Francis de Sales (1567–1622), Pascal (1623–62), J. S. Bach (1685–1750), Billy Sunday (1863–1935), A. Schweitzer (1875–1965), R. Bultmann (1884–1976), Billy Graham (1918–), and Schüssler Fiorenza (1938–). What would be a faithful way of reading the various writings in this multi-authored book? All the words of all the authors are in English. The book falls under one title, say, 'A Compendium of Christian Thought'. All of the writers in the book are from within the Christian tradition. In these respects this hypothetical book manifests a certain unity. Does that unity mean that we can pick and choose at random a line from here and another from there without taking seriously into account the time and setting that informs the texture of the various

---

[7] See the discussion in Chapter 5.

[8] Called in Greek, *kalamos*, a reed split at one end like the nib of a metal pen.

[9] More than a thousand, if we accept the tradition that Moses wrote much of the Pentateuch (Torah).

texts of the different writers? Along with the unifying factors there is great diversity among the writers by virtue of the particular social-cultural and religious world that nurtured their respective thoughts. To read such a composite book as this requires attentive, sensitive concern for the difference in time and custom and thought in the texture of the various texts.

Is there an analogy here to the Bible? I think there is. The single story of redemption traceable throughout the documents of the Bible is, at the same time, multidimensional and multicultural. Here we have the story of the giving and receiving of law, and there stories about nation building; here wise sayings, and there a prophetic oracle; here a collection of musical poems, and there an apostolic letter. Each of these in turn comes out of a time and place and culture peculiar to their life-situation. One writer lives at a time of building the nation of Israel out of a band of nomadic clans; another at a time of the kingdom's strength and glory. One writes at a time of oppression and destruction and another at restoration after destruction. One writes from inside the nation of Judah and another from exile in Babylonia. Some wrote under one imperial rule and some under another. Most of the writers of the Bible wrote before the Easter experience of the Christian Church while a number wrote after Easter.

With every external change comes also an internal change in outlook and understanding and self-identity. All of these facets of social and spiritual life show up in the texture of the biblical texts and constitute the fabric of their intended sense. Linked to this time-place-culture tapestry in the biblical texts are, of course, the literary types: judicial narrative (in Exodus and Deuteronomy), sacred-political narrative (in Joshua through Kings), prophetic oracle (in the prophetic books), wisdom sayings (in Proverbs), wisdom drama (in Job), a love song (Canticles), religious-political-personal Psalms, gospel narratives, church narrative (Acts), personal and community letters, (as in Galatians and Philemon), general epistles (as in Hebrews and 1 Peter), and apocalyptic (Daniel and Revelation). A more complete listing of the documents of the Bible comes up in the next chapter.

Who were these writers of the various documents of the Bible? And how many people had a hand in the composition of each of the documents as they appear in their present form in our Bible? Although these two questions have less currency in biblical studies now than they used to, they still continue to surface with vigour, as illustrated in Professor Friedman's 1997 edition of *Who Wrote the Bible?*[10]

Meet the Writers in Their Writings

Before proceeding too far into the discussion, we need to consider first if there is a point to the questions. What does it matter if we can attach a personal name to a document of Holy Scripture? Does it make a difference if we are able to say a man named Moses wrote this and a man named Matthew wrote that? What does the ancient Egyptian name 'Moses' or the Palestinian Jewish name 'Matthew' mean to us today? Really very little, apart from the symbolic freight they carry in the Jewish and Christian traditions respectively. We have not met Moses or Matthew personally. We have come to know them symbolically through the tradition to which we belong – less so through the actual documents of the Bible. There were many writers of Scripture whose proper names we do not know. Yet their writings are among the most treasured in our Bible. That being so, we do well to have the writers introduce themselves to us through their writings. It matters little if we do not hear their proper names coming through, but more that we sense their interests, their time in history, their vision of God and their culture, the nature of their quest for reality. Getting to know the writers from their own writings is not a quick and easy flick of the pages. It requires diligent observation as we read, consultation with other readers, rereading what we thought we knew already. The more of that kind of activity we do the more we get to know 'the faces' of the inspired writers of the Bible.

As illustrated from reading the Pentateuch

What better body of biblical literature from which to illustrate the process than the celebrated Pentateuch ('five rolls': Genesis, Exodus, Leviticus, Numbers, Deuteronomy)? From the last four of these books we learn of Moses, mediator of God's Law (*Torah*) to the ancient Hebrews. From the Jewish tradition we know him as the *writer* of all five books. The evidence in the Hebrew Scriptures is resoundingly clear that a figure called Moses, raised in the Egyptian court, led the Hebrew people out of slavery in Egypt, and mediated God's laws to them, in

---

[10] Richard Elliott Friedman, *Who Wrote the Bible?* (San Francisco: HarperSanFrancisco, 1997).

particular the Ten Commandments carved in stone *with the finger of God* (Exod. 31.18), to govern their nomadic lives in the wilderness, and later their settled lives in the promised land of Canaan.

That much firmly acknowledged, it is quite another matter to claim, as the Jewish-Christian tradition does, that Moses wrote every word contained in the five rolls of the law in their entirety during the forty years wandering in the wilderness, including the account of his own death and burial (Deut. 34.1–12). The internal evidence from the Pentateuch itself speaks against the traditional claim on several counts.

First, as indicated already, the idea that Moses would write about his own death and burial is strained to breaking point. So also his writing of accolades about his own outstanding character, humble spirit, and unequalled leadership: *Never since has there arisen a prophet in Israel like Moses* (Deut. 34.10). Clearly, this narrative comment assumes that Israel as a nation has been around for a long time, and that prophets have preached in Israel long after Moses' death. The statement must come from the hand of someone living in a much later period.

Second, at several points in the last four books of the Pentateuch the narrator refers to Moses as having done certain deeds, including especially writing down laws that he received from God, and creating a tent-of-meeting for the worship of God. It would be strange indeed for Moses to write about himself in the third person as doing certain deeds, especially the writing of God's laws for the people, while at the same time withholding his identity as the writer of the present version of the same laws and deeds.

Third, there are numerous allusions in the Pentateuch to events, places and people who lived many years after Moses' time. For example, Genesis 36.31 alludes to kings who had reigned over Israel, a situation unknown to Moses; Genesis 14.14 knows of a city in the north called Dan to which Abraham pursued his enemy, even though the place called Dan did not get its name until years after Moses' death (Judg. 18.29); Genesis 21 and 26 mention the Philistines, who came to prominence after 1200 BCE, some years after Moses.[11]

The trail of internal evidence through the Pentateuch against a single Mosaic authorship of the five books could go on endlessly. For our present purposes, we may simply pay tribute to the torrent of

---

[11] Barclay, *Introducing*, 26–7.

investigation of the Pentateuch over the last two centuries,[12] and touch on the presence of writers in the intricate texture of the Pentateuch. In turn, this window into the writing of the Pentateuch should provide insight into the process of the writing of other documents in the Bible. Bear in mind, again, the reason for highlighting the writing of the biblical texts: *to alert the reader of the Bible to the interconnection between conditions surrounding the writers and the intricately meaningful tapestry displayed in the various texts.*

Strong evidence exists in the biblical tradition that Moses, educated in the Egyptian court, was equipped to write and that he did write foundational material (Exod. 2.1–10; 17.14; 34.28).[13] But what? We do not know for certain. We do know that his character as prophetic leader and mediator of law pervades Exodus through Deuteronomy, but we also know now that several (perhaps many) writers had a hand in the composition of the five books traditionally attributed to Moses.[14] Who they were exactly no one knows for certain. Neither do we know precisely when they wrote. We can only detect their presence as we read through the final form of the five books. From these different texts, combined with other pieces of evidence, we can say something about the circumstances that conditioned their texts, something of their interests, their style of writing and their theology.

Four literary strands in particular are woven into the texture of the five books. From this observation Old Testament scholars have concluded that distinct sources underlie the present shape of the Pentateuch.[15]

A uniform style, certain preferences of vocabulary and theme, and its own chronological framework mark each of the four sources. It is the

---

[12] For a good summary of research up to 1961 see John Bright, 'Modern Study of Old Testament Literature', in *The Bible and the Ancient Near East: Essays in Honour of William Foxwell Albright*, ed. G. Ernest Wright (Garden City NY: Doubleday, 1961), 13–31. Cf. Brevard S. Childs, *Introduction to the Old Testament as Scripture* (Philadelphia: Fortress Press, 1979), 109–35, and Robert B. Coote and Mary P. Coote, *Power, Politics, and the Making of the Bible: An Introduction* (Minneapolis: Fortress Press, 1990), 25–73.

[13] Note Childs' point to this effect, *Introduction*, 132–5.

[14] David Ewert, *From Ancient Tablets to Modern Translations: A General Introduction to the Bible* (Grand Rapids: Zondervan, 1983), 66. 'The divine inspiration of the Pentateuch does not rule out the participation of other authors, or later editors, in the production of the Pentateuch.'

[15] Julias Wellhausen established this hypothesis towards the end of the nineteenth century. 'There have been all kinds of shifts within hypothetical construction over the course of the last hundred years, but on the whole, down to most recent times it has only be [*sic*] questioned by some outsiders.' Rolf Rendtorff, *The Old Testament: An Introduction* (Philadelphia: Fortress Press, 1986), 157.

unresolved clashes between the four, mutually incompatible presentations that make the Pentateuch so bewildering to the casual reader.[16]

Since the personal identity of the writers is unknown, the four literary types have had letters of the alphabet assigned to them to identify their character: *J, E, P* and *D*. The first three, *J, E* and *P*, find their place at various points in the first four books of the Pentateuch (Genesis, Exodus, Leviticus and Numbers). The *D* source appears only in Deuteronomy.[17]

J signifies the source that prefers using the divine name, *Yahweh* (transliterated Jehovah = LORD).[18] He is often referred to as the *Yahwist.* Showing particular interest in locations in the southern kingdom, the writer(s) seems to hail from the Judah some time after the United Kingdom of Israel had divided in 922 BCE.[19] His interest in culture – from the origin of musicians and metalworkers (Gen. 4.21–22) to the possibility of huge construction projects (Gen 11.3) – is marked by a prevailing world-view: humanity, plagued with mistrust and pride, suffers pain, discord and anxiety, is hemmed in by the hand of Yahweh. At the same time humanity can live in hope of blessing in the future. The blessing to humankind will come from Israel. Yahweh is never far away from his creation (Gen. 3.8).[20]

E identifies the writer (or school) who consistently uses the Hebrew title *Elohim* for God. His interest in the northern kingdom of Israel hints that this source comes from that region, possibly during the reign of Jeroboam in the north.[21] This source is often referred to as the *Elohist.* The *Elohist* links narratives together and gives summary statements (Gen. 50.20). He accents the witness of the patriarchs who point the way for God's people to travel (Gen. 22.1–12). The message of the *Elohist* is that the fear of God will enable the people to obey

---

[16] John Barton, 'Source Criticism', *ABD*, 6 (1992), 164.

[17] It should be noted that there is not agreement in the details about the source hypothesis for the Pentateuch. In this section I merely want to point out that the Pentateuch is made up of different kinds of material from different times and settings. Further reading is indicated throughout. See, e.g. the discussion in Rendtorff, *Old Testament*, 157–63.

[18] *J* could be a school, not a single author. If the source had a single author he would almost certainly have been male, hence the masculine pronoun. The same is true for the other sources.

[19] Friedman, *Bible*, 62–7. Rendtorff, *Old Testament*, 159, says *J* 'was usually dated in the early monarchy'.

[20] Hans Walter Wolff, *The Old Testament: A Guide to Its Writings*, trans. Keith R. Crim (Philadelphia: Fortress Press, 1973), 27–8.

[21] So Coote and Coote, *Making*, 41–2.

the divine will: *God has come to prove you, and that the fear of him may be before your eyes, that you may not sin* (Exod. 20.20).

P is assigned to the texts that bear the mark of a Priestly source centred in the temple of Jerusalem, and following in the tradition of Aaron, priest of Moses, during a period of reform and impending danger from hostile powers, especially Babylon. The *P* source contributed more to the Pentateuch than any of the other three. Some have argued that *P* is more redactor than source, in that *P* seems to know the two earlier sources and wraps a context around them.

Childs believes that *P* could have contributed source material as well as edit the other sources.[22] At least there is evidence of a different kind of material from the other two. Its cultic interest is unmistakable. The people of Israel are to enter into relationship with God, as Abraham did (Gen. 17.8). They are to remember the tent of meeting and the arc of the covenant where they met God (Exod. 25.10ff.; 29.42ff.; 40.1ff.). 'As its vital message for its day, the Priestly Document stressed the first of the two statements in the covenant formula: I am your God, you are my people.'[23]

D refers to the material characteristic of Deuteronomy. The source, whether a single writer or a school, is called the Deuteronomist. The book of Deuteronomy served as theological reference for a whole Deuteronomistic history recorded through Joshua, Judges, Samuel and Kings. Deuteronomy itself has a series of sermons that interpret the laws. The Ten Commandments (Decalogue) appear early (chapter 5) and set up the interpretation in the sermons that follow (chapters 6–11). 'Its origin is to be sought in the circles of Levitical preachers who spiritually were very close to the prophet Hosea,' says Wolff.[24] The theological emphases are not hard to trace. At the centre are the gifts of Yahweh that call for a response of obedience from the people (Deut. 12.15; 15.14). Above all, the people of Israel in Deuteronomic thinking are to be *holy to the Lord your God* (7.6; 14.2; 16.18). The theme of judgement, announced earlier by the prophets, rings out in the Deuteronomic school with clarity. 'They issued a concrete call to the people to forsake the innumerable cultic sites in the land and gather in the one place which Yahweh had chosen as the place where his name would dwell (12.2ff.; 16.1ff.).'[25]

[22] Childs, *Introduction*, 123.
[23] Wolff, *Old Testament*, 34.
[24] Wolff, *Old Testament*, 40.
[25] Wolff, *Old Testament*, 42.

This outline – that is all it is – of sources within the Pentateuch simply illustrates the complexity of the writing process in this collection of five books. The job of locating the various contributions of the four writers, or schools of writers, within the books is like the work of a detective in discovering clues to a mystery. Within the constraints of this chapter the most we can do in exploring specific texts is to illustrate[26] the presence of two of these sources in the composite story of Noah and the Flood in Genesis.

The two sources are *J* and *P*. Using Friedman's analysis in locating the two in Genesis 6.5–8.22, we find two fairly coherent stories about Noah and the Flood, each one marked by its own vocabulary and style, its own interests, and its own narrative details. When each of the two stories is set out and read by itself it constitutes a complete story in its own right. In Illustration 6.1 the two merged versions of the flood story are set out, *J* in regular type and *P* in *italics*.[27]

Figure 6.1   J and *P* Flood Narratives

Genesis 6

5 The LORD saw that the wickedness of humankind was great in the earth, and that every inclination of the thoughts of their hearts was only evil continually. 6 And the LORD was sorry that he had made humankind on the earth, and it grieved him to his heart. 7 So the LORD said, 'I will blot out from the earth the human beings I have created – people together with animals and creeping things and birds of the air, for I am sorry that I have made them.' 8 But Noah found favor in the sight of the LORD.

9 These are the descendants of Noah. Noah was a righteous man, blameless in his generation; Noah walked with God. 10 And Noah had three sons, Shem, Ham, and Japheth. 11 Now the earth was corrupt in God's sight, and the earth was filled with violence. 12 And God saw that the earth was corrupt; for all flesh had corrupted its ways upon the earth. 13 And God said to Noah, 'I have determined to make an end of all flesh, for the earth is filled with violence because of them; now I am going to destroy them along with the earth. 14 Make yourself an ark of cypress wood; make rooms in the ark, and cover it inside and out with pitch. 15 This is how you are to make it: the length of the ark three hundred cubits, its

---

[26] With the help of Richard Friedman's detective work, *Bible*, 54–9.

[27] The translation is from the NRSV, except for the word 'expire'/'expired' in Genesis 6.17; 7.21. Friedman provided his own translation.

width fifty cubits, and its height thirty cubits. 16 Make a roof for the ark, and finish it to a cubit above; and put the door of the ark in its side; make it with lower, second, and third decks. 17 For my part, I am going to bring a flood of waters on the earth, to destroy from under heaven all flesh in which is the breath of life; everything that is on the earth shall expire. 18 But I will establish my covenant with you; and you shall come into the ark, you, your sons, your wife, and your sons' wives with you. 19 And of every living thing, of all flesh, you shall bring two of every kind into the ark, to keep them alive with you; they shall be male and female. 20 Of the birds according to their kinds, and of the animals according to their kinds, of every creeping thing of the ground according to its kind, two of every kind shall come in to you, to keep them alive. 21 Also take with you every kind of food that is eaten, and store it up; and it shall serve as food for you and for them.' 22 Noah did this; he did all that God commanded him.

Genesis 7

1 Then the LORD said to Noah, 'Go into the ark, you and all your household, for I have seen that you alone are righteous before me in this generation. 2 Take with you seven pairs of all clean animals, the male and its mate; and a pair of the animals that are not clean, the male and its mate; 3 and seven pairs of the birds of the air also, male and female, to keep their kind alive on the face of all the earth. 4 For in seven days I will send rain on the earth for forty days and forty nights; and every living thing that I have made I will blot out from the face of the ground.' 5 And Noah did all that the LORD had commanded him.

6 Noah was six hundred years old when the flood of waters came on the earth.

7 And Noah with his sons and his wife and his sons' wives went into the ark to escape the waters of the flood.

8 Of clean animals, and of animals that are not clean, and of birds, and of everything that creeps on the ground 9 two and two, male and female, went into the ark with Noah, as God had commanded Noah.

10 And after seven days the waters of the flood came on the earth. 11 In the six hundredth year of Noah's life, in the second month, on the seventeenth day of the month, on that day all the fountains of the great deep burst forth, and the windows of the heavens were opened. 12 The rain fell on the earth forty days and forty nights.

13 On the very same day Noah with his sons, Shem and Ham and Japheth, and Noah's wife and the three wives of his sons entered the ark, 14 they and every wild animal of every kind, and all domestic animals of every kind, and every creeping thing that creeps on the earth, and every bird of every kind – every bird, every winged creature.

15 They went into the ark with Noah, two and two of all flesh in which there was the breath of life.

16 And those that entered, male and female of all flesh, went in as God had commanded him;

and the LORD shut him in. 17 The flood continued forty days on the earth; and the waters increased, and bore up the ark, and it rose high above the earth. 18 The waters swelled and increased greatly on the earth; and the ark floated on the face of the waters. 19 The waters swelled so mightily on the earth that all the high mountains under the whole heaven were covered; 20 the waters swelled above the mountains, covering them fifteen cubits deep.

21 And all flesh expired that moved on the earth, birds, domestic animals, wild animals, all swarming creatures that swarm on the earth, and all human beings;

22 everything on dry land in whose nostrils was the breath of life died. 23 He blotted out every living thing that was on the face of the ground, human beings and animals and creeping things and birds of the air; they were blotted out from the earth. Only Noah was left, and those that were with him in the ark.

24 And the waters swelled on the earth for one hundred fifty days.

Genesis 8

1 But God remembered Noah and all the wild animals and all the domestic animals that were with him in the ark. And God made a wind blow over the earth, and the waters subsided; 2 the fountains of the deep and the windows of the heavens were closed,

the rain from the heavens was restrained, 3 and the waters gradually receded from the earth.

At the end of one hundred fifty days the waters had abated;

4 and in the seventh month, on the seventeenth day of the month, the ark came to rest on the mountains of Ararat. 5 The waters continued to abate until the tenth month; in the tenth month, on the first day of the month, the tops of the mountains appeared.

6 At the end of forty days Noah opened the window of the ark that he had made

7 and sent out the raven; and it went to and fro until the waters were dried up from the earth.

8 Then he sent out the dove from him, to see if the waters had subsided from the face of the ground; 9 but the dove found no place to set its foot, and it returned to him to the ark, for the waters were still on the face of the whole earth. So he put out his hand and took it and brought it into the ark with him. 10 He waited another seven days, and again he sent out the dove from the ark; 11 and the dove came back to him in the evening, and there in its beak was a freshly plucked olive leaf; so Noah knew that the waters had subsided from the earth. 12 Then he waited another seven days, and sent out the dove; and it did not return to him any more.

13 In the six hundred first year, in the first month, the first day of the month, the waters were dried up from the earth;

and Noah removed the covering of the ark, and looked, and saw that the face of the ground was drying.

14 In the second month, on the twenty-seventh day of the month, the earth was dry. 15 Then God said to Noah, 16 'Go out of the ark, you and your wife, and your sons and your sons' wives with you. 17 Bring out with you every living thing that is with you of all flesh— birds and animals and every creeping thing that creeps on the earth— so that they may abound on the earth, and be fruitful and multiply on the earth.' 18 So Noah went out with his sons and his wife and his sons' wives. 19 And every animal, every creeping thing, and every bird, everything that moves on the earth, went out of the ark by families.

20 Then Noah built an altar to the LORD, and took of every clean animal and of every clean bird, and offered burnt offerings on the altar. 21 And when the LORD smelled the pleasing odor, the LORD said in his heart, 'I will never again curse the ground because of humankind, for the inclination of the human heart is evil from youth; nor will I ever again destroy every living creature as I have done. 22 As long as the earth endures, seedtime and harvest, cold and heat, summer and winter, day and night, shall not cease.'

As the *J* and *P* versions of the Noah story are carefully compared the differences stand out. The vocabulary is different. *P* calls the deity

'God' consistently, whereas *J* uses 'Yahweh'. *P* uses male and female to designate the sex of the animals. *J* uses 'man' and 'woman' as well as 'male' and 'female'. *P* says everything on the earth 'expired' while *J* says everything 'died'. Observe also how the two differ in the details of the story: one pair of every kind of animal/seven pairs of clean and one pair of unclean; the flood lasts a year/the flood lasts forty days and forty nights; Noah sends out a raven/Noah sends out a dove. Each of the two has a different way of understanding how the deity works: the deity in *J* regrets past action, grieves in his heart, closes the door of the ark, and smells Noah's sacrifice. In *P* God is above these human qualities and very much in control of all things.

> The two flood stories are separable and complete. Each has its own language, its own details, and even its own conception of God. And even that is not the whole picture. The J flood story's language, details, and conception of God are consistent with the language, details, and conception of God in other J stories. The P flood story is consistent with other P stories. And so on. The investigation found each of the sources to be a consistent collection of stories, poems, and laws.[28]

Returning to Deuteronomy for a moment, the story of its composition is still a bit of a mystery. It is now widely believed that Deuteronomy ('second law', Deut. 17.8) is connected somehow with the reform program carried out by King Josiah in the seventh century BCE (2 Kings 22–23). The story in 2 Kings 22 about the discovery of the book of the law in the temple of Jerusalem may correspond more or less to the time of its composition. Judging from the temple context associated with appearance of the book of the law at the time of Josiah's reform, a priest, or group of priests, may have been responsible for bringing Deuteronomy to its present form. In whatever manner the book of Deuteronomy may be a seventh-century production, it contains layers of ancient traditional material. The present form derives 'from a long period of historical development'.[29] Its form as a whole bears the marks of the seventh-century restoration of dedicated temple worship, with an emphasis on the centralization of the service (chapter 12). The design of the book is clearly theological, not merely cultic. 'There is probably no other book in the Old Testament of which this could be said so clearly.'[30]

[28] Friedman, *Bible*, 60.
[29] Childs, *Introduction*, 206.
[30] Rendtorff, *Old Testament*, 155.

It lays out a view of Israel's faith in one God, and of the relationship of God to the people.

When Josiah heard a reading of this book of the Law found in the Temple he tore his clothes in repentance. He perceived the covenant enjoined in this book of the law to have been broken. The central sanctuary was in serious disarray. As king of the chosen nation, he was responsible for bringing the people into right relationship with God. The event of finding *the book of Torah* (2 Kings 22.8)[31] in the temple was the beginning of a new day for temple religion in Judah, and for the reading of the law in the hearing of the people. The majority opinion is that the book associated with Josiah's reform was most likely Deuteronomy, in that the reforms that followed the discovery and reading follow very much the lines laid down in Deuteronomy.[32]

As indicated earlier, the book of Deuteronomy exerted a significant influence on the writing of Israel's story from the conquest of Canaan to the end of the monarchy (Joshua—2 Kings). This Deuteronomistic history, as it is called, has the theological imprint of Deuteronomy stamped at several junctures in the narrative. This is not to suggest that the writer, or school, responsible for Deuteronomy is the same one responsible for the Deuteronomistic history.[33] The personal, nominal identity of the writer, or the school, responsible for any of Deuteronomistic literature remains hidden. Not so the character, social context, and theological orientation. These we find within the literature itself, which in the end is quite enough.

The question with which we conclude this discussion of the writers of the Pentateuch focuses on the final combination of all the parts into the five rolls of the Law (Torah). Who was responsible for bringing the rich heritage of Moses up to date, and into its five-part written form for future generations? Again, an unequivocal answer is not forthcoming. Friedman suggests Ezra, the priestly scribe of the post-exilic Second Temple in Jerusalem, as the most likely candidate (Ezra 7.6).[34] Possible but not easily demonstrated. There is some evidence that Ezra brought *the book of the law of God* (Neh. 8.18) to Jerusalem, perhaps from exile in Babylonia. That he assembled the parts into a five-scroll Torah is not

[31] 'This expression otherwise appears only in the closing chapters of Deuteronomy (e.g. Deut. 30.10; 31.26)', so Rendtorff, *Old Testament*, 155.

[32] W. David Stacey, *Groundwork of Biblical Studies* (Minneapolis: Augsburg, 1979), 268.

[33] Cf. Friedman, *Bible*, 125–7, who posits Jeremiah as the most likely candidate for the composition of the Deuteronomistic history.

[34] Friedman, *Bible*, 223–6.

at all evident. Even though Ezra was viewed as a second Moses in Jewish tradition, an Aaronid priest who called the people together around the new altar and Temple, who read the Law of Yahweh to the people, there is nothing in the tradition that says he compiled the Pentateuch.

Writers of the biblical texts do show their hand, as it were, in their texts. And in doing so they allow us, readers, to discover the distinctive texture of their thought and life in relation to our own. The writers do not make meaning for us to ingest. They generate meaning in us by our meeting with them in the reading of their respective texts.

As illustrated from reading the Gospels

Whereas Moses, mediator of the Torah of Yahweh, occupied centre stage in the unfolding drama of Israel's story of redemption in the Old Testament, at the heart of the New Testament documents stands the figure of Jesus of Nazareth, Messiah of God. Coming from the post-Easter Church as they did, the writers of these documents[35] confess Jesus of Palestine variously as the suffering servant of the Lord (Acts 8.32), the Son of God (Mark 1.1), Lord (Rom. 10.9), Saviour (Phil. 3.20), New Adam (1 Cor. 15.22ff.), Son of David (Matt. 1.1; Rom. 1.3), resurrected Messiah whose Spirit resides in the community of believers (Rom. 8.1–9).

It should come as no surprise, therefore, that such reflective confession of faith in the person of Jesus of Nazareth produced a number of Gospels that tell the story of his transforming word and work.[36] We have no less than four of these 'gospel' (good news) books in the New Testament that tell the story of this one figure, Jesus: Matthew, Mark, Luke, and John. One Gospel writer is not trying to outdo the other in this foursome. Each of them has his own interests, insights, purposes and social situation in telling the story of the one Jesus of Nazareth.[37] Does this sound like an echo of four other sources (*J, E, P, D*) involved in producing the Pentateuch? There we had each

[35] Even the epistle of James, which otherwise makes no mention of Jesus, twice calls Jesus 'Lord ... Christ' (1:1) and 'glorious Lord ... Christ' (2.1).

[36] Many more gospels than the four of the New Testament came out during the first three centuries of the Church. Most of them are brought together in one volume, edited by Robert J. Miller, *The Complete Gospels: Annotated Scholars Version* (Sonoma CA: Polebridge Press, 1992).

[37] For a helpful synopsis of the character of each of the four Gospels see Christian E. Hauer and William A. Young, *An Introduction to the Bible: A Journey into Three Worlds* (fifth edition, Upper Saddle River NJ: Prentice Hall, 2001), 264–92.

of the four writing the story about Israel's God, and about God's earthly agent of deliverance and direction in Israel, Moses. There we found the first three (*J, E, P*) interwoven throughout the first four books of the Pentateuch. Here in the New Testament the four Gospel writers stand apart from each other in separate books. Each of the four evangelists, in his own way, draws on available tradition (including oral tradition and written sources) about Jesus and weaves it into a distinctive Gospel.[38] The result is a tension between the four presentations of the one Jesus. For example, John sets the clearing of the Temple at the beginning of Jesus' ministry, whereas the other three have it at the last week. Matthew has Jesus deliver his great sermon on a mountain but Luke places it on a plain. Luke has an abundance of material about Jesus that is not found in the others. In the first three Gospels Jesus asks God to take the cup of suffering from him, but in John Jesus unequivocally accepts the pain of the cross. In the first three a man named Simon of Cyrene carries Jesus' cross, but in John Jesus carries his own cross. Even where the Gospels give the same story their vocabulary and details in presentation vary.

Before long, some people in the early Church, upon feeling the tension between the four versions of the story of the one Jesus, sought to resolve the tension. One man in particular, Tatian in the second century, harmonized the various parts of the four into one consistent Gospel, called the Diatessaron (lit. 'through four'), for his church in Syria.[39] His effort availed little. The four separate Gospels prevailed in their individuality, and with their individuality also the *differences* between their presentations of Jesus of Nazareth.

The four Gospels may be further grouped into two: (1) Matthew, Mark and Luke, all three together called Synoptic (lit. 'seen together'), and (2) John, which is quite distinct from the other three. Because the Synoptic Gospels view the ministry of Jesus more or less in common with each other, their commonality implies a line of tradition from which they drew their information and insight. The obvious name given to the line is 'synoptic tradition'. By further implication, the Gospel of John is said to draw on a different line of tradition about Jesus, appropriately called the Johannine tradition. It is time now to

---

[38] Werner Georg Kümmel gives a comprehensive introduction to the Gospels in his *Introduction to the New Testament*, revised edition, trans. Howard Clark Kee (Nashville: Abingdon Press, 1975), 35–150; 188–247.
[39] See Ewert, *Tablets*, 165–6.

meet each of the four writers by reading examples from their respective texts and drawing some comparisons between them.

A word of counsel might be in order at this point. This brief introduction to the writers of the Gospels is still a long way from a fully-fledged conversation[40] with them in their writings. That will come in due course.

First, the Synoptic Gospels. It is now generally held that Mark is the earliest of the synoptic evangelists,[41] written somewhere between 65 and 70 CE, and that Matthew and Luke independently used Mark as a primary source for their own rendition of the story of Jesus. Both Matthew and Luke follow Mark's general order of events, often use Mark's words, sometimes use their own words, add some details of their own, and sometimes skip some of Mark's details or alter them in some way. Table 6.1 illustrates the phenomenon in the threefold rendition of the transfiguration of Jesus on a mountain. Compare the vocabulary and details in each of the three and get to know each one from their way of telling the story.

To help facilitate the reading of this passage, and others like it in the Synoptic Gospels, here are a few guideposts:

1. The vocabulary and word order in the narrative parts are sometimes exactly the same from one Gospel to the other. For example, Mark has the line, *And he was transfigured before them.* Matthew has exactly the same words and word order.

2. One writer may add or delete a word or phrase found in Mark's wording. For example, Mark writes, *and led them up a high mountain apart, by themselves.* Matthew omits the redundant word, 'apart'. Luke changes the wording more radically: *and went up on the mountain to pray.*

3. One writer will include a phrase here and there in accordance with the concerns in his mind and heart, as in the following examples. Matthew says Jesus' *face shone like the sun.* Neither Mark nor Luke has that particular phrase. From other indicators in this Gospel we see that Matthew is concerned to show Jesus as a new Moses whose face shone when he approached the Lord on the mountain. Here in Matthew the face of Jesus shone when he

---

[40] See above, p. 89.

[41] A minority still hold that Matthew was written before Mark, exemplified especially in the work of William R. Farmer, *The Synoptic Problem: A Critical Analysis* (Dillsboro, NC: Western North Carolina Press, 1976).

Table 6.1

Matthew 17.1–5	Mark 9.2–7	Luke 9.28–35
Six days later, Jesus took with him Peter and James and his brother John and led them up a high mountain, by themselves. 2 And he was transfigured before them, and his face shone like the sun, and his clothes became dazzling white. 3 Suddenly there appeared to them Moses and Elijah, talking with him.	Six days later, Jesus took with him Peter and James and John, and led them up a high mountain apart, by themselves. And he was transfigured before them, 3 and his clothes became dazzling white, such as no one on earth could bleach them. 4 And there appeared to them Elijah with Moses, who were talking with Jesus.	Now about eight days after these sayings Jesus took with him Peter and John and James, and went up on the mountain to pray. 29 And while he was praying, the appearance of his face changed, and his clothes became dazzling white. 30 Suddenly they saw two men, Moses and Elijah, talking to him. 31 They appeared in glory and were speaking of his departure, which he was about to accomplish at Jerusalem. 32 Now Peter and his companions were weighed down with sleep; but since they had stayed awake, they saw his glory and the two men who stood with him. 33 Just as they were leaving him, Peter said to Jesus,
4 Then Peter said to Jesus, 'Lord, it is good for us to be here; if you wish, I will make three dwellings here, one for you, one for Moses, and one for Elijah.' 5 While he was still speaking, suddenly a bright cloud overshadowed them, and from the cloud a voice said, 'This is my Son, the Beloved; with him I am well pleased; listen to him!'	5 Then Peter said to Jesus, 'Rabbi, it is good for us to be here; let us make three dwellings, one for you, one for Moses, and one for Elijah.' 6 He did not know what to say, for they were terrified. 7 Then a cloud overshadowed them, and a from the cloud there came voice, 'This is my Son, the Beloved; listen to him!'	'Master, it is good for us to be here; let us make three dwellings, one for you, one for Moses, and one for Elijah' – not knowing what he said. 34 While he was saying this, a cloud came and overshadowed them; and they were terrified as they entered the cloud. 35 Then from the cloud came a voice that said, 'This is my Son, my Chosen; listen to him!'

approached the Lord on the new mountain. In Luke the face of Jesus changed *while he was praying*. Luke repeatedly shows Jesus in a praying mode when the other writers do not, as here.

4. Sometimes a particular text will prompt a writer to add a sizeable portion to the narrative to accent his interest and intention. In this section of the Synoptic Gospels, seen in Table 6.1, Luke adds this long statement not found in the other two: *[Elijah and Moses] appeared in glory and were speaking of his departure, which he was about to accomplish at Jerusalem. 32 Now Peter and his companions were weighed down with sleep; but since they had stayed awake, they saw his glory and the two men who stood with him*. By citing the 'glory' in the persons of the two notable figures from the sacred history and the 'glory' that appeared on Jesus, Luke demonstrates continuity between Jesus and the story of Israel past. Further, he adds that Peter and his companions saw the 'glory' of Jesus as also the 'glory' of the two men from the past. Peter and company will be able to carry the 'glory' of God's salvation forward into the Church, as we see in the book of Acts written by this same hand.

Another fascinating aspect of the Synoptic Gospels comes to the fore where Matthew and Luke share material that does not appear anywhere in Mark. The shared texts are mostly sayings without much narrative. For that reason, perhaps, the shared texts appear at different places in the structure of each of the two Gospels of Matthew and Luke. This observation of parallel sayings in Matthew and Luke has led to the conclusion that these two writers took over text material from a document, since lost, and incorporated the texts independently of each other. The lost document is commonly called Q, from the German word *Quelle* meaning 'source'. Table 6.2 has a sampling of Q from Matthew and Luke.[42]

Without going into detail on each saying, suffice it to point out that Luke manifests a strong social conscience throughout his Gospel.[43] Not surprisingly he pleads the cause of the poor and the hungry in his rendition of the beatitudes. In Luke blessing comes to *you who are poor for yours is the kingdom of God*. In Matthew it comes to the *poor in spirit*

[42] For a concise essay on the debate about Q in the Sermon on the Mount (Matthew) and the Sermon on the Plain (Luke) in recent scholarship see Hans Dieter Betz, 'The Sermon on the Mount and Q', in *Gospel Origins and Christian Beginnings: In Honor of James M. Robinson* (Sonoma CA: Polebridge Press, 1990), 19–34.

[43] As also in Acts; see e.g. Robert M. Grant, *A Historical Introduction to the New Testament* (New York: Harper & Row, 1963), 138–47, and Hauer and Young, *Introduction*, 277–8.

Table 6.2

Matthew 5.3–12	Luke 6.20–23
Blessed are the poor in spirit, for theirs is the kingdom of heaven.	Blessed are you who are poor, for yours is the kingdom of God.
4 Blessed are those who mourn, for they will be comforted.	
5 Blessed are the meek, for they will inherit the earth.	Blessed are you who weep now, for you will laugh.
6 Blessed are those who hunger and thirst for righteousness, for they will be filled.	21 Blessed are you who are hungry now, for you will be filled.
7 Blessed are the merciful, for they will receive mercy.	22 Blessed are you when people hate you, and when they exclude you, revile you, and defame you on account of the Son of Man.
8 Blessed are the pure in heart, for they will see God.	
9 Blessed are the peacemakers, for they will be called children of God.	
	23 Rejoice in that day and leap for joy, for surely your reward is great in heaven; for that is what their ancestors did to the prophets.
10 Blessed are those who are persecuted for righteousness' sake, for theirs is the kingdom of heaven.	
11 Blessed are you when people revile you and persecute you and utter all kinds of evil against you falsely on my account.	
12 Rejoice and be glad, for your reward is great in heaven, for in the same way they persecuted the prophets who were before you.	
Matthew 6.9–13	**Luke 11.2–4**
Our Father in heaven, hallowed be your name. 10 Your kingdom come. Your will be done, on earth as it is in heaven. 11 Give us this day our daily bread. 12 And forgive us our debts, as we also have forgiven our debtors. 13 And do not bring us to the time of trial, but rescue us from the evil one.	Father, hallowed be your name. Your kingdom come. 3 Give us each day our daily bread. 4 And forgive us our sins, for we ourselves forgive everyone indebted to us. And do not bring us to the time of trial.

for theirs is the kingdom of God. The blessing in Luke belongs to those who are *hungry now for you will be filled,* whereas in Matthew blessing is afforded *those who hunger and thirst for righteousness for they will be filled.* Righteousness is thematic in Matthew as compared to Luke.

Behind both sets of sayings in Matthew and Luke lies the same Q source,[44] but each of the two Gospel writers incorporates the sayings into his Gospel as befits his vision of the Church and the world, and of God's new work in both spheres through the Spirit of Jesus the Christ.

Besides apparent reliance on specific traditions in common, each of the writers of the Synoptic Gospels had material exclusive to his own gospel story. Matthew's special material is spread throughout his Gospel, while Luke's special material comes together in two places in particular: in the introduction (chapters 1 to 2) and in the 'journey narrative' (chapters 9 to 18).[45]

A good instrument for discovering the features of these three fascinating, synoptic pictures of Jesus of Nazareth is generally called 'Gospel parallels', available through several publishers. Each section from the three is set out in parallel columns for comparative study, exemplified in Tables 6.1 and 6.2 above. Where one writer has special material found only in his Gospel, then only one column will appear under the respective name.

Figure 6.2 illustrates the suggested flow of material from Jesus through the post-Easter proclamation and tradition about Jesus into the written documents. Let it be understood, however, that the writers did not merely collect traditional material and piece it together in a Gospel. They were writers with purpose and concern. Their distinctive vision and inspiration comes through in the texture of their texts.

Second, the Gospel of John. If we were to put the Fourth Gospel into Figure 6.2 it would sit slightly below the line of Matthew and Luke, being written perhaps some time between 85 and 95 CE. John would have its own line flowing from the 'Traditions of Jesus in the Churches', with a dotted line running from the other three Gospels to indicate John's awareness of their existence in the churches.

The Gospel of John has attracted attention from scholars and church people of all descriptions through the centuries to the present time.[46]

---

[44] Some would argue for a $Q^{Matt.}$ and a Q^{Luke} to account for the difference between the Sermon on the Mount and the Sermon on the Plain, although the majority of scholars see only one Q behind both Matthew's Sermon and Luke's, Luke's being the closest to the Q version; see Betz, 'Sermon ... Q': 19–20, 32–4.

[45] Other Lukan material is fitted into Mark's schema, e.g. the post-resurrection narrative of 24.12–53; see Kümmel, *Introduction*, 130–47.

[46] Out of the long list of monographs on the Fourth Gospel I select three from this century, different yet complementary works, for further consideration beyond this brief meeting with the author's text. C. H. Dodd, *The Interpretation of the Fourth Gospel* (Cambridge: Cambridge University Press, 1953); David Rensberger, *Johannine Faith and Liberating Community* (Philadelphia: Westminster John Knox Press, 1988); Raymond E. Brown, *The Community of the Beloved Disciple* (New York: Paulist Press, 1979).

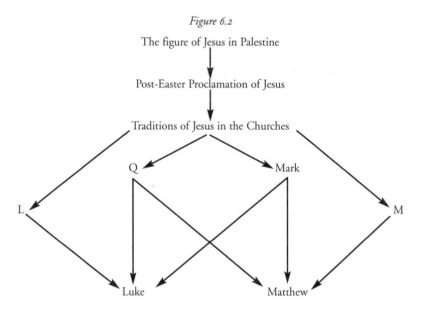

Figure 6.2

The figure of Jesus in Palestine

Post-Easter Proclamation of Jesus

Traditions of Jesus in the Churches

Q → Mark

L

M

Luke

Matthew

Its portrait of Jesus is sculpted distinctively for people faced with all kinds of alternate religions and faith communities in the Greco-Roman world. It was written *so that you may come to believe that Jesus is the Messiah, the Son of God, and that through believing you may have life in his name* (John 20.31). The Fourth Gospel is more Hellenistic (Greek-oriented) than any of the other three. It opens with a highly sophisticated prologue about the Word (*logos*) of God that created the world and entered it in the human form of Jesus (John 1.1–18). The large block of material (chapters 2 to 12) that follows the introduction consists of 'signs' and their significance. Following the block of 'signs' texts is the passion discourses (13 to 17) and the passion narrative (18 to 20).

The acts of Jesus, from the changing of water into wine to the raising of Lazarus from the dead, are all called 'signs' (*semeia*) of the higher reality of spirit present in the world of flesh. The signs in Jesus' ministry in John are not themselves the higher reality. They embody it and point to it, but do not constitute it totally in themselves. The ultimate sign that incorporates all the other signs in itself is the crucifixion of Jesus on behalf of the world of humankind.[47] Out of that sign of the self-giving Messiah, lifted up in crucifixion, flows the higher reality from the other world of the true God to this world of mortal humankind (John 3.14; 8.28; 12.32–4; 19.30–4).

Woven into the tapestry of the Gospel of John is an abundance of symbolic nuance and ironic gesture: Nicodemus the Israelite teacher comes to Jesus *by night* (3.1–15), while a woman of Samaria comes to Jesus *at noon* (4.4–29). The former should know the way to God but does not. The latter should be blind to the light of life in Jesus but sees it and calls others to come to it. Peter should be the ideal apostle, but an anonymous disciple *whom Jesus loved* (13.23) is the ideal disciple and apostle instead. Similar kinds of literary subtleties can be traced throughout this Fourth Gospel.[48] In short, when you read the Gospel of John you meet a very different writer from those of the other three Gospels.

Conclusion

The key point coming out of all these illustrations, from the writing/reading of the Pentateuch and from the writing/reading of the four Gospels, is that you meet the writers primarily from reading their own work. The writer is not someone we reconstruct from tradition or from modern critical investigation. The biblical writers are always making themselves known to us through *our* repeated, reverent, attentive, reflective reading of *their* writing. Knowing their names might be interesting to us, but it is not crucial to our understanding of the book.

The proper names given to the four Gospel writers (Matthew, Mark, Luke, John), for example, are not revealed by the writers themselves in their own writings. The nominal identity of the writers comes out of the later tradition, when it was deemed important to know who were the real writers of sacred books being used in the life of the orthodox communities. With the raising of this topic about 'which books', we are led right away into the next chapter.

---

[47] See further in Dodd, *Interpretation*, 383–9.
[48] See further in Paul Duke, *Irony in the Fourth Gospel* (Atlanta: John Knox Press, 1985), 7–156; and R. Alan Culpepper, *Anatomy of the Fourth Gospel* (Philadelphia: Fortress Press, 1983), 101–202.

Objective

To understand and appreciate the concept of 'canon' as this term was
applied to the collections of books of the Bible in their extant form.

Lead Questions

1. What might lead to the Bible being viewed superstitiously as a book
   of magic?
2. Explain how the term 'canon' was used before it was applied to the
   list of authoritative books for believing communities, and define the
   term 'canon' as it came to be applied to the books of the Bible.
3. What does the 'extant form' of a book imply?
4. To what extent were the pre-canonical forms authoritative for the
   believing communities?
5. In what sense is the 'canon' both closed and open?
6. What are the names in order of the Hebrew Bible, the Protestant
   Christian Bible, and the Catholic Christian Bible?
7. What are the books on Eusebius' list, and how are they categorized?
8. What does the canonical shape of a book say about the faith of the
   believing community that accepted the book as canonical? Use
   Isaiah and John to illustrate.
9. How might the 'canon' contribute in some measure to a misuse of the
   text of the canonical books? Use the compositions of Mozart to illustrate.
10. What is the earliest evidence of a Jewish 'canon' of Scripture? When
    and where was the question of the Hebrew 'canon' settled?
11. What is considered the earliest collection of New Testament
    documents? What might have prompted their collection?
12. Who was the first to list New Testament documents? Why was he
    considered a heretic? What documents were on his list?
13. Which were the last books of the New Testament 'canon' to be
    accepted by the Christian communities?
14. Which bishop first listed the books of the New Testament as we have
    it today? When did he do that? Which council 'ratified' the list,
    (with some reordering)?
15. How far did the Reformers go in reopening the question of 'canon'?
    What is 'canon within the canon'?

7

These Books as a Rule

The canonical process created a flexible framework.
(Brevard S. Childs)

Protestant Christian Bibles have sixty-six books, thirty-nine in the Old Testament[1] and twenty-seven in the New Testament. Catholic Christian Bibles have forty-six in the Old Testament[2] for a total of seventy-three. Why this many in each case, not more or less? And why these books in a particular order? We could give a very short and simple answer to both questions: God willed it that way! For many people of faith that short answer is sufficient. In my experience, however, most people who ask these kinds of questions of us find such axiomatic replies not enough, nor should they be enough.

The question of which books were destined to become sacred Scripture, and therefore authoritative for the believing communities that adopted them, is not easily accessible even after intensive research and endless debates on the subject. Still, after centuries of probing the subject this way and that,[3] scholars have left us a legacy from their labours, the benefit of which helps answer our two questions: Why this number of books? Why these in a particular order?

The multi-volume Bible is not a book of magic. Owning it does not protect us from misfortune nor guarantee us a happy life. Inspired writers in the ancient communities of faith produced the books one by one out of a long tradition of life under God, not thinking at the time of writing that their books would one day be revered as Scripture, much less part of a book of magic. They produced their works to be read and studied, not merely to be placed on a coffee table, or even on

---

[1] Based on the Hebrew Bible.

[2] Based on the Latin Vulgate and the Greek Septuagint (translation of the Old Testament carried out in Egypt). The additional books in the Catholic Bibles are 'known to Catholics as "deuterocanonical" and are regarded as an integral part of the canon of the Old Testament;' from the 'Introduction' to *The Holy Bible: Revised Standard Version Containing the Old and New Testaments, Catholic Edition* (London: Thomas Nelson & Sons, 1966), vi.

[3] See especially the review of the literature in Brevard S. Childs, *Introduction to the Old Testament as Scripture* (Philadelphia: Fortress Press, 1979), 46–83; and his *The New Testament as Canon: An Introduction* (Philadelphia: Fortress Press, 1985), 3–33.

a communion table. Just as the Bible is not a magical relic, neither did the collection of books magically appear on the religious scene in a single flash.

After many years of extensive use in the various communities of faith each of the books in its final form proved itself to be a faithful guide, along with others, for the life and thought of successive faith communities. The books having proved themselves thus were catalogued as authoritative Scripture, the Word of God. The list of books became an abiding guide for generation after generation of Christian faith communities. The books on the list, in addition to their use as a guide for living faithfully, formed the basis for doctrine and church order.

The official act of 'listing' the authoritative books is known as their *canonization*, and the 'list' itself the *canon* of Scripture. The subject of the canon of Scripture evokes much more than historical interest in how a 'list' came about. The notion of a canon has profound theological significance as well. It tells us about the life and thought of a particular people, and about the transmission of that life and thought to successive generations of the faithful, including our own generation.

Canon

A few days ago I heard an announcer on radio use the word 'canon' in connection with the renowned eighteenth-century composer, Mozart. The announcer spoke of a 'Mozart canon' by which he meant a musical form and compositional technique that follows the principle of imitation. An initial melody is imitated at a particular interval. Although related to the original sense of 'canon', this musical use is not the original meaning, any more than the current use of 'canon' in connection with the Bible is original.

Tracking the term

Before the word found its way into English, it lived in Greek as *kanôn*; before that in the Semitic languages (Assyrian *qanû;* Ugaritic *qn;* Hebrew *qaneh*); and before that in Sumarian.[4] In its earliest known use the word meant a straight *reed* that grows by a river (e.g. Job 40.21) that one could use as a ruler for drawing straight lines. Gradually its

---

[4] R. K. Harrison, *Introduction to the Old Testament* (Grand Rapids: Eerdmans, 1969), 260.

meaning took on figurative notions. In Greek *kanôn* came to mean 'anything straight and upright' such as 'a rule, standard, paradigm, model, boundary, chronological table and tax assessment'.[5] Some early church leaders used *kanôn* to refer to Church doctrines, an exemplary life, a table of contents and the like.

There is no direct evidence for the application of the Greek word *kanôn* to the list of books of the Bible before the latter part of the fourth century CE. Bishop Athanasius used the word in one of his Easter letters (*c.* 367) to his flock to mean a list of books of the Church deemed worthy for keeping the congregations on the right track. The twenty-seven that Athanasius listed for the New Testament are precisely the twenty-seven of the New Testament today. Not only was this the first time the word *kanôn* was applied to a list of authoritative books for the Church, but also the first time for these twenty-seven to appear together on a list.

Working definition

More on the story of the New Testament canon shortly. At this point we do well to consider the role the canon of Scripture has played and still plays in the life of the people of God.

The canon can mean different things to different people at different times. To facilitate our discussion in this part of the chapter let me offer a working definition of the canon of the Christian Scriptures, drawn from the faith tradition on the one hand, and from the scholarly community on the other: *The Christian canon of Scriptures is an official list of books in their extant form and particular order, comprising the Old and New Testaments, used to define the thought, life, and doctrine of the community of faith in Jesus Christ.*[6]

Like all definitions, this one leaves plenty of room for expansion and inquiry. The cluster of questions it raises could take us far beyond the scope of this chapter. Some of the more salient ones can be treated here briefly: Why is the extant form of a listed book the canonical form? Is the list, produced at a particular time, for example, 367 CE, closed or open? What does the shape and order of the books on the list say about the faith and life of the community that adopted the list? Does the canonization of books affect the way people read them? We will address

---

[5] Harrison, *Introduction,* 260.
[6] The essence of this definition applies also to the Hebrew Bible of the Jewish people, who did not adopt the list of twenty-seven distinctively Christian books.

these four questions in order briefly before proceeding to a synopsis of the drama that led to the current Jewish and Christian canons.

Four questions about canon

1. *Why is the extant form the canonical form?* The extant form is simply the form that survived, not the earlier versions of it, or the sources incorporated into the particular book. We have seen already from our review of the composition of the Pentateuch and the four Gospels that earlier writings are woven into the shape of the extant books. When we read the first four extant books of the Pentateuch we detect the earlier *J*, *E*, and *P* woven into the final form of Genesis, Exodus, Leviticus and Numbers. In the Synoptic Gospels we discerned *Q* and *M* in Matthew and *Q* and *L* in Luke. These earlier writings were used to foster faith and life in the communities that produced them, otherwise they would not have found their way into the surviving documents. Could these earlier compositions not also be viewed as 'canonical' in their own right? Can we not study them as reflections of the life of faith and understanding they represent, even though they did not survive independently? I think the answer is yes.

In their own right, the earlier documents that did not survive independently were 'canonical'. The community that produced them recognized their value as instruments of divine guidance. In that sense they were canonical. We can study these incorporated writings on their own terms, and thus appreciate the community's experience of God's action in the world at that particular time and place and circumstance prior to the composition of the extant form.

However, for the later Christian communities, as for Jewish communities, the final form is the canonical form. We study the final form as well, the form that survived as a book in our Bible, the form that became canonical. Its shape and purpose over all reflects the life and thought of the community that produced it and used it and recognized it as the Word of God.

2. *Is the list (canon) of books closed or open?* This is a sticky question. It will be noted in Table 7.1, for example, that the number and/or arrangement of books in the list for the Old Testament is not the same from one stream of the tradition to the other. In the case of the New Testament, Table 7.2, the list from the early part of the fourth century is not the same as the list at the end of the same century. As later discussion will illustrate, the lists currently in use for both testaments

developed from earlier lists of books for instruction and worship.[7] The point here is that the canons of both Old and New Testaments were open for centuries before circumstances and councils moved to bring closure to the listing of books that could be read as Scripture. More on the circumstances and councils in a moment.

Closing the canon was expedient for the Church's ongoing life in the world. The perpetual addition of books composed out of new experience and insight from various parts of the Church could only lead to confusion and lack of cohesion in the community of faith. One might say in this respect, as Walter Brueggemann does, that the canon has served as a model for biblical education in the life of the Church.[8] Its diversity was matched and ameliorated by its unity of faith, just as the diversity in the Church's life in the world revolved around a coherent centre of faith in the revelation of the Redeemer-God in the person of Jesus Christ.

The creeds and confessions that welded the churches together rested on a vision of a closed canon. Creeds and confessions of faith are open, as also interpretation of the various parts of the canon is open. Interpretation is subject to revision. The canon is not. As an educational model the canon teaches the divine virtue of oneness in spirit while acknowledging the different experiences and insights from one writer to another within the canon. That quality of unity-in-diversity emanates from the character of the canon. In the Old Testament, Deuteronomy and Exodus, while different in outlook, intention, and focus regarding the law of the Lord, stand together in one household of faith in the promise-keeping God, Yahweh. In the New Testament, the letters of Paul and the epistle of James, although quite different in perspective, purpose, and rhetoric regarding faith and works, stand together in one household of faith in the God who saves us from sin and death through Jesus Christ the Lord.

In short, the canon is both closed and open: closed in that the list of books is not subject to addition or deletion any more; open in that the texts in the various books in the canon are subject to further

---

[7] See additional canons in the appendices in Arthur G. Patzia, *The Making of the New Testament: Origin, Collection, Text and Canon* (Downers Grove: InterVarsity Press, 1995), 151–6.

[8] Walter Brueggemann, *The Creative Word: Canon as a Model for Biblical Education* (Philadelphia: Fortress Press, 1982), 3f. 'Attention to the process and shape of canon may tell us something about education in ancient Israel. In addition, it may provide clues for our own educational task, which I suggest is aiding communities and their members in the ongoing task of canon construction and canon criticism.'

Table 7.1 The Canon of the Old Testament

HEBREW BIBLE (24 books)	ENGLISH BIBLE Protestant (39 books)	ENGLISH BIBLE Catholic (46 books)
Torah (5 books)	**Law** (5 books)	**Law** (5 books)
Genesis	Genesis	Genesis
Exodus	Exodus	Exodus
Leviticus	Leviticus	Leviticus
Numbers	Numbers	Numbers
Deuteronomy	Deuteronomy	Deuteronomy
Prophets (8 books)	**History** (12 books)	**History** (14 books)
Former Prophets	Joshua	Josue (*Joshua, Judges, Ruth*)
Joshua	Judges	1 Kings (1 Samuel)
Judges	Ruth	2 Kings (2 Samuel)
Samuel (1 book)	1 Samuel	3 Kings (1 Kings)
Kings (1 book)	2 Samuel	4 Kings (2 Kings)
	1 Kings	1 Paralipomenon (1 Chron.)
Latter Prophets	2 Kings	2 Paralipomenon (2 Chron.)
Isaiah	1 Chronicles	Esdras-Nehemiah (Ezra, Neh.)
Jeremiah	2 Chronicles	Tobias (Tobit)
Ezekiel	Ezra	Judith
The Twelve (treated as 1)	Nehemiah	Esther
Hosea	Esther	
Joel		**Poetry and Wisdom** (7 books)
Amos	**Poetry** (5 books)	Job
Obediah	Job	Psalms
Jonah	Psalms	Proverbs
Micah	Proverbs	Ecclesiastes
Nahum	Ecclesiastes	Canticle of Canticles
Habakkuk	Song of Songs	Wisdom of Solomon
Zephaniah		Ecclesiasticus (Sirach)
Haggai	**Major Prophets** (5 books)	
Zecharia	Isaiah	**Prophets** (20 Books)
Malachi	Jeremiah	Isaias (Isaiah)
	Lamentations	Jeremias (Jeremiah)
Writings (11 books)	Ezekiel	Lamentations
'Emeth (Truth) (3 books)	Daniel	Baruch
Psalms		Ezechiel (Ezekiel)
Proverbs	**Minor Prophets** (12 books)	Daniel
Job	Hosea	Osee (Hosea)
Megilloth (Scrolls) (5)	Joel	Joel
Song of Songs	Amos	Amos
Ruth	Obediah	Abdias (Obediah)
Lamentations	Jonah	Jonas (Jonah)
Ecclesiastes	Micah	Micheas (Micah)
Esther	Nahum	Nahum
Daniel	Habakkuk	Habacuc (Habakkuk)
Ezra-Nehemiah	Zephaniah	Sophonias (Zephaniah)
Chronicles (1 book)	Haggai	Aggeus (Haggai)
	Zecharia	Zecharias (Zechariah)
	Malachi	Malachias (Malachi)
		1 Machabees (1 Maccabees)
		2 Machabees (2 Maccabees)

Table 7.2 Canon of the New Testament – Fourth Century

EUSEBIUS (323 CE)	ATHANASIUS (367 CE)	COUNCIL OF CARTHAGE (397 CE)
Acknowledged by all Gospels (Matt. Mark, Luke, John) Acts Paul (14 with Hebrews?) 1 John 1 Peter (Revelation?) **Disputed by some** James Jude 2 Peter 2 John 3 John **Rejected by all** Shepard of Hermas Didache Barnabas Acts of Paul Apocalypse of Peter	Gospels (4) Acts **Catholic Epistles** James 1 Peter 2 Peter 1 John 2 John 3 John Jude **Paul's Epistles** (14 including Hebrews) Revelation	Gospels (4) Acts **Paul's Epistles** (13 excluding Hebrews) Hebrews 1 Peter 2 Peter 1 John 2 John 3 John James Jude Revelation

interpretation in light of new information, new situations in life, and new understanding.

3. *What does the canonical shape of the books, and their arrangement on the list, say about the faith and life of the community that put the books on the list?* We may use the book of Isaiah from the Old Testament and John from the New Testament to illustrate how the canonical shape of a book tells something of the life of the community that adopted it thus. It is generally accepted that the extant scroll (or book) of Isaiah has three clearly identifiable parts, referred to as First (1—39), Second (40—55) and Third Isaiah (56—66). First Isaiah contains the oracles and historical context of the eighth-century prophet, Isaiah of Jerusalem. Second and Third Isaiah contain the oracles of fifth-century exilic prophets without historical context (apart from an oblique reference to Emperor Cyrus (44.28—45.1)). That is, the theological

message of Second and Third Isaiah is placed within the canonical context of First Isaiah.

First Isaiah relates a vision of a holy God and an unclean people (chapter 6) who are subject to the judgement of God. Second Isaiah holds out forgiveness and healing to repentant Israel through redemptive suffering for sin (e.g. 53.1ff.).[9] The city of Jerusalem in First Isaiah gives way in Third Isaiah to a new Jerusalem within a new heaven and a new earth, greater than the *former things* of First Isaiah.[10] The significance of collecting the oracles of Isaiah of Jerusalem and joining them together with the oracles of the later prophets of the exile (or post-exile) into the present canonical form is that the messages from all of them apply to Israel for all time.

The impending judgement of God in First Isaiah is balanced with the good news of forgiveness and mercy coming from the same God to exiled Israel when the people turn from their sinful ways. The canonical shape of Isaiah presents the theme of promise and fulfilment, sin and repentance, judgement and forgiveness. Literary and historical tensions remain in the canonical form, but the multifaceted theme exists by uniting the three in one, not in their independence from each other.[11]

The Gospel of John is not as diverse as Isaiah. Yet this book too has three rather distinct parts: the prologue (1.1–18), the main body consisting of the signs narrative-discourse (1.19—12.50), and the passion discourse-narrative (13.1—20.31), and an appendix (21.1–25). For our present purposes I want to focus particularly on the relation of the 'appendix' to the body of material in chapters 1 to 20.

First of all, the Gospel of John does not exist in any manuscript tradition apart from chapter 21, so this chapter must have been attached to the rest of the Gospel at a very early stage. Yet clearly this last chapter 21 is an addition to the argument of the first twenty chapters, which comes to an apt conclusion after the resurrection appearances in the statement of purpose: *Now Jesus did many other signs in the presence of his disciples, which are not written in this book. But these are written so*

---

[9] On the problems associated with the servant songs in Second Isaiah see Childs, *Introduction*, 334–6.

[10] The phrase, 'former things', appearing only in Second and Third Isaiah, probably points to the prophecy of First Isaiah, so Childs, *Introduction*, 328–30. See also James M. Efird, *The Old Testament Writings: History, Literature, and Interpretation* (Atlanta: John Knox Press, 1982), 184–9.

[11] See Childs, *Introduction*, 325–36. Studies currently going forward in Isaiah are many. The view represented here is only one, dependent largely on Childs' research and insight.

*that you may come to believe that Jesus is the Messiah, the Son of God, and
that through believing you may have life in his name* (20.30–31).

Curiously enough, in chapters 1 to 20 Peter does not fare nearly as
well as the anonymous disciple whom Jesus loved. In the end Peter
denies Jesus outright three times. Nor does he shed tears of repentance
in this Gospel when he hears the cock crowing after the third denial
(18.27; cf. Matt. 26.74 par.). When the same two disciples in chapter 20
run to see the empty tomb the Beloved Disciple outruns Peter and
believes upon seeing the empty tomb (20.8). Nothing is said of Peter's
faith when he saw the tomb empty. Chapter 21 picks up the problem of
Peter's unresolved denial from chapters 1 to 20, and attempts to resolve
the breach between him and Jesus. Jesus meets Peter on the beach, has
breakfast with him and the others – following their miraculous catch of
fish – and tests Peter's love for him (21.15–17). Peter passes the test, not
with a perfect score, but passes nonetheless. He is absolved of his sin of
denial from the earlier chapters, and is shown to be the Christian
witness and martyr that the tradition says he was (21.19).

Without chapter 21 the reader of the Fourth Gospel is left with the
rather negative impression that Peter's discipleship and apostleship were
at best second rate and at worst false, as compared to the completely
unsullied character of the Beloved Disciple. Chapter 21 vindicates Peter,
presents him forgiven and commissioned as pastor *along with* the more
trustworthy Beloved Disciple. In a nutshell, chapter 21 of John holds
out forgiveness to one so foolhardy and guilty as Peter, and at the same
time demonstrates the unity of calling and mission between the
Johannine and Petrine branches of the Church. Without the last
chapter of the Fourth Gospel the reader would be left wondering about
the trustworthiness of this Christ-denying Peter, and about the Church
that developed under his influence.

The canonical shape of the Gospel of John retains the tension
between Peter who denies Jesus at the end of chapters 1 to 20 and Peter
who loves Jesus in chapter 21, and demonstrates at the same time the
overflowing grace of Jesus in welcoming both Peter and the Beloved
Disciple together into the forgiven community to serve in accordance
with the will of God (21.20–23). This is what we mean by the canonical
shape of the books on the list.

As for the overall arrangement of the books on the list(s), we begin
with the canon of the Hebrew Bible. As we have it now, the Hebrew
Bible (on which the Protestant Old Testament is based, Table 7.1)
consists of three parts arranged in order of importance: (1) the Torah

(instruction for life and thought, Law), (2) the Prophets, and (3) the Writings. The first and most important part for the Jewish community from its inception to the present time is the Torah. The Torah reveals the will of God for the people called to serve the Lord in freedom. Their way of life rests on their knowing and obeying the will of God expressed in the Torah. Without appropriation of its laws their life and world degenerate into chaos, resulting in the judgement of God on the nation. Obedience to Torah, on the other hand, results in the gracious blessing of God.

Opening with a book about origins (Genesis), the Torah invites probing questions about the universe and about our place in the scheme of world history, but announces all the while that a supreme Creator, Redeemer, Sustainer lives and moves in all aspects of existence. The remaining four books of the Torah (Exodus, Leviticus, Numbers, Deuteronomy) tell the story of deliverance from bondage and provide direction for an ordered life in the redeemed community. As such, therefore, the Torah is foundational to all other books in the canon and appears first on the list.

Following the Torah the former prophets (see Table 7.1) relate the story of Israel's efforts to live under the rule of God in their place in the world. Sometimes they measure up, but often they do not. The story in these historical-prophetic books warns against disobeying the will of God, and points the right way forward. The oracles of the latter prophets (Isaiah, Jeremiah, Ezekiel and The Twelve) generate the same effect.

The third group of books called the Writings (*kethubim*) is 'a miscellaneous collection of everything else in the Old Testament'.[12] Of all the books on this list, the book of Psalms has held a prominent place in the hearts of the people of God. The collection of these one hundred and fifty poems became the hymnbook of the restored community after exile. With just about equal authority to the Psalms, the books of Job and Proverbs addressed the intellectual and practical issues of life in the community and the world. The rest of the books in the third division of the Hebrew Bible were less important, judging by the frequency of quotation from them in the relevant sources in formative Judaism and early Christianity.

In sum, the order of the three-part canon of the Hebrew Bible teaches (1) that the gift of God's instruction (Torah) forms the

---

[12] Brueggemann, *Creative Word*, 9.

foundation of life and thought in the redeemed community, (2) that the voice of God has spoken and continues to speak through the prophets to direct the community in its ongoing life in the world, and (3) that sages and songsters and visionaries in the *kethubim* foster good thoughts and feelings and behaviour. The canon of the Hebrew Bible was (and is) the authoritative textbook from which the Israel of God could reach intellectual, moral and religious decisions beyond those addressed in the canon itself. In this sense the closed-and-open canon is *a model* for education in the faith community.

The shape of the Christian Old Testament is somewhat different from that of the Hebrew Bible. The Hebrew canon recognized the narrative writings (Joshua, Judges, Samuel and Kings) as Former Prophets, and the more oracular prophetic writings as the Latter Prophets. The two lists appear in sequence. The Christian canon of the Old Testament inserts the Poetical and Wisdom writings (Job, Psalms, Proverbs, Ecclesiastes, and Song of Songs) between the narrative writings (Former Prophets) and the more oracular Prophets. This Christian shape of the canon of the Old Testament seems to follow the pattern: origins (Pentateuch), story of the people (Historical Books), life and thought (Poetry and Wisdom), and vision for the future (Prophets). A similar pattern can be observed in the shape of the New Testament canon.

The New Testament of the Christian Church gives first place to the Gospels (see Table 7.2). Even though Paul's letters were the earliest compositions of the new Christ-community, they do not have pride of place in the canon of the New Testament. The Gospels, like the Torah of the Hebrew canon, constitute the foundation of the new faith community. They tell the story of the founder of the new movement, including a synopsis of his teaching. Each of the Gospels in its own way gives an account of how Jesus lived and died, and of what he expected from his disciples in their own living and dying in the world until the kingdom of God comes in its fullness.

But the Gospels about Jesus are not the end of the story. Acts gives an account of the community formed out of the Easter experience, of its mission and its mode of life in the name of Jesus. Acts may be compared to the role of the narrative writings in the Old Testament canon. Following Acts, the canonical position of the Letters of Paul (as compared to their chronological priority in the New Testament) extends the story of Acts into the heart and soul of the communities formed out of the Paul's Gentile world mission. Paul's letters could be considered the anti-type of the Wisdom and Poetry of the Old Testament, which kept the community in line with the will of God for life in the world.[13] The remaining books comprising the General Epistles and Revelation offers encouragement to the faithful, judgement on the wicked, and hope for the future. In this respect these books correspond more or less to the Prophets of the Old Testament. Their acceptance came slowly, and not without debate.[14]

In both canons, the Christian Old Testament and the New Testament, we find what may be called a canon within a canon. The idea is that some books are more beloved by the community, more read, and become in the process more authoritative than the others. That is true of the Torah and the Prophets in the Hebrew Bible and of the Gospels and the Letters of Paul in the New Testament.

4. *Does the canonical status of the books affect the way people read them?* The answer cuts both ways, it would seem. The positive effect the books had on the faith communities before they found their place in the canon was the impetus that led to their placement on the list. Once listed, then the books took on a special significance for all succeeding communities of faith by virtue of their presence in the canon. A book in the canon was no longer a single book with its own status and merit in a world of many religious books in circulation. A canonized book possesses a new quality of life that affected the way people read it for ever after.

The Bible as canon is not like a novel with a plot, or a dissertation with an argument. A reader of the Bible does not begin at the first line and follow a plot line, or a line of argument, from start to finish. Some people decide to read through the Bible in a year as a discipline, but they do not experience a coherent, non-repetitive body of literature as they read. When they have finished, they have read a collection of different books each with its own character, context and purpose. More often than not, the reading of the Bible right through in a given period, as though it were a single book, does little to bring the canonical word to life. The canonization of the books of the Bible was never intended to rob the books of their individual life. On the contrary, the books

---

[13] The parallel is far from perfect. Paul's letters are laced with prophetic insight, warning of judgement, etc.

[14] Luther, for example, considered James a 'right strawy epistle'; Calvin thought Revelation defied responsible interpretation. Hebrews, believed for a long time to be an epistle of Paul, continued to elicit questions about its place on the list.

were canonized as books, not dissolved into a collection of phrases or verses to make one big book.

When people read bits and pieces of the Bible, a verse here and there, a chapter here and there, a passage selected at random, they are not reading the Bible as canon, however much they think they are. Reading the Bible as canon takes seriously the right of each book to communicate its message by its own parameters and purpose. Reading the Bible as canon means reading the small parts of a book – sentences, paragraphs, favourite lines, etc. – as integral parts of the whole book to which they belong.

Returning to Mozart for a moment by way of illustration, how should one listen to his musical compositions? Would it do justice to the genius of the composer to listen to a few bars from a concerto, or to a few phrases from various arias of his operas? A composition of Mozart does not have 'too many notes', as the prudish director of the opera in Vienna said in the movie, *Amadeus*. Mozart's compositions have just as many notes as they require, neither more nor less. It would violate the Mozart canon to pluck a line from an opera, one from a symphony and another from a concerto and string them together into a pattern of our own. Yet the Church has done just that with the canon of Scripture. Just as a Mozart aria has integrity within itself and within the larger composition in which it appears, so too does an argument of Paul, a parable of Jesus, a Psalm of David or an oracle of Jeremiah have integrity within its composition.

Take a narrative parable in a Gospel, for example. A parable is a whole unit. Its meaning resides in the intertwining of the parts to make the whole parable, not in the disintegrated parts by themselves. And the parable as a whole lives in the context of the particular Gospel in which it appears.

What has led to this random reading of the Bible? There is probably no single, simple answer. In part, at least, I think the idea of the canon has contributed, although not intentionally, to this slipshod way of reading the books and their integrated parts. Because the many books of the Bible are on one official list, or bound together in one volume singularly called The Bible, people of faith feel justified in random reading. But random reading can become reckless reading and wrongful construction of meaning. One has only to listen to some TV preachers who pick and choose a verse from here and a verse from there to construct their own vision of reality, or their own program of 'the last days'. The canon does not give believers a license to plunder the texts for props in support of a preferred system of thought and behaviour.

Responsible interpretation demands that we take the character of the canon to heart. Its centre of gravity in one God who reconciles the world to the divine mind does not thereby render the individuality and integrity of each of the books null and void. Quite the opposite. The canon as canon teaches us that the Word of God continues to live when the texts are read with integrity intact, their own and ours.

The Story in Brief

As I have indicated earlier, both Israel and the Church had sources of authority guiding their way of thinking and living prior to the extant forms of the books in the canon. The laws in the Pentateuch existed in Israel in some form before the composition of the Pentateuch as we know it. Stories and oracles in oral or written form also circulated in the community of Israel before they found their way into the books that now make up our Bibles. Some of the later writings of the Old Testament appeal to these earlier sources as authoritative. Similarly, the tradition of Jesus existed in oral and (very probably) written form before any of the writings that make up the New Testament canon. And again the writings of the New Testament make reference to these earlier traditions as authoritative (e.g. 1 Cor. 11.23–5; 7.10; 9.14).

Our concern at this point is to observe briefly the steps by which the books of the Bible found their way there.

Old Testament

In the last chapter I inferred that someone, or a group, was responsible for bringing together the five books of Torah into one collection in the present form. While there is no direct evidence from the late fifth century BCE that the five books were listed and treated as canon, the evidence from the centuries following assumes the existence and authority of the collection. Their translation from Hebrew into Greek in the middle of the third century presupposes their authority.[15] That evidence is still indirect.

From Ben Sira to Jamnia

More concrete data comes from the second century BCE, from the pen of one Ben Sira. Ben Sira knows and uses all the passages having to do

---

[15] Childs, *Introduction*, 64.

with the prescriptions of the Law in all five books. His familiarity with all the prescriptions points to the canonical status of the five books of the Pentateuch.

The same Ben Sira of the second century knows another body of literature called the Prophets citing 'all the prophetic books in a canonical order (46.1—49.13) and even the title of the Book of the Twelve'.[16] Accordingly, it appears that a set of prophetic books had the stamp of authority on them by the beginning of the second century or earlier. The collection and canonization of the five rolls of the Law may have influenced the collection of the prophetic writings. Or the presence of the prophetic books in the communities may have prompted the canonization of the books of Torah. Be that as it may, Ben Sira speaks of a bipartite body of literature called the Law and the Prophets, which bear the stamp of authority on them and thus constitute a canon. Down to the time of writing the books of the New Testament the same two-part canon of the Law and the Prophets held the day (see Matt. 7.12; 11.13; Luke 16.16; cf. 24.44; Acts 13.15; Rom. 3.21). In Luke 24.44 we find the Psalms added to the Law and the Prophets as a third body of authoritative Scripture.

The third collection, the Writings, has less support from the second century BCE, although Ben Sira does add the phrase, 'and the remaining books', after his twofold category, Law and Prophets. It sounds more like a throwaway phrase than a marker for a canonized collection of books. Many such books were in circulation in the Jewish communities, including the Jewish community in the desert south east of Jerusalem at Khirbet Qumran near the Dead Sea, from the third century BCE onwards. A number of these books were translated into Greek and included with all the others in the Septuagint for the Greek-speaking Jewish community in Egypt. From the Septuagint – the Bible of the early Jewish Christian missionaries as well – these writings made their way into the early Christian canon of the Old Testament.

Coming from the same period of formative Judaism,[17] and reflecting the politics and religion of the times, is a fairly large body of literature called the Pseudepigrapha, literally 'false writings' (Table 7.3). That is, the books were written under an assumed name from the treasured tradition. One of the chief characteristics of many of these writings is

---

[16] Childs, *Introduction*, 64.

[17] I use the designation, 'formative Judaism', to indicate the period from post-Ezra to the establishment of the post-Temple school of the Rabbis at the turn of the first century CE.

apocalyptic, 'unveiling'. Apocalyptic paves a symbolic path out of the turmoil and suffering of the present. When the divine clock strikes, God will intervene through his agents to judge the wicked who inflict the injustice, and to bless those who remain faithful to the will of God. This apocalyptic genre, which begins in Ezekiel and Daniel, blossoms in many books of the Pseudepigrapha (and in the War Scroll of the Dead Sea Scrolls from the same period), and from there enters the writings of the New Testament as well.[18] But the Pseudepigrapha also contains testaments, prayers, poetry and oracles in addition to apocalyptic (Table 7.3). Valued as they were in Jewish life and thought of the time, these pseudepigraphal writings remained apart from any official list of authoritative books.

Numerous factors doubtless influenced (1) *the production* of this literature in the period of Second Temple of Judaism, and (2) *the limitation* of the books to those that provided succour and stability to the Jewish communities in Palestine and beyond. Not least among the factors was the Maccabean Revolt of the mid-second century BCE when a band of Jewish loyalist militants mounted an effective resistance against the domination of Hellenistic Syria. Greek forces under Antiochus IV of Syria threatened the cultural and religious identity of the Jewish people in Palestine. The literature of the time reflects the political, religious and cultural turmoil. The books produced out of that turmoil, and after it, spoke to the hearts of the many Jewish people affected by the onslaught of Greek and Roman domination in their lives. That was in the second century BCE.

Closure at Jamnia

Under Roman domination in the first century CE the descendants of those who suffered in the Maccabean period also suffered when the Roman legion under General Titus sacked the city of Jerusalem, pillaged and burned the holy Temple, and slaughtered a mass of people in the streets.[19] The only Jewish leaders to survive the devastation in the city of Jerusalem were the Pharisees. Rome allowed them to relocate at Jamnia, a city on the southern coast of Palestine, and to make their educational (not cultic) headquarters there.

---

[18] Apocalyptic appears also in the Synoptic Gospels of the New Testament (Mark 13 par.), in the letters (e.g. 1 Thess. 5; 2 Thess. 2; 2 Pet. 3), and constitutes the whole of Revelation, otherwise called The Apocalypse of John.

[19] Josephus devoted Book V of his *Wars of the Jews* to the siege and destruction of Jerusalem.

Table 7.3 The Books of the Pseudepigrapha of formative Judaism

Apocalyptic Writings	*Wisdom and Philosophy*
1, 2, 3 Enoch	Ahiqar
Sibyline Oracles	Pseudo-Phocylides
Treatise of Shem	3 and 4 Maccabees
Apocryphon of Ezekiel	The Sentences of the Syriac Menander
Apocalypse of Zephaniah	Aristobulus
4 Ezra	Demetrius the Chronographer
Questions of Ezra	Aristeas the Exegete
Revelation of Ezra	
Apocalypse of Sedrach	*Poems, Odes, Psalms and Prayers*
2 and 3 Baruch	Additional Psalms of David (151–155)
Apocalypse of Abraham	Prayer of Manasseh
Apocalypse of Adam	Psalms of Solomon
Apocalypse of Elijah	Hellenistic Synagogue Prayers
Apocalypse of Daniel	Prayer of Joseph
	Prayer of Jacob
Testaments	Odes of Solomon
Testaments of the Twelve Patriarchs	Philo the Epic Poet
Testament of Job	Theodotus
Testament of the Three Patriarchs	
Testament (Assumption) of Moses	*Oracles*
Testament of Solomon	Orphica
Testament of Adam	
	Drama
Legends and Additions to Books	Ezekiel the Tragedian
Letter of Aristeas	
Jubilees	*History*
Martyrdom and Ascension of Isaiah	Eupolemus
Joseph and Asenath	Pseudo-Eupolemus
Life of Adam and Eve	Cleodemus Malchus
Pseudo-Philo	
Lives of the Prophets	*Romance*
Ladder of Jacob	Artapanus
4 Baruch	Pseudo-Hecataeus
Jannes and Jambres	5 Maccabees
History of the Rechabites	
Eldad and Modad	*Fragments*
History of Joseph	Pseudo-Greek Poets

In their new home in Jamnia the Rabbis, as they were called from then on, held meetings on many matters. One such meeting in *c*. 90 CE dealt (in part at least) with the kind and number of books that could be admitted into the Hebrew canon. The Rabbis considered many of the writings that came out of the Greek and Roman periods of Jewish history 'apocryphal' (hidden), and therefore not suitable for the canon of sacred writings. A number of these 'apocryphal' books remained in the canon of the Greek Septuagint despite the decision at Jamnia, and from the Septuagint found their way into the early Christian canon of the Old Testament. Allusions to some of these 'apocryphal' books appear in early Christian literature in support of arguments (cf. Jude 9, 14–15). But the rabbinic house of Jamnia radically removed the 'apocryphal' books from the Hebrew canon, perhaps because the books tended to foster sectarian interests among other things.

The Writings that passed the scrutiny of Jamnia are those that now appear in the Hebrew Bible on which the Protestant Old Testament is based (see Table 7.1). Not all of them passed without question. The Song of Songs was deemed too erotic to be Scripture; Ruth extolled the virtues of a Gentile woman; Lamentations was negative, as was Ecclesiastes; Job's story seemed to contradict the tenor of Torah that promised blessing to the upright; Esther does not contain the name of God, but does institute the Festival of Purim not prescribed in the Torah. The questions surrounding these books were settled not so much by explaining away the problems associated with them, but by attributing their composition to heroic figures from the pre-Maccabean period of Israel's history:[20] The Song of Songs was attributed to Solomon, Ruth to Samuel, Lamentations to Jeremiah, Proverbs and Ecclesiastes to Solomon, Job to Moses, the whole collection of Psalms to David (even though Psalm 72.20 says *the prayers of David, the son of Jesse, are ended*), Ezra-Nehemiah to Ezra, and Esther to the men of the Great Synagogue, or to Mordecai himself.[21]

By 90 CE, following a 'council' session of the Rabbis at Jamnia, the Palestinian Jewish canon of the Hebrew Bible was fixed. Josephus affirms as much. Writing towards the end of the first century CE, this Jewish historian 'implies a concept of divinely inspired writings, fixed in number, originating within a limited period of time, with an established text'.[22] Fixed it was, but not fossilized. The Jewish people continued to work out the implications of their Scriptures in life and world, nowhere more evident than in their written interpretations,

---

[20] See Barclay, *Introducing*, 39ff. for a concise discussion of the principle of inclusion of the books in the Hebrew canon.

[21] So Josephus, *Antiquities* XI, 6, 1.

[22] Childs, *Introduction*, 50 (with reference to Josephus, *Contra Apionem* I, 42f.).

most notably the Babylonian Talmud consisting of Mishnah (instruction) and Gemera (completion of instruction).

The New Testament

The Scriptures of the first Christians were the same Scriptures in use among the Jewish people. The first Christians were, after all, Jewish. It would not have occurred to them right away to create a new body of sacred literature to replace the Scriptures of their heritage. Nor did they think to add anything to the existing books. That came a generation later. In the meantime the earliest Christians preached Jesus Christ, first in Jewish Palestine and then also in the Gentile world around the north Mediterranean. Their missionary endeavours, especially those of Paul, took them into the heartland of Greek thought and religion. In such a Hellenistic climate the most useful Bible was not the Hebrew edition of Palestine, but the Greek translation associated primarily with Egypt (called the Septuagint, abbreviated LXX).

The LXX had been around for over two hundred years already and was read in the synagogues dotted around the Greco-Roman world. Written in the Greek language it was the Bible best suited to the world mission of the early Christians. Paul quotes from it exclusively in his letters to his mission churches.

The Letters of Paul and Acts

Our story of the making of the New Testament begins with this apostle Paul. His letters, comprising the largest collection of writings in the New Testament, are the earliest writings of the Christian Church to survive until the present time. It is generally agreed that Paul wrote his earliest letter (probably 1 Thessalonians) around 49/50 CE; the others within the next decade of his mission. But what happened during the twenty-year gap between the death and resurrection of Jesus (29/30 CE) and the writing of Paul's first letter?[23] We do not have any surviving records from the period. But from the later accounts we can be sure that the early believers in Jesus were active in preaching the word about Jesus wherever they went.

---

[23] On this question see especially Martin Hengel, *Between Jesus and Paul: Studies in the Earliest History of Christianity* (London: SCM Press; Philadelphia: Fortress Press, 1983), 1–29; and Ben F. Meyer, *The Early Christians: Their World Mission and Self-discovery* (Wilmington: Michael Glazier Inc., 1986), 53–104.

The launching of the Gentile world mission, with Paul at the helm, marked also the first stages of the making of the New Testament. Paul's letters were personal and communal, not public and literary. They answered questions his churches asked after he had moved on to his next destination. They dealt with issues that arose on the spot (1 Cor. 5–7); they commended missionaries who went out in the name of Christ (Rom. 16); they appealed for right behaviour in keeping with the law of Christ (Gal. 6); they expounded matters of faith that were misunderstood (1 Thess. 4; 1 Cor. 15); and they defended Paul's mission and preaching against attacks from various quarters (2 Cor. 10–13).

When a church in Thessalonica or Corinth or Philippi or Rome received a letter from Paul the people did not there and then treat it as Scripture on a par with the ancient Scriptures of Israel. Paul's letters did not achieve that status until much later, after his death, and after his letters had been collected at the end of the first century.

Someone living near the end of the first century CE, probably in Ephesus, decided to collect as many of Paul's letters from his mission churches as he could find[24] and then had them copied, perhaps even combining fragments of letters onto one roll of papyrus,[25] for use in all the churches. The collection and distribution of Paul's letters did not mean their instant authority as sacred Scripture. But the collection did carry something of the heart and soul of the apostle who had served the cause of Christ so admirably in his time. In their way the letters brought the apostle to life again to encourage and guide the churches facing hard times in the hostile environment of Roman domination.

As likely as not, the event that may have prompted the collection of Paul's letters was the publication of Acts around 90 CE.[26] Acts extols the outstanding missionary vision and character and work of Paul in establishing the churches in the Gentile world. With Acts now in circulation Paul's letters would have become immediately valuable to the churches, especially so since Acts makes no mention of them,[27] nor of the cross-theology that so permeates the letters.

---

[24] According to his own statement in 1 Cor. 5.9 (cf. 2 Cor. 2.4), Paul wrote more letters than those listed in the New Testament; how many more we do not know for sure.

[25] Scholars have detected the presence of at least two fragments in 2 Corinthians. See my *2 Corinthians Believers' Church Bible Commentary* (Scottdale: Herald Press, 1998), 263–6; cf. Kümmel, *Introduction*, 287–93 and on Romans 314–20.

[26] Barclay, *Introducing*, 47.

[27] They were probably not available to the author of Acts at the time of writing his second treatise.

With the appearance of the collection of Paul's letters, however many there were in the earliest collection,[28] came also letters from disciples of the apostle written under his name as a way of invoking his authority. In addition to non-canonical letters under Paul's name, some scholars have argued that the canonical Pastoral Epistles (1 and 2 Timothy and Titus) and Ephesians bear the marks of Pauline disciples from a later time and situation. In these letters Paul is invoked to speak to the new issues of the day as though present.

Writing under the name of a traditional figure of authority was common practice in the ancient world of Judaism and Christianity. During the next three centuries the Church hierarchy, sensing the need to defend the Church against heresies, set itself the task of separating what it considered the genuine from the spurious. In the final analysis what mattered most was (1) the extent to which a letter was in use in the churches, and (2) the degree of orthodoxy and moral integrity inherent in the letter. This twofold rule would apply to other books in use in the Church from the beginning of the second century onward.

Gospels

Gospels also began to circulate by the end of the first century. These writings gave an account of the work and word of Jesus. Gospels arose out of a need to keep the apostolic witness to Jesus alive and active in the churches scattered around the Mediterranean. As the apostles of Jesus died, the risk of losing the story and teaching of Jesus increased for the communities of faith remaining in the world. Many more Gospels than the four we have in our New Testament existed at the turn of the first century. Some of the better known of these are the Gospel of Thomas, of Mary, of Peter, of the Hebrews, and of the Nazoreans.[29] But the four Gospels of the New Testament were more widely used in the churches. They measured up better to the standard of orthodoxy in the Church of the second century than the others.

It must be admitted, though, that the Gospel of John was questioned for some time. Orthodox Church leaders were ambivalent about its language and thought pattern, which tended to accommodate

---

[28] According to Patzia, the 'seven churches' edition 'arranged according to the principle of decreasing length'. 1–2 Corinthians (1), Romans, Ephesians, 1–2 Thessalonians (1), Galatians, Philippians and Colossians (*Making*, 109).

[29] See the collection in Robert J. Miller, ed., *The Complete Gospels: Annotated Scholars Version* (Sonoma, CA: Polebridge Press, 1994).

the Gnostic mind-set that had begun to find a place in the life of the Church in the second century. Gnosticism (Greek: *gnosis* = 'knowledge'), which took various forms in both Judaism and Christianity, held that matter and spirit do not co-mingle. Matter is evil. The good God did not create matter. Sin and suffering are related to the material universe. God is spirit and therefore good, separate from matter.

The Gnostics believed that salvation involved initiation of one form or another into the realm of the Spirit through a kind of spiritual knowledge (*gnosis*). God provided mediators of this knowledge from above. The human being had only to grasp the significance of the signs that the mediator acted out, and thus be transported into the fullness of the divine mind and the secrets of the universe. This is an over-simplified version of Gnosticism, of course, but it will serve to illustrate the problem the orthodox church had with the Gospel of John. Notice the classic Gnostic terms of reference: 'fullness', 'knowledge', 'spirit', 'matter/flesh', 'above/below'. The Fourth Gospel accents these terms of reference. In short, this Gospel became tentatively suspect among orthodox Christian leaders of the second and third centuries, not least because a champion of Gnostic thought, Valentinus, produced 'the earliest commentary on the Fourth Gospel'.[30] The Gospel of John was probably the last of the four to be written, around 90–95 CE, Mark the first at 65–70 CE, and Matthew and Luke between these two at around 80–90 CE. By the beginning of the third century these four together occupied a place of privilege in all the churches.

Other writings

The other writings of the New Testament, the General Epistles and Revelation, came into use in various quarters of the Church over the second, third and fourth centuries. But they did not appear together on any list until the fourth century. The earliest list of authoritative books came not from the orthodox side of the Church, but from the Gnostic side, from one Marcion (*c.* 100–165 CE).

From Marcion to the Council of Carthage

Marcion led a large contingent of Christians into a Gnostic way of thinking about faith and life in relation to Jesus Christ. By 144 CE the

---

[30] Kümmel, *Introduction*, 489.

orthodox branch of the Church expelled him for his heretical views, especially those related to the Old Testament. Marcion considered the God of the Old Testament of lower status, and the writings about that God unworthy of the Church that accepted the Spirit of Jesus Christ. Moreover, he rejected the Jewish Scriptures, believing them to have been fulfilled in the coming of Jesus and the Spirit.

In place of the Jewish Scriptures, it would seem, Marcion drew up a list of strictly Christian books already in circulation in the churches. His list, dating from the middle of the second century, included ten letters (excluding 1 and 2 Timothy and Titus) under Paul's name and a version of the Gospel of Luke. This Marcionite canon is the earliest list of writings of the New Testament, intended to guide the Marcionite congregations in their thought and life.

Another witness to an early canon comes from a codex (book form) manuscript dating around 200 CE. The binding together of a group of writings creates the same effect as listing the books to be read. This codex, numbered $\mathfrak{P}^{46}$, belongs to a group of manuscripts known as the Chester Beatty library.[31] Some pages of $\mathfrak{P}^{46}$ are missing, but we gather from what remains that the codex consisted of the ten letters under Paul's name (apart from the Pastorals) and Hebrews. Here then is a second indication of an early canon for the churches.

Yet another early sign of a canon of the New Testament comes from a list appearing in what is now called the Muratorian Fragment.[32] This fragment, dated at about 200 CE according to many scholars, contains twenty-two of the twenty-seven books in the present New Testament. Here for the first time we have the three Pastoral Epistles mentioned among the letters under Paul's name. Metzger's judgement is this: 'Perhaps the most that can be said is that a member of the Roman Church, or of some congregation not far from Rome, drew up in Greek toward the close of the second century a synopsis of the writings recognized as belonging to the New Testament in his part of the Church.'[33]

The story of the listing of authoritative books can hardly ignore the work of a notable bishop of Caesarea, Eusebius (260–340 CE). His access to records in the well-stocked library of Caesarea afforded him the opportunity to write a history of the Church to that time, including

---

[31] Located in the castle in downtown Dublin, Ireland. See further in Chapter 8.

[32] So named after the Italian historian who discovered it in the eighteenth century, L. A. Muratori.

[33] Bruce Metzger, *The Canon of the New Testament: Its Origin, Development, and Significance* (Oxford: Clarendon Press, 1987), 194.

his insights into the making of the New Testament. He seems quite unaware of any official list of authoritative books of the Church. Instead, he scoured the sources in the libraries of Caesarea and Jerusalem and registered his findings about which books had gained the most positive recognition in the Church, especially in the East where he works, and which ones were rejected by the same authors representing the churches. He ends up with a three-part classification of the books (see Table 7.2): (1) books that all his sources acknowledged as authoritative; (2) books that were questioned by some of his sources; (3) books rejected by all as spurious.

Perhaps most puzzling about the list is the third class, the books rejected by all. The books in this class must have been sufficiently well known and used by some branches of the Church to make it on to the list at all. We know now that such books as the *Shepherd of Hermas*, the *Epistle of Barnabas*, and the *Didache* (teaching of the Twelve) were quite popular among the churches of the West. At least one codex manuscript of the New Testament from the same period as Eusebius includes the so-called spurious *Shepherd* and *Barnabas*.[34]

However much we might wish to pursue the attempts at closing the canon in the churches in the East and the West from 200 to 400 CE,[35] we must bring closure to this survey by referring to two events that effectively closed the canon for about one thousand years. The person responsible for the first of these events was 'the most celebrated theologian of the fourth century, Athanasius of Alexandria (*c.* 296–373)'.[36]

It was customary for the bishop of Alexandria to write an annual Festal Letter to the churches and monasteries of Egypt informing them of the date of Easter for that year, among other things. The Thirty-Ninth Festal Epistle of 367 CE also provided a list of the books of the Old and New Testaments. For the first time, the list in Athanasius' Festal Epistle of 367 contains precisely the twenty-seven presently in our New Testament, although not in the same order as our New Testament. The sequence in Athanasius' letter is: Gospels, Acts, the seven Catholic Epistles, the Pauline Epistles (including Hebrews between 2 Thessalonians and 1 Timothy), and the Revelation of John.

---

[34] Codex Sinaiticus. See Chapter 8 for more detail.
[35] For a full discussion of these attempts see Metzger, *Canon*, 209–47.
[36] Metzger, *Canon*, 210.

Other churches East and West relied on Athanasius for the date of Easter, and were doubtless also influenced by his list of authoritative books to be read in the public service. He declared these twenty-seven to be the *kanōn* (canon) for the Church's faith and life. This was the first time the word *kanōn* was used for a list of books that could be read as New Testament Scripture in public worship.

So far there has not been any official conciliar pronouncement on which books would be in or out of the New Testament canon. Thus we come to our second event that attempted to close the canon. As far as we can tell, the Third Council of Carthage held in 397 CE was the first Church Council to make a pronouncement on the books that could be read in public worship in the Church. Not surprising, the list produced by the Council of Carthage in 397 had exactly the same books as those listed in the Festal Epistle of Athanasius in 367, but not in the same order (see Table 7.2). The list of the Council of Carthage puts the thirteen Pauline letters immediately after Acts, and transfers Hebrews from the Pauline corpus to the General Epistles ahead of 1 Peter.

For the most part the list of books coming out of the Council of Carthage was accepted throughout the Latin Church of the West. Several Synods of the Greek Church in the East continued to use books beyond the twenty-seven of the Council of Carthage in worship, and do so to this day.

Criteria

What guided the selection of the books during this period? How did the churches judge a book's eligibility for canonisation? Three criteria seemed to be operative.

First, a book had to pass the test of the *rule of faith*. It had to prove itself orthodox before it could be deemed worthy of the list of authoritative books to be read in the Church. Second, a book had to make *connection with a living apostle*. This rule was difficult enough to execute, because the listing of the authoritative books happened long after the death of the apostles. Some Christian leaders had already begun to write under the name of an apostle before the notion of a New Testament canon came to the fore. The test of apostolicity meant that (1) an apostle of Jesus wrote the book, or (2) the writing was connected in some way to an apostle. For example, the Gospel of Luke passed this second test by assigning the third Gospel to Luke the physician and friend of Paul (Col. 4.14). Otherwise the third Gospel is anonymous, like many other writings of the New Testament. Third, a book had to find *acceptance in the Church at large* to qualify for the canonical list of New Testament books.[37]

The Reformers

The Reformation brought with it renewed interest in which books of the New Testament could be considered authoritative. The Epistle of James suffered most at the hands of Martin Luther. Luther considered the very limited reference to the work of Christ a serious weakness in James, which rendered it 'a right strawy epistle'. It mattered not to Luther who wrote the book, but whether Christ was central in the text: 'Whatever does not teach Christ is not apostolic, even though St Peter or St Paul does the teaching. Again, whatever preaches Christ would be apostolic, even if Judas, Annas, Pilate, and Herod were doing it.'[38] Luther put four books in a group of lesser value, according to his test, than the other twenty-three. The four were Hebrews, James, Jude and Revelation. Here we see Luther's signature effectively declaring a 'canon within the canon'.

To conclude, the Church found it necessary to mark out the bounds of Scripture by excluding some books and including others in what came to be called 'the canon' of Scripture. The declared canon had the stamp of authority on it, making it nothing less than the Word of God for the people of God gathered in the name of Jesus Christ. The canonized books became normative for personal faith and life, and for the organizing of Christian community in the world. In this sense also the canon is an educational model. Its instruction sets the standard for separating truth from error (theology/doctrine), and for determining what constitutes right and wrong behaviour (morality/ethics).

[37] See further in Metzger, *Canon*, 251–3; Patzia 102–3; and F. W. Beare, 'Canon of the New Testament' *IDB*, 525–32.
[38] Cited in Metzger, *Canon*, 243.

On Course...

Objective

To know what was involved in the transmission of manuscripts of the Scriptures up to the printed versions of the Bible, and to be able explain the aims and procedures of textual criticism.

Lead Questions

1. Of the many cultural innovations, which three mark critical turning points for the development of history and literacy?

2. When was the European printing press invented? By whom?

3. What was the first book to be published using the printing press?

4. What were some of the problems encountered in the practice of copying the biblical texts by hand?

5. What are four ways by which a change in wording could occur in the process of copying?

6. What is meant by the 'Masoretic text'?

7. List five important bodies of manuscript material that have survived.

8. What is meant by a 'critical text'? Name one critical text of the Septuagint?

9. What is the importance of Westcott and Hort, and Nestle, for the study of the New Testament texts?

10. Explain the 'family tree' of New Testament manuscripts (with reference to Westcott and Hort).

11. What is the character of the Western type text?

12. What are the Greek Papyri, and how are they identified?

13. What are three major Uncials?

14. To which text is the term textus receptus applied? What does it mean?

15. What is the aim of textual criticism? What are the two kinds of evidence used in the procedure of textual criticism?

8

Behind the Printed Text

We possess an uncommonly rich Christian literature.
(Eberhard Nestle)

One of the earliest memories I have from my primary education in the Armstrong School in Armagh, Northern Ireland, comes from working in my 'transcription book'. That exercise book helped to guide the pupils into a proper style of writing. The transcription book had one line of beautiful script at the top of the page. We had to copy the shape of the letters exactly several times. As I recall we started out transcribing with pencil, then later graduated to pen and ink.

If the same kind of transcription books are assigned in primary school these days, I doubt if that will long be the case. Instead of instruction on how to use the once universal pen and ink to write properly, young school children now learn to use the all-in-one communication tool, the computer. Those of us in later life have had to develop some computer skills to survive in this brave new world. Now at the beginning of the twenty-first century I resonate with the words of a nineteenth-century British Prime Minister, William Gladstone: 'The world of today is not the world in which I was bred and trained and have principally lived.'[1]

Today when I want to insert a passage from the Bible into a chapter such as this one, I do not even need to key the words into my document, much less copy them with pen and ink. I have the Bible stored in my computer in multiple languages and versions. I simply click on the Bible program in my computer, block the passage I want, and paste it into the document I am writing. This is the world in which we now live. The Bible today is not only a *printed text*, but also now a *digital text*. To get behind the printed/digital text of the Bible to the practice of copying every letter of every word with pen and ink by the light of a candle or oil lamp requires something of an intellectual conversion on our part. Try to imagine the enormous, and surely

---

[1] Quoted in F. H Hinsley, ed., *The Cambridge Modern History*, Volume XI (Cambridge: Cambridge University Press, 1962), 408.

monotonous task of writing copies of the Bible for use in all the places of worship multiplying in the world.

The task before us now is to discover how the copies, handwritten over fifteen hundred years ago, or more,[2] relate to our printed text. How many handwritten copies have survived the ravages of time? What does a comparative study of the surviving copies reveal? Which handwritten copy (or copies) form the basis for the printed text? How do the people responsible for printing the Bible decide on which text to use? We will discuss these related issues (in a limited way within the scope of this chapter) under four headings: (1) the cultural revolution following the printing press, (2) the practice of copying text by hand, (3) manuscripts that have survived, and finally (4) textual criticism.[3]

The Cultural Revolution Following the Printing Press

Devices for imprinting images existed long before the European invention of movable type. Seals were used in the imperial courts, for example, centuries before the invention of movable type in Europe. Even the European invention itself may have taken its cue from a similar invention evident already in China and Korea. The real cultural breakthrough for the world at large, however, is credited to Johann Gutenberg of Strasbourg, who put the movable type to full use in his hand-operated press in 1436/1437. The raised metal letters were set in place within a fixed form, ink was rolled over the surface of the raised letters, and the form was then pressed against a sheet of paper. The procedure could be repeated over and over again, producing copy after copy of pages in short order.

Gutenberg's first complete book-size publication of a printed text, and the earliest printed from movable type in existence in the West, was the text of the Bible printed in Mainz, Germany in 1455. The three-

---

[2] Longer for the manuscripts of the Old Testament.

[3] Some helpful resources on the subject of textual studies are as follows: Bruce M. Metzger, 'History of Editing the Greek New Testament', *The Bible and the Church: Essays in Honour of Dr David Ewert*, ed. A. J. Dueck, H. J. Giesbrecht and V. George Shillington (Winnipeg: Kindred Press, 1988), 29–44; Bruce M. Metzger, *A Textual Commentary on the Greek New Testament* (New York: United Bible Societies, 1975); Patzia, *Making*, 112–49; F. F. Bruce, *The Books and the Parchments* (Old Tappan: Fleming H. Revell, 1984), 166–210; Ralph W. Klein, *Textual Criticism of the Old Testament: The Septuagint After Qumran* (Philadelphia: Fortress Press, 1974), 1–84; Ernst Würthwein, *The Text of the Old Testament*, trans. Erroll F. Rhodes (Grand Rapids: Eerdmans, 1979), 3–119; Eberhard Nestle, *Introduction to the Textual Criticism of the Greek New Testament*, trans. William Edie (New York: G. P. Putnam's Sons, 1901), 1–335.

volume work, in majestic Gothic Latin text, was printed in 42-line columns. The first copy of Gutenberg's Bible was placed in the library of Cardinal Mazarin in Paris, hence the name given to it thereafter, the Mazarin Bible. No one knows exactly how many copies of the Mazarin Bible were printed in 1455. Forty copies of it still exist in various libraries in Europe and the United States.

The point of the story is this: with the invention of movable type for the printing press a cultural revolution was unleashed upon the world. No longer did scribes need to spend long hours copying important texts. Reformers in the century after Gutenberg could spread their word far and wide via the printed text. Literacy increasingly moved from the educated priests and nobility to the rank and file. More people could own books and learn to read. Newspapers became commonplace. The world changed for ever with the invention of the printing press, more so than with the innovation of the computer I suspect.

With respect to biblical studies the invention of the mechanical printing press meant that the reproduction of the Bible was no longer subject to the human proclivity that comes with copying by hand. But we cannot simply pass lightly over the long practice of copying by hand. Printed Bibles are only five hundred years in production, whereas copied Bibles boast a history of some fifteen hundred years.[4] What is important to note here is that printed copies of the Bible rely on the hand-copied texts, hereafter called manuscripts (MSS), and for that reason we do well to explore what was involved in hand-copying the biblical texts that pre-date the first printed Bible, and how those manuscripts lie behind the current text of our modern printed Bibles.

The Practice of Copying Text

Texts that exert influence on culture are worth copying. That is true for classics such as the writings of Homer and Virgil, Aristotle and Plato, Augustine and Luther. How much more so for the text of the Bible that shaped the life and thought of Jewish and Christian faith communities in the world. Each new community wanted to hear the prophetic, apostolic word in their own time and situation. With the canonization of a book came also greater demand for copies of the book. And the only way to meet the demand was to have the text copied and recopied and always by hand with pen and ink.

---

[4] Longer for the Old Testament.

Copying was a specialised skill developed among some of the members of the ancient communities. The copyists, or scribes, carried a mandate in principle to reproduce the text they received with integrity. Still, the copyists were human, and subject to weaknesses and propensities to which human nature is heir. The job itself, while valuable to the faith communities, was not abounding in personal reward. The copyist merely reproduced the text on another piece of papyrus or parchment as needed. The source text may have suffered damage from wear and tear and thus needed to be copied before it became too illegible to read. Or a new community may have requested a new copy of the Bible for its life and worship. In any case, the copyist was fully employed in the trade of transmitting the manuscripts he had received. What is noteworthy here is that the surviving manuscripts do not all share exactly the same rendering of the words of the text. Variants appear from one text to the other – or from one group of texts to the other. These variants can be explained from the practice of copying.

Changes in the wording of a biblical text happened in at least four ways: (1) weariness of the copyist and therefore inattention to the details of the text; (2) a psychological propensity to read one word for another; (3) recreating illegible words from a damaged source text; and (4) deliberate addition of text material to make the meaning more clear or more telling.

To the first point, a weary copyist of the Hebrew Bible may read the letter ד (d) for ר (r), or ה (h) for ח (hch) or vice versa. The two letters are similar in appearance, but one cannot be interchanged for the other without changing the meaning of the word. Similar mishaps occurred in copying the New Testament. For example, ἔβαλον (I/they threw) can be confused with ἔλαβον (I/they received), two quite different words. Moreover, words can suffer corruption by inadvertently substituting some letters for those in the source text. In addition, the eye of the copyist can slip to another line or to another phrase that begins with the same words as the phrase being copied, thus missing the intermediate words. This happens from weariness or simply from insufficient attention.

Second, a new word can be read in place of the one in the source text.[5] For example, in English 'the sword of the Lord' could easily be

---

[5] I have illustrated in Chapter 2 above this phenomenon of reading something in a text that does not actually appear in the text.

read as 'the word of the Lord'. By the same token, a word in the source text can be inadvertently overlooked, resulting in a change of meaning. Consider the difference between 'Thou shalt not commit adultery' and 'Thou shalt commit adultery'. This error actually appeared in one of the early printed versions of the English Bible, subsequently banned as 'the wicked Bible'.

Third, often the manuscript from which a copyist was obliged to reproduce the new manuscript had suffered damage. Manuscripts were put to good use in the churches, but in the process of such repeated use the script became illegible, especially words at the edge of the columns. The copyist, consequently, had to decide which word to use to replace the illegible one in the source text. Sometimes the decision was in error, as we know now from a comparative analysis of surviving manuscripts.[6]

Finally, a copyist, out of faith conviction, sometimes inserted material deliberately to make the text more clear or more telling in its effect. A Christian copyist, for example, living at a time when the doctrine of the Trinity was established in the Church, might feel inclined to insert a Trinitarian statement at 1 John 5.7–8, where the writer points to three witnesses whose testimony agree. We now know that a copyist did just that. This kind of change to a text in the practice of copying is *intentional*. But intentional change should not be construed as coming from evil intent. The additions are inserted out of genuine faith conviction.

With the broad array of variants in the surviving manuscripts of the two testaments the question of which manuscript is most reliable becomes acute. 'Most reliable' needs explanation. If our intention is to study the writings of the documents that were first adopted by the faith communities as authoritative texts for the life and thought of the community then we need a text that fairly represents the actual words of the text that was first adopted. The importance of this matter for theology cannot be overestimated. The theologian or preacher has to decide which wording of a text to use in creating a discourse or sermon. The matter comes up for discussion below under 'Textual Criticism'.

Manuscripts that Have Survived

Meanwhile, we do well to take some stock of the manuscripts that have survived for both testaments. Only the most important ones for each testament can be cited within the scope of this chapter.

---

[6] See the discussion of textual criticism below.

Old Testament manuscripts

The books of the Old Testament have come down through the centuries in several languages and recensions (extant copies from a line of earlier texts) other than Hebrew, the original language of the Old Testament. For good reason, though, we begin with the Hebrew MSS: they are copies in the original language of the Israelite community and constitute the primary basis for modern printed versions of the Old Testament, from which modern translations are made.

The Masoretic Text. The surviving Masoretic manuscripts, called after the name of their scribes, the Masoretes, are few and relatively recent. The earliest complete Masoretic MSS of the Old Testament are dated 1008–1050 CE. For the Old Testament that is recent. The Masoretes were intent on preserving the Masora, the scholarly notes about how the sacred consonants should be pronounced etc. Eventually (500–900 CE) these Masoretic Jewish scribes, operating from their headquarters in Tiberias in Galilee, produced vowel pointing to appear integrally with the consonantal text rather than in marginal notes or endnotes. Here is an example of a printed Masoretic vowel pointing on the Hebrew consonantal text of Psalm 23.1.[7]

יְהוָה רֹעִי לֹא אֶחְסָר׃

The handwritten Hebrew manuscript on which this printed text is based was copied in 1008 CE. Lodged in the Leningrad Public Library and coded B19[A], this manuscript (Codex Leningradensis) has no equal when it comes to a primary complete manuscript (MS) of the Old Testament. It is the oldest complete MS of the Old Testament from the well-known Ben Asher family of Masoretic scribes. Its close companion, also from the same Ben Asher family and labelled the Aleppo Codex (now in Jerusalem), is a later copy but still from the first half of the eleventh century.

In the latter part of the nineteenth century some fragments of the Hebrew Bible were discovered in the *Geniza* (hiding place) next to a synagogue in Cairo. These partial texts pre-date Codex Leningradensis by two to three hundred years, and are thus valuable for possible emendation of the Leningrad MS.

Why so few Masoretic copies of the Hebrew text of the Old Testament? It seems that the Jewish Masoretic scribes viewed the

---

[7] Hebrew text reads from right to left.

consonants as sacred. To avoid profaning the sacred text they hid the source text in a secure room (*Geniza*) until the new copy was established. Once established as a genuine copy, the source text was ceremonially buried to protect it from profanity. Unfortunately the buried MSS decayed, thus destroying valuable evidence of the Masoretic text pre-dating the B19[A] copy.

Dead Sea Scrolls. Without other significant Hebrew MSS from an earlier time there was no way to verify the reliability of the Masoretic copies of the eleventh century CE. That changed dramatically with the accidental discovery of the Dead Sea Scrolls in 1947. Of the many fragmentary MSS of all the books of the Hebrew Bible found in the eleven caves, none was as complete as the large scroll of Isaiah from Cave 1 (1QIsa[a]). This scroll of Hebrew Isaiah (like the others from the Qumran caves) pre-dates the Leningrad copy by about one thousand years. An examination of the text of the Qumran scrolls alongside the Masoretic text has revealed many variants, as might be expected given the number of copies made between the writing of the Qumran scrolls and the writing of the Masoretic texts of the eleventh century CE. These texts from the caves of Qumran at the northwest corner of the Dead Sea are a treasury of textual inventory of the Old Testament.

The Samaritan Pentateuch. The Samaritans descended from the northern tribes of Israel. In their reoccupation of their territory after exile in Assyria they established themselves in their headquarters in the old city of Shechem. Between the returned Samaritans and the returned Judeans there was not much social or political interaction. Any there was came to an abrupt end in the second century BCE when John Hyrcanus destroyed Shechem and ravaged the Samaritan shrine on Mount Gerizim. The Samaritans at that time had the Pentateuch. They kept it to themselves and copied it for themselves. Thus we have in the surviving copies of the Samaritan Pentateuch a separate Hebrew recension of the five books of the Law. There are some six thousand variants between the Masoretic Pentateuch and the Samaritan Pentateuch, many of them not very significant. Some of them can be traced to Samaritan interest in their own cult.

Most of the copies of the Samaritan Pentateuch date from the thirteenth century CE and later. The oldest copy, a codex manuscript in the Cambridge University Library, was written some years before 1150 CE, the date of sale noted in the manuscript. Valuable as a Hebrew recension of a major part of the Old Testament, the use of the Samaritan Pentateuch for recreating an older Hebrew text of the

Pentateuch is limited by its close tie with the Greek version (see below) and by its Samaritan cult interest.

In addition to copies of the Old Testament in Hebrew, such as the Samaritan Pentateuch and the Dead Sea Scrolls, we have versions of the Old Testament in a number of translations. While translations are useful witnesses in reconstructing an older text of the Hebrew Bible, they are at best witnesses to a language form other than Hebrew. Translations (as the next chapter explains) are in some measure also interpretations. That factor in itself reduces their value in coming up with an older text of the Hebrew Bible. Having said that, we do well to note some of the principal handwritten versions of the Old Testament that have been used variously to reconstruct an older Hebrew text.

The Aramaic Targums. 'Targum' is the Aramaic word for a translation. When the Judeans came back to Palestine from exile in Babylon they picked up the Aramaic language from their Syrian neighbours. As generation followed generation Aramaic became more and more the language commonly spoken in Palestine. Demand for an Aramaic translation of the Hebrew text used in the synagogue service grew. As a rule, the Aramaic version could be spoken in the service but not read lest the sacred Hebrew text be profaned or replaced. Outside the synagogue service the Targums were committed to writing. A good many of these have survived. Principal among the surviving Targums are *Targum Onkelos* comprising the Pentateuch and *Targum Jonathan* comprising the Prophets. These two Targums were established in Babylon in the fifth century CE as the official and authoritative Targums of Judaism. 'Both Targums attempt to reproduce the Hebrew text quite literally.'[8] Besides these two, and less well known, the *Palestinian Targum* seems to be related to these two official Targums. The *Palestinian Targum* is more a paraphrase of the Hebrew text, with added explanation and interpretation. These and other fragmentary Targums bear witness to the Hebrew text. They do not always agree with it, but neither do they provide substantial evidence for emending the Masoretic text, by the fact that they are translations.

The Septuagint (LXX). The story of the translation of the Hebrew Bible into Greek is long and legendary. A compressed version of the story, beginning with the legend, must suffice here. Reference to the translation appears first in the Letter of Aristeas, a purportedly non-Jewish proponent of the translation, who lived in the court of the king

[8] Würthwein, *Text*, 78.

of Egypt (285–247 BCE). As the story goes, one day Demetrius, legendary director of the famous library of Alexandria at the time, announced to his king, Ptolemy II Philadelphus, that the Jewish law (Pentateuch) deserved a place in the royal library of Alexandria, but that it should be in Greek instead of Hebrew. The king approved, and sent word immediately to Eleazar the high priest in Jerusalem to arrange for the translation. Eleazar appointed seventy-two scribes (six to represent each tribe of Israel) and sent them to Alexandria to complete the work of translation.

Secluded on the island of Pharos, the scribes separately translated the Hebrew text into Greek in seventy-two days. Their translations all agreed perfectly. The translation was read first to the Jewish community in Alexandria 'who pronounced it beautiful, pious, and accurate'.[9] The legend promulgated thus by Aristeas was repeated and expanded by Jewish historian Josephus, by Jewish philosopher Philo, and by early Christian leaders of the Church, who viewed the LXX as the authoritative Old Testament of the Church. 'However legendary and improbable the details, many still believe that some accurate historical facts about the LXX can be distilled from Aristeas: (1) the translation began in the third century BC[E]; (2) Egypt was the place of origin, and (3) the Pentateuch was done first.'[10]

It is now believed that the writer of the letter in question lived at least a century after the reign of Ptolemy Philadelphus. The motive for the translation was not to enhance the collection in the royal library of Alexandria, but to accommodate the Greek-speaking Jewish community living in Alexandria. The translators were most likely not Aramaic-speaking Judean scribes, but Greek-speaking Jewish scholars of Alexandria who could read Hebrew. The need for the Greek translation in Alexandria was similar to the need for the Aramaic Targums in Palestine: the congregations understood Greek in Alexandria better than Hebrew, and wanted Greek to be used in their synagogue services.

The LXX became the Bible for the Jewish world outside Palestine, and most especially for the Christian Church in the world. It was the Bible of St Paul in his Gentile world mission, and remained the Old Testament Bible of the Church until Jerome's Latin Vulgate (common edition) effectively replaced it. The LXX translation of the Hebrew Bible is not the product of one family of copyists, much less that of one

---

[9] Würthwein, *Text*, 50. See Klein's version of the story in *Textual Criticism*, 1–2.
[10] Klein, *Textual Criticism*, 2.

hand. It reflects a number of hands, the translation of the Pentateuch being most closely related to the Masoretic Hebrew text.

Adopted by the Christians as their sacred Scriptures, the LXX lost its sanction in the rabbinic Jewish community. Jewish authorities banned it from use in their synagogues, and produced Greek translations, notably those of Aquila, Symmachus, and Theodotion, to replace it. Copying the LXX from then on became the responsibility of the Christian Church. Numerous MSS of the LXX (most of them partial) have been discovered over the last several centuries. The text of most of them was written on papyrus in codex format. Some of the earliest and best partial MSS reside in the John Rylands Library in Manchester, the Chester Beatty Library in Dublin Castle,[11] the University of Michigan, the British Library,[12] and the Vatican Library in Rome.

But by far the most valuable recensions of the LXX are contained in three significant Greek MSS of the Bible in codex (book) form.[13] The most valuable of these for the LXX is one called Codex Vaticanus from the fourth century, but also Codex Sinaiticus and Codex Alexandrinus, from the fourth and fifth centuries respectively. These recensions of the LXX seem to have largely escaped the revisions common to many other manuscripts of the LXX.[14] Their value is that they are much earlier than the surviving Masoretic Hebrew text of the Old Testament. In that respect they provide a useful check on the later Masoretic recension of the Hebrew text. Beyond that, though, their usefulness as a check on the Masoretic text is curtailed by the fact that they are Greek translations originating in Alexandria of Egypt.

Several critical editions of the LXX exist and should be noted here. The Göttingen Septuagint developed over many years (c. 1931–1967) with many contributors to the various parts.[15] The Old Greek text of the LXX is printed at the top of the page with critical apparatus appearing at the bottom. Each volume in the series has a full introduction in German, explaining how the text was reconstructed.

---

[11] The Chester Beatty collection was moved from its place in a special library in the suburbs of Dublin to the Castle in the centre of the city in 1998.

[12] Manuscripts housed for many years in the British Museum were transferred to the British Library in the summer of 1998.

[13] Discussed in more detail later under 'New Testament Manuscripts'.

[14] Other recensions of the LXX exist in other Codices dated earlier than the eleventh century. These are listed in the Introduction to the Göttingen Septuagint, and cited in Würthwein, *Text*, 70–2.

[15] Under the title *Septuaginta: Vetus Testamentum Graecum auctoritate Societatis (Academiae) Litterarum Gottingenis edition*.

The Cambridge Septuagint[16] has three volumes. In each the text of Vaticanus appears at the top with three sections of apparatus below giving the readings from other recensions. As one reviewer puts it, '[The Cambridge LXX] gives all the material and is indispensable for the master mariner of LXX research; for the cabin boy, however, and also for the seaman, it is but a roaring sea of variants in which he perishes.'[17] Still, for text critical purposes this LXX is valuable for reconstructing a text of the Hebrew Bible.

A third edition of the LXX, edited by A. Rahlfs,[18] has two volumes and contains the entire Old Testament. Its reconstructed text and critical apparatus rely very much on the texts of fourth- and fifth-century codex manuscripts – Vaticanus, Sinaiticus and Alexandrinus. The narrow survey in this edition limits its usefulness in reconstructing a critical text of the Hebrew Bible.[19]

Other Early Versions of the Old Testament. Other versions of the Old Testament pre-date the Masoretic recension of the eleventh century. Their early date gives them the right to mention. Their reliability as witnesses to the integrity of the Masoretic text, however, has to be weighed by the integrity of the translators, a factor sometimes difficult to determine. The most that can be done here is to list the better known of these versions of the Old Testament.[20] (1) The Syriac Version, called the Peshitta ('simple' or 'plain'), is a rather loose and uneven translation of questionable origin. (2) The Old Latin Version is a translation of the Septuagint. As a secondary translation its value as witness to the Hebrew text is seriously diminished. (3) The Latin Vulgate, translated by St Jerome under the auspices of Pope Damasus I (366–384), was translated from a Hebrew recension available to Jerome in the fourth century. This quality of the Vulgate makes it a highly valuable witness to the Masoretic text. (4) Coptic Versions written in the common language of Egypt for the Christian churches in the area are from an early period.

In addition to these, the Ethiopic Version from the fourth century is a rendering out of Hebrew or Greek or Syriac, or a combination of these for the population of the area. The Armenian Version of the Old

---

[16] Under the title *The Old Testament according to the text of Codex Vaticanus.*
[17] Ludwig Koeler, quoted in Klein, *Textual Criticism*, 52.
[18] Under the title *Septuaginta: id est Vetus Testamentum Graece iuxta LXX Interpretes.*
[19] For fuller discussion of the editions of the LXX see Klein, *Textual Criticism*, 51–4, and Würthwein, *Text*, 72–4.
[20] For a fuller description of these witnesses to the Hebrew Bible see Würthwein, *Text*, 80–100.

Testament appeared shortly after the invention of the Armenian alphabet in the fifth century. Arabic Versions began to appear with the rise of Islam and the spread of the Arabic language. Their use for the textual criticism of the Old Testament is very slight.

These, then, are the chief textual witnesses to the integrity of the Masoretic text of the Hebrew Bible on which the printed text is based. We turn now to the surviving MSS of the New Testament that pre-date the printed text.[21]

New Testament manuscripts

New Testament manuscripts have a family history. From the beginning of the eighteenth century, textual scholars have studied and grouped manuscripts of the New Testament by the character of copying evident in the text. Since I will be referring to the text family, or type, it would be well to tell the story in brief here. More will follow under textual criticism.

Family Tree. Johann Jakob Griesbach (1745–1812) inquired into the kinds of MSS of the New Testament available to him, and concluded that three kinds of copying could be identified in relation to a particular locale in the church: Alexandrian, Western, and Byzantine. The idea was to identify which family type exercised the most restraint and care in transmitting the text.[22]

By the end of the nineteenth century, and after many years of work on the MSS, two Cambridge scholars, B. F. Westcott and F. J. A. Hort (hereafter WH), published a two-volume work on the text of the New Testament (1881). The first volume was a critical edition of the Greek New Testament, and the second an introduction to the analysis they had conducted in their effort to reproduce as nearly as possible the earliest text of the New Testament. WH identified *four families* of text they had encountered in their investigation: Syrian, Western, Alexandrian, and Neutral. From their research they concluded that the Neutral text had less corruption than any of the other three families. In 1924, however, English scholar B. H. Streeter, less assured of an unmixed text, revised the labels of WH. For him there was no 'neutral' text. The result that stands today is still four families of New Testament

---

[21] The first printed Greek text, also called the Received Text (discussed below), is foundational to the early printed editions of the English Bible, including the King James Version.

[22] J. H. Greenlee, *Introduction to New Testament Texture Criticism* (Grand Rapids: Erdmans, 1964), 81.

MSS under new names. The WH Neutral type was changed to *Alexandrian*; the Syrian became *Byzantine*; Alexandrian was identified as a *Caesarean* text, originating in Alexandria, and brought to Caesarea perhaps by Origen; the Western type remained *Western* (Rome). Of these four types the Alexandrian represents the strictest copying practice and the Western the most liberal. With these family names in place, we can now proceed with an overview of the principal witnesses to the New Testament text.

As with the Old Testament, so also the New, not a single fragment of an original manuscript of the New Testament exists today. But we do have numerous copies of copies of the originals, at least 5000, from different parts of the ancient world, and written by different Christian scribes in different parts of the Mediterranean basin. These treasured copies are grouped according to two kinds of writing and two kinds of writing material.

First, the two kinds of writing. *Uncial* letters are large and free standing, similar to English upper case lettering. *Minuscule* letters are of a smaller, cursive style. People of the Roman period used the cursive style for everyday writing – letters, receipts, announcements – but not for literary documents. Paul's personal letters to churches and individuals may have been written in the cursive style, although no hard evidence to this effect exists. All the early MSS of any part of the New Testament are in uncial lettering, with little or no punctuation, not even spaces between words, much less verses and chapters. Uncial writing was reserved for books up to the ninth century CE, at which time the minuscule cursive style was adopted for literary works as well. Hence, all of the minuscule MSS of the New Testament are later than 900 CE.

Second, the two kinds of writing material. *Parchment*, made from treated skins of animals, provided very durable material for text. A number of the major Uncial MSS of the New Testament are on parchment. *Papyrus*, (plural, *papyri*) made from the soft centre of the papyrus reed, had become a popular material on which to write text. Although not as durable as parchment, papyrus material had the capacity to survive for a long time in dry conditions, as in the sands of Egypt or in the sealed jars of Qumran. The letter form in the early papyrus MSS is uncial. However, the term 'Uncial MSS', or simply 'Uncials', is reserved for the great parchment manuscripts, even though they are not the earliest MSS of the Greek New Testament. The earliest surviving MSS are the papyri type. For this reason they are first on our list of witnesses to the New Testament text.

Greek Papyri of the New Testament. The nineteenth century witnessed the discovery of many papyri, especially in Egypt, consisting of various kinds of religious and everyday texts. Even more astounding were the discoveries in the first half of the twentieth century. Among the finds of various MSS, was a number of the New Testament. Some were small fragments containing a few verses. Others were large portions of whole books bound together in codex form.

The *Papyri* of the New Testament are coded by the upper case (or archaic) 𝔓 followed by a superscript number (e.g. 𝔓¹³). What follows is a list of the most valuable MSS for textual study of the New Testament. The numbering sequence is in the order of discovery and editorial verification.

The Chester Beatty collection is among the most valuable MSS of the Greek New Testament. Housed mostly in Dublin Castle, the Chester Beatty MSS were copied in the third century CE. Sir Frederic G. Kenyon evaluated and edited the collection soon after Chester Beatty announced his discovery in the early 1930s.[23]

𝔓⁴⁵ is the first of these. It has 30 leaves of an original 220 from a book (codex) containing the four Gospels and Acts. Of the thirty surviving leaves, thirteen belong to Acts, the rest to Mark (six) and Luke (seven). Two fragmentary leaves belong each to Matthew and John.

𝔓⁴⁶ is another. Copied in the early part of the third century, it is perhaps the most valued codex manuscript containing originally nine letters of St Paul and Hebrews in the following order: Romans, Hebrews, 1 and 2 Corinthians, Ephesians, Galatians, Philippians, Colossians, 1 and 2 Thessalonians. All of 2 Thessalonians was missing, and parts of Romans and 1 Thessalonians. The Pastoral Epistles (1 and 2 Timothy and Titus) were not in the original codex. The anonymous Epistle of Hebrews was obviously considered a writing of Paul judging from its place in the codex.

𝔓⁴⁷ is also among the collection. This one has ten leaves of an original thirty-two of Revelation, consisting of 9.10—17.2. The MS was copied in the second half of the third century.

Old as the Chester Beatty papyri are (all of them from some part of the third century), the oldest papyrus text of the New Testament is 𝔓⁵². This fragment measures only 2½ by 3½ inches, and contains the text of

---

[23] Frederic G. Kenyon, *The Chester Beatty Papyri, Description and Texts* (London: 1933–37), cited in Metzger, *Text*, 37.

John 18.31–33; 37–38. Found in Egypt in 1920 by Bernard P. Grenfell, this tiny fragment of John did not come to prominence until 1934 when C. H. Roberts recognized its script as coming from the first half of the second century. Other noted scholars agreed with the early date, proving that the Gospel of John had made its way into the Egyptian churches within forty or fifty years after its first appearance. The fragment belongs to the John Rylands Library Collection in Manchester.

The second substantial collection of early papyri MSS of New Testament are called the Bodmer papyri, after Martin Bodmer who acquired them.

$\mathfrak{P}^{66}$ has 104 leaves containing John 1.1—6.11 and 6.35—14.15 and dated at about 200 CE. The text exhibits at least two styles of copying, coming from two parts of the Mediterranean. The text type is therefore mixed.

$\mathfrak{P}^{72}$ is the earliest copy of Jude and 1 and 2 Peter. Included also in this codex are a number of other sundry texts, all of them copied in the third century by four copyists.

$\mathfrak{P}^{74}$ copied in the seventh century, contains portions of Acts, James, 1 and 2 Peter, 1, 2, and 3 John, and Jude. The pages are fragmentary, and the text difficult to read.

$\mathfrak{P}^{75}$ has 102 of 144 original leaves preserving large parts of Luke and John. Its editors date it between 175 and 225 CE.

These are the most important papyri witnesses to the text of the Greek New Testament, and each of them bears a somewhat different testimony to the degree of corruption of the text in transmission through the ages. We turn attention now to the most important parchment MSS.

Greek uncials of the New Testament. All of the Uncial MSS are codex form, the earliest of them coming from the fourth century. The codes are made up of both a capital letter and a number for each MS.[24]

א/01, Codex Sinaiticus has pride of place because of its antiquity, evidence of good copying practice, and its completeness. Discovered in the monastery of St Catharine on Mount Sinai by Constantin von Tischendorf in the middle of the nineteenth century,[25] this codex contains the entire New Testament and much of the LXX, the only uncial codex able to make this boast. Included in the codex with the

---

[24] Except for Codex Sinaiticus, which was given the first letter of the Hebrew alphabet, א.

[25] The story of Tischendorf's discovery of Codex Sinaiticus is fascinating, but complicated. See Metzger, *Text*, 42–6 for details.

twenty-seven New Testament books and the LXX are two others known and used in the Church at the time: the Epistle of Barnabas and the Shepherd of Hermas. The text of ℵ/o1 was copied in the fourth century. Its text family is Alexandrian. There are, in places, also signs of the Western influence, which took more liberties in copying. Today Codex Sinaiticus resides in the British Library in London.[26]

A/o2, Codex Alexandrinus is a fifth-century copy, originally containing the LXX and New Testament. Parts of Matthew, John and 2 Corinthians were damaged or lost. This codex exhibits two types of copying (Byzantine and Alexandrian). Along with Codex Sinaiticus, Codex Alexandrinus is the property of the British Library.

B/o3, Codex Vaticanus, considered the most valuable of all Greek MSS of the New Testament (as also of the LXX, including the books of the Apocrypha, except the Maccabees), was copied in the middle of the fourth century. Unfortunately, Vaticanus is missing everything from Hebrews 9.14 through Revelation. As its name implies, this uncial MS has been housed in the Vatican Library in Rome since the fifteenth century. The Library withheld it from textual scholars until about 1890. Since then Vaticanus has served as a basic source for revising the Greek text of the New Testament, representing as it does the best of the Alexandrian text type.

C/o4, Codex Ephraemi is a fifth-century MS, although not nearly as valuable for textual editing as the ones already cited. The parchment material was used twice. The first text, the Greek New Testament, was erased in the twelfth century and the parchment reused for a translation of some sermons and treatises of St Ephraem of the Syrian church (fourth century). Using a chemical mixture, Tischendorf was able to make visible the underlying Greek text of the New Testament. Its text type is largely Byzantine, not considered as valuable as the Alexandrian type. In the letters of Paul, however, the text manifests more of an Alexandrian hand than a Byzantine.

D/o5, Codex Beza, so called after the French scholar, Theodore Beza, who presented it to the library of Cambridge University in 1581, contains the four Gospels and Acts and part of 3 John. What distinguishes this MS from the others mentioned already is its diglot form. It has the Greek text on the left page and the Latin translation on the right. One of the notable characteristics of Codex Beza is the free and

---

[26] The manuscript was moved with others from the British Museum to the British Library in 1998.

easy way the scribe inserted words or sentences into the copied text. The text family is clearly Western. Its usefulness in textual editing of the New Testament has to be conducted cautiously.

D/06, Codex Claromontanus from the sixth century contains only the Letters of Paul and Hebrews. This MS, like Codex Beza, is a Greek-Latin diglot of the Western text type. It is judged that nine different correctors had a hand in its final production.

W/032, the last of our sampling of Uncial MSS of the New Testament,[27] was discovered in 1906 by Charles L. Freer of Detroit. It is sometimes referred to as the Freer Codex, or Codex Washington. It is located in the Smithsonian Institution in Washington, D. C. Its early date makes it valuable for textual analysis, but the text is a mixed type, as though copied from different source texts. One of the notable marks of Codex W/032 is the longer post-resurrection ending of Mark (16.9–20).[28]

Greek minuscules of the New Testament. Of these there are many, all of them copied from the tenth through to the sixteenth century. Even though they are late their family connection makes them worthy witnesses to the text of the New Testament. At the same time their lateness calls for caution in using them to emend the text to represent the earliest publication. I will mention only two, out of the large number of medieval minuscules, to illustrate how corruptions had crept into the Greek text of the New Testament by the time of the invention of the printing press in the fifteenth century.

In 1868 Professor Ferrar of Dublin University first discovered that four MSS that had come to the fore exhibited the same type of copying. Later this small Family 13 expanded to include at least twelve.[29] Copied some time between the eleventh and the fifteenth century, one striking feature of Family 13 minuscules is the insertion of the story about the adulterous woman after Luke 21.38, which then leads into the plot to kill Jesus at Passover in Luke 22. The pericopé (unit of text) appears at John 7.53—8.11 in other MSS, as also in the KJV and other English versions since.[30] The best MSS of John or Luke do not have the story.

---

[27] See further in Greenlee, *Textual Criticism,* 36–42; Metzger, *Text,* 42–61; and Kümmel, *Introduction,* 513–25.

[28] Jerome mentions texts that have the longer ending. The earliest and best MSS of Mark end at 16.8.

[29] Numbers 13, 69, 124, 346 (Ferrar's four), 230, 543, 788, 826, 828, 983, 1689, 1709.

[30] The pericopé in John is not well supported by the best Greek MSS. See the Appendix at the end of this chapter.

From another minuscule MS (61) copied in the early sixteenth century comes the notable insertion about the Trinity at 1 John 5.7. It appears in Jerome's Vulgate, but in no other Greek MS except this single minuscule. When Erasmus published his third printed edition of the Greek New Testament in 1522 he was required by his critics to include the insertion about the 'the Father, the Word and the Holy Ghost'. Hence it appears in the King James Version of 1611.[31]

Other witnesses. Besides the Greek copies of parts or all of the text of the New Testament there are three other witnesses that bear testimony: (1) quotations of the New Testament in Greek writings of the Church Fathers, otherwise called *Patristics*; (2) *translations* of the New Testament, and (3) *Lectionaries.*

The Patristic quotations are many and varied, and are useful especially for their age. They come from the third, fourth and fifth centuries and from different locales in the Church. Greek MSS and translations can be checked against a quotation found in these Patristic quotations.

The early translations also offer testimony to the Greek text behind the translation. Their testimony is valued for the age of the text primarily. If the translations were made directly from a Greek MS of the New Testament, not from another translation, then their value increases. There exist a number of Syriac versions, Old Latin versions from Africa and Europe, the Latin Vulgate of Jerome, Coptic, Gothic, Armenian, Ethiopic, Georgian, and Old Slavic versions (among others). Each of these in its own way, and by informed comparison with other resources, speaks to the wording of the books of the Greek New Testament that first appeared in the Church and the world.

The third group called to testify is the Lectionaries of the Church. Lectionaries are collections of scriptural readings taken from different parts of the Bible for use in public services. Some of the surviving Lectionaries go back to about the sixth century. Others, of course, are much later. What makes these witnesses important is not only their age, but also their official status as 'readings for worship' in the Church, and their representation of different text families.

Textual Criticism

'Criticism' has such a negative tone to it! Nobody likes to be criticized. Why use this negative label to identify what biblical scholars do with

---

[31] See further in Metzger, *Text*, 99ff.

biblical texts? Like many words in any language, this one has negative connotations in one context but not in another. In the scholarly discipline of biblical studies it has quite a positive side.

Biblical scholars simply want to know the truth of the matter, whatever matter happens to be under review at the moment. In this sense 'criticism' is genuinely positive. When scholars engage in some kind of biblical criticism, therefore, they are making certain kinds of *judgement* on contending issues in a given area of biblical study to reach a *decision* on the truth of the matter.[32] The English word 'criticism' comes from a set of cognate Greek words: *krinō* (verb, 'evaluate, judge, prove'), *krisis* (noun, 'evaluation, judgement, proof'). 'Criticism' is negative when the judgements are made rashly, with evil intent, or without sufficient basis in fact. But sound judgements are good all around. They lead to truth and righteousness, and as such are positive. So it is with the various categories of biblical criticism: when its aim is truth and goodness and its method reasonable and responsible, then its practice is thoroughly justified.

Of the several subcategories of biblical criticism – to be discussed later – this section will attend specifically to *textual criticism*. That is, the evaluation of the surviving manuscripts of the Bible as to their effectiveness as witnesses to the texts that first appeared in the ancient faith communities. The aim of textual criticism is to reconstruct as nearly as possible the text of the documents of the two testaments when they were first received in the communities of faith in their final form. The goal is achieved by applying scientific methods with a good resource of informed insight to the study of the available manuscript evidence. In the words of the eminent textual scholar of a century ago, Eberhard Nestle:

> [T]he task of the textual critic resembles that of the physician, who must first of all make a correct diagnosis of the disease before attempting a cure. Manifestly the first thing to do is to observe the injuries and the dangers to which a text transmitted by handwriting is liable to be exposed.[33]

In a sense textual criticism has gone on for as long as texts have been copied. When some Greek orators would quote the classics in ways that

---

[32] I allude here to the 'circuit of knowing' discussed in Chapter 1: from experiencing to understanding, to judging to deciding.

[33] Eberhard Nestle, *Introduction to the Textual Criticism of the Greek New Testament* (London: Williams & Norgate, 1901), 234.

suited themselves, intelligent 'critics' would call an orator to account for misrepresenting the classical text. In the early Church theologians such as Origen and Jerome were aware of some of the problems of copying text, and made a concerted effort to rely on a text that seemed to them to represent the source text more accurately. By the time of the Renaissance and Reformation the awareness of corruption in MSS had become still more acute. The intent always was to find a MS judged to be more closely related to the original. The urge to find such a MS had its own problems, especially for Church authorities.

Agreement on the superiority of one over another of the competing MSS was generally not forthcoming. Tradition continued to play a part in the selection of the best text to use for copying, for translation, and for other uses. For the Old Testament the traditional text for all the possible functions in the faith communities was the Masoretic text. For the Christian Church a traditional text of the New Testament was not as readily at hand. There were many Greek texts of the New Testament competing for acceptance as the single source text.

Textus Receptus (Received Text), as it came to be called, was the title of honour and publicity given to the first printed edition of the Greek New Testament. The task of coming up with a Greek text for the printing of the New Testament rested with Dutch scholar, Erasmus of Rotterdam (1469–1536). After a rather hasty editing process, Erasmus published his first edition of the Greek text of the New Testament in 1516. One of the problems Erasmus faced in bringing the Greek New Testament to print was the partial Greek MSS he had available to him. He incorporated several different types into his Greek edition, in particular 'two rather inferior manuscripts ... both dating from about the twelfth century'.[34] His editing process included translating parts of the Latin Vulgate back into Greek to arrive at a complete Greek text in print.

There was great demand for Erasmus' Greek Testament, although not everyone accepted his Greek text without question. Some of the criticisms were caustic and without solid foundation. One in particular is striking. In Erasmus' first two editions he omitted the Trinitarian words of 1 John 5.7–8[35] because he did not find them in any of the Greek MSS available to him, although the words were in the

---

[34] Metzger, *Text*, 99.
[35] 'The Father, the Word and the Holy Ghost: and these three are one. And there are three that bear witness in earth.'

long-standing Latin Vulgate. Erasmus promised his critics that if a single Greek MS could be found with these words in 1 John 5 he would include them in his third edition. Someone conveniently found such a MS (believed to have been written in 1520 in Oxford during the debate over Erasmus' printed Greek text). Erasmus kept his promise and included the Trinitarian statement in his third edition. This Greek New Testament of Erasmus, resting as it did on inferior MSS, most of them late, was promoted as *Textus Receptus* and widely adopted. It became the basis for the growing number of translations that appeared in the sixteenth century, including Luther's German translation and the English King James Version of 1611.

With the acceptance and use of Erasmus' Greek New Testament, *Textus Receptus* became a virtual dogma in church circles. The Latin phrase, first used to advertise Erasmus' Greek edition, has the sense of generally received. By extension *Textus Receptus* means the 'standard text'. A standard text might be fine if the said text is the result of thoroughgoing critical research and well-founded judgement. But that was not at all the case with Erasmus' Greek text of the New Testament. Still his text held its 'standard' position for many years, despite the ongoing discoveries and critical textual research over the next several centuries.

> So superstitious has been the reverence accorded the Textus Receptus that in some cases attempts to criticise or emend it have been regarded as akin to sacrilege. Yet its textual basis is essentially a handful of late and haphazardly collected minuscule manuscripts, and in a dozen passages its reading is supported by no known Greek witness.[36]

What then is the purpose and program of textual criticism? In short, it is the production of a *critical text* of the Scriptures. 'By means of textual criticism [scholarship] attempts to ferret out all the alterations that have occurred and recover the earliest possible form of the text.'[37] But the earliest possible form is still not equal to the original wording of the sentences of Scripture when they were first written; that is, before their extant form. But the earliest possible wording does mean the wording of the documents when they became canonical. For the Old Testament that time would have been somewhere between 400 and 200 BCE.[38] For the New Testament about the middle of the second century CE.

---

[36] Metzger, *Text*, 106.
[37] Würthwein, *Text*, 103.
[38] So Würthwein, *Text*, 103; cf. Childs, *Introduction*, 101, where he suggests the recovery of a text at about 100 BCE is attainable.

Textual criticism of the Old Testament usually starts with the Masoretic Text tradition as the line of testimony. The process continues with the examination of available manuscripts related to the tradition down to the Masoretic Text extant in the Dead Sea Scrolls. Of course, deciding on which text belongs to the tradition, and which is close to the tradition, is not an easy matter. But much work has already been done and more is forthcoming. Massive work has been carried out on the Dead Sea Scrolls, for example, and the results are becoming more available to the textual scholar.

Critical versions also, particularly the Göttingen Septuagint, provide significant textual resource for establishing the traditional text of the Hebrew Bible. The wording of a version cannot be taken at face value. The LXX provides a good textual resource, but the Greek text has to be translated back into Hebrew. This procedure is called retroversion. 'A recurring difficulty in retroversion is that a given Hebrew word can be translated by many different Greek words. Thus the Hebrew word "to give" (*ntn*) is rendered by some thirty different words in the LXX.'[39]

Critical editions, such as the Göttingen Septuagint, 'provide a valuable guide through the mass of variants when used with discretion'.[40] The challenge for the textual critic is to reach a decision about the traditional Hebrew text of the Old Testament after careful comparison following appropriate principles and procedures, which are essentially the same for both Old and New Testaments, and are set out in a section below. In the final analysis, however, 'there is no precisely defined method for Old Testament textual criticism',[41] as there is not for New Testament textual criticism.

For the New Testament there seems to be more manuscript evidence to sift through. Over the past two hundred years New Testament textual scholars have refined their method of dealing with the many MSS before them. I have already mentioned the landmark work of WH at the end of the nineteenth century in establishing four text families for the Greek New Testament. That work marked a major achievement for textual criticism of the New Testament. The committee for the English Revised Version (RV) of the King James Version relied substantially on the critical text of WH for their revision. Criticisms against WH, and also against the RV, became fast and

---

[39] Klein, *Textual Criticism*, 64.
[40] Würthwein, *Text*, 113.
[41] Würthwein, *Text*, 111.

furious. The four-hundred-year-old *Textus Receptus* continued to raise its head even at the end of the nineteenth century. But the forward movement of scientific study of the texts of the New Testament could not be stopped.

Eberhard Nestle, using the materials of textual criticism available to him at the end of the nineteenth century, and by engaging rules of internal and external evidence (outlined below), produced a critical edition of the *Greek New Testament* with notes that would serve as a basis for all future critical editions of the twentieth century.[42] Kurt Aland has continued to revise the Nestle text in light of new evidence since Nestle's time.

In 1966 a committee appointed by the United Bible Societies (UBS) produced its first edition of the Greek New Testament to serve as the text for translators around the world. The result is an eclectic text, using the best textual evidence and skill to emend, always with the aim of arriving at the wording of the Greek text first acknowledged by the communities of faith. As new discoveries and additional insights occur over the years new editions appear. The UBS's *Greek New Testament* is now in its fourth revised edition (1993). Meanwhile, revision of the Nestle text, with full critical apparatus, continues into the twenty-first century. Both of these critical texts – of UBS and Nestle – are now virtually identical.

Principles and procedures. To close the discussion of this chapter, a brief summary of ground rules of textual criticism would be appropriate. 'Of the approximately five thousand Greek manuscripts of all or part of the New Testament that are known today, no two agree exactly in all particulars.'[43] On what basis do the textual scholars decide which wording to incorporate into their edition of the Hebrew and Greek texts of the Bible? In broad terms, judgements are made using two kinds of evidence: external and internal.

External evidence comes from examining the extant manuscripts using appropriate principles of investigation. There are essentially three that come into play. (1) The age of the manuscript speaks to the number of copies that have gone before it. The older the copy the more likely it is to be free of corruption through repeated copying. This principle cannot be applied in isolation from the others. (2) The geographical spread of the manuscripts is taken into account. If copies

---

[42] See his discussion of the materials available and his 'theory and praxis' of doing textual analysis in his *Introduction*, 28–246.

[43] Metzger, *Textual Commentary*, xxiv.

of a text come from different locations of the faith communities, and if they were copied independently, then their joint testimony carries some weight. (3) Text type, or family, has to be considered, not merely the number of witnesses. One reading may be found in twenty manuscripts, all from the same source manuscript. The source manuscript may have been corrupt to begin with. Having twenty witnesses that have the same reading is therefore not telling. Another reading with only two manuscripts may come from a better text type and by that principle be more likely.

Internal evidence takes into account the *human tendency* in scribal copying. Here there are five guiding principles of discernment. (1) The more difficult reading is preferred over a simple reading. A scribe would be more inclined to simplify than to make a reading more difficult. (2) The shorter reading is preferred, because a scribe would be more inclined to elaborate than to abbreviate. This assumes that the scribe has not missed something in the text accidentally. (3) A reading that is out of harmony with another passages is preferred over a reading that is harmonious. A believing scribe is more inclined to bring harmony to a document than discord. (4) Unfamiliar wording and awkward wording is preferred over familiar, smooth wording. A scribe is more inclined to smooth out a sentence than to make it rough. (5) Judgement is sometimes made on the wording of a specific text from the context, or from the style of an author in the whole document. These are the basic rules for textual analysis.[44]

Conclusion

In the end a human judgement has to be made between contending readings in the available manuscripts. Scholars do not always reach exactly the same decision from the textual evidence. However, when a committee of well-qualified scholars works on the material, the joint decision has much more to commend it than the decision of one, as in the case of Erasmus with *Textus Receptus*. Today we can read the Hebrew text of the Old Testament, the Greek text of the Septuagint, or the Greek text of the New Testament, with a high degree of confidence that we have in our hands a critical facsimile of the documents of the Bible as they were first received in the faith congregations of the ancient world.

[44] See further in Klein, *Textual Criticism*, 62–84; Würthwein, *Text*, 111–19; Nestle, *Introduction*, 156–246.

Appendix to Chapter 8
Examples of Variants in the KJV
that Lack Support

Listed below are some well-known texts in the KJV New Testament that lack support in the better manuscripts now available. The newer versions in English have the emended text, or the KJV text set off in a footnote or a square bracket.

John 7.53—8.11, the text about the adulterous woman and Jesus writing in the sand, appears in the KJV. The pericopé seems to have existed in the early Jesus tradition, but was probably not published in the earliest text of the Fourth Gospel. It is missing from such important MSS as 𝔓⁶⁶, ⁷⁵ ℵ B L N T W X Y Δ Θ Ψ 0141 0211 22 33 and many others. In deference to the possibility that this is a likely story from the tradition of Jesus, the UBS Greek New Testament has included it inside square brackets.

Mark 16.9–20 appears in the KJV, but is missing from the oldest and best manuscripts, ℵ and B, and from the writings of Clement and Origen, both of Alexandria. Eusebius and Jerome say that the passage is missing from the Greek MSS known to them. Some MSS include some words after verse 8, while others include other words. The most likely ending of Mark when it first circulated came at verse 8. Because of the rather negative tone of verse 8, and lack of a commission from the resurrected Jesus, copyists were inclined to bring the ending of Mark in line with the positive endings in other Gospels. Mark 16.8 reads: *So they went out and fled from the tomb, for terror and amazement had seized them; and they said nothing to anyone, for they were afraid.*

1 John 5.7–8 contains the Trinitarian insert in the KJV: *in heaven, the Father, the Word, and the Holy Ghost: and these three are one. And there are three that bear witness in earth.* This insertion comes from a few late sources. It appears in some later copies of the Latin Vulgate and in a few Greek MSS that are translations out of late copies of the Latin Vulgate. It is certain that these Trinitarian words were not in the earliest text of 1 John.

Luke 2.14 has *Glory to God in the highest, and on earth peace, good will toward men* in the KJV. The NRSV has *Glory to God in the highest heaven, and on earth peace among those whom he favors!* The difference comes from the ending of one Greek word, *eudokias,* rather than *eudokia.* The first is a genitive ending (NRSV) and the second a nominative (KJV). The genitive (NRSV) means that the peace comes to people of good will, or those whom God favors. The nominative means that peace and good will come to everyone, good and bad. The genitive is supported by the oldest Greek MSS. The change may have happened as a result of oversight on the part of some copyists. In the days of uncial writing style, missing one letter, such as 'ς', at the end of a word was easy to do, especially so if the meaning made sense without the final letter.

Colossians 1.14 in the KJV reads: *In whom we have redemption through his blood, even the forgiveness of sins.* The NRSV omits the phrase, through his blood, simply because it is not in the oldest and best MSS, such as ℵ and 𝔓⁴⁶. The omission is not (as some would have us believe) from a theological bent of the modern versions, but from lack of textual warrant. A later scribe may have inserted the phrase as a parallel to the same phrase in verse 20, attested in the most trustworthy MSS.

The Doxology of Romans is the last, and rather complicated, example of a difference between the KJV and the recent translations. The KJV has a benediction at Romans 16.24 followed by a doxology and second benediction (vv. 25–27), whereas the NRSV does not have verse 24, but does have verses 25–27. Some MSS have a benediction at the end of chapter 14 in addition to 16.24–27, and still others have a doxology at the end of chapter 15 but not after 16.23.

The variants in the MSS related to the ending of Romans can be grouped into five categories as follows:

(1) 1.1—16.23 + doxology (24–27)	𝔓⁶¹ ℵ B C 81 1739, and some copies of the Vulgate, a Syriac and Coptic version.
(2) 1.1—14.23 + doxology + 15.1—16.23 + doxology	A P 5 33 104
(3) 1.1—14.23 + doxology + 15.1—16.24	L Ψ 0209 181 326 330 614 1175 and some translations.
(4) 1.1—16.24	F G 629
(5) 1.1—15.33 + doxology + 16.1—23	𝔓⁴⁶
(6) 1.1—14.23 +16.24 + doxology	Vulgate MSS, An Old Latin version.

In light of these variant endings to Romans, and in the knowledge that Marcion's Romans (*c.* 150–175) did not have chapters 15 and 16, some scholars have judged that Paul wrote Romans (1) in two versions, a long one and a short one, (2) that chapter 16 was originally part of another letter, which was later attached to the ending of Romans. Whatever the literary argument, clearly there was some confusion on the part of the various copyists as to the placement of the doxology and benediction.

Two Jars from Cave 1 at Qumran
(From Würthwein, *Text*, 137)

The First Isaiah Scroll (IQIsa^a)
(Isa. 38.8–40.20)
(From Würthwein, *Text*, 141)

The Second Isaiah Scroll (IQIsa^b)
(Isa. 48.17–49.7)
(From Würthwein, *Text*, 145)

Codex Leningradenis
(Gen. 28.18–29.22)
(From Würthwein, *Text*, 169)

167

ΜΙΝ ΤΟΝ ΛΙΘΟΝ ΕΚ ΤΗϹ
ΘΥΡΑϹ ΤΟΥ ΜΝΗΜΕΙΟΥ
ΚΑΙ ΑΝΑΒΛΕΨΑϹΑΙ ΘΕΩ
ΡΟΥϹΙΝ ΟΤΙ ΑΝΑΚΕΚΥ
ΛΙϹΤΑΙ Ο ΛΙΘΟϹ ΗΝ ΓΑΡ
ΜΕΓΑϹ ϹΦΟΔΡΑ ΚΑΙ ΕΛ
ΘΟΥϹΑΙ ΕΙϹ ΤΟ ΜΝΗΜΕΙ
ΟΝ ΕΙΔΟΝ ΝΕΑΝΙϹΚΟΝ
ΚΑΘΗΜΕΝΟΝ ΕΝ ΤΟΙϹ
ΔΕΞΙΟΙϹ ΠΕΡΙΒΕΒΛΗΜΕ
ΝΟΝ ϹΤΟΛΗΝ ΛΕΥΚΗΝ
ΚΑΙ ΕΞΕΘΑΜΒΗΘΗϹΑΝ
Ο ΔΕ ΛΕΓΕΙ ΑΥΤΑΙϹ ΜΗ
ΕΚΘΑΜΒΕΙϹΘΕ ΙΝ ΖΗΤΕΙ
ΤΕ ΤΟΝ ΝΑΖΑΡΗΝΟΝ ΤΟ
ΕϹΤΑΥΡΩΜΕΝΟΝ ΗΓΕΡ
ΘΗ ΟΥΚ ΕϹΤΙΝ ΩΔΕ ΙΔΕ
Ο ΤΟΠΟϹ ΟΠΟΥ ΕΘΗΚΑ
ΑΥΤΟΝ ΑΛΛΑ ΥΠΑΓΕΤΕ
ΕΙΠΑΤΕ ΤΟΙϹ ΜΑΘΗΤΑΙϹ
ΑΥΤΟΥ ΚΑΙ ΤΩ ΠΕΤΡΩ
ΟΤΙ ΠΡΟΑΓΕΙ ΥΜΑϹ ΕΙϹ
ΤΗΝ ΓΑΛΙΛΑΙΑΝ ΕΚΕΙ ΑΥ
ΤΟΝ ΟΨΕϹΘΕ ΚΑΘΩϹ ΕΙ
ΠΕΝ ΥΜΙΝ ΚΑΙ ΕΞΕΛΘΟΥ
ϹΑΙ ΕΦΥΓΟΝ ΑΠΟ ΤΟΥ
ΜΝΗΜΕΙΟΥ ΕΙΧΕΝ ΓΑΡ
ΑΥΤΑϹ ΤΡΟΜΟϹ ΚΑΙ ΕΚ
ϹΤΑϹΙϹ ΚΑΙ ΟΥΔΕΝΙ ΟΥ
ΔΕΝ ΕΙΠΟΝ ΕΦΟΒΟΥΝ
ΤΟ ΓΑΡ· ⳽

ΚΑΤΑ
ΜΑΡΚΟΝ

B Codex Vaticanus
(Mark 16.3–8. Verses 9–20 are absent)
(From Nestle, *Textual*, Plate IV)

Codex Sinaiticus
(1 Macc. 9.12f. 9.20–22; Jer. 9.2f. Tob. 6.5–7; 6.11f.)
(A sampling of three scribes, from Würthwein, *Text*, 187)

Chester Beatty Papyrus 967
(Ezek. 16.57–17.1)
(From Würthwein, *Text*, 183)

Minuscule Evv. 274 of the tenth century CE
(Mark 16.6–15, with the shorter conclusion in the lower margin)
(From Nestle, *Textual*, Plate X)

Objective

To be conversant with some of the principles of translation and with the story of the English Bible, and to evaluate the merits and demerits of a translation.

Lead Questions

1. *Why have new translations of the Bible generated attacks against translators?*

2. *Define translation, using the derivative etymology from Latin.*

3. *Why do translators continue to translate the Scriptures into contemporary language?*

4. *What does it mean for a translator, or committee of translators, to be 'faithful' to the original text?*

5. *How might 'bias' be held in check in the process of translating the text of Scripture?*

6. *What is the difference between a 'paraphrase' and a 'version'?*

7. *What importance would you attach to the translation work of Wycliffe, Tyndale, and Coverdale in preparing the way for the authorization of an English translation of the Bible for use in all the churches?*

8. *Why was the Geneva Bible so named? And likewise the Douai-Rheims?*

9. *How do you explain the long, unrivalled tenure of the version authorized by King James I of England?*

10. *What explanation would you offer for the proliferation of revisions to the KJV, and new translations, appearing in the twentieth century?*

11. *State five positive guidelines for choosing a translation.*

12. *What are two features of the New Revised Standard Version that were not present in its predecessor, the Revised Standard Version?*

13. *Name four widely recognized versions and five private translations published in the twentieth century.*

9

In Other Words

There can never be an absolutely final translation.
(Robert M. Grant)

Translating the Bible has proven to be a risky business. Retranslating it equally so. People of faith react negatively to reading or hearing the Bible in words other than the familiar and traditional. For this reason, among others, translating and retranslating the Bible is risky. Ask some of the key players in the history of translation.

Saint Jerome (c. 400) was sharply denounced for his Latin Vulgate translation, even by such a stalwart Christian thinker as St Augustine. John Wycliffe's translation into Middle English, edited later by his followers the Lollards, so enraged the church authorities that they dug up Wycliffe's bones forty years after his death and burned them (1415). Cambridge scholar William Tyndale was strangled and his body burned for providing a new translation of the Bible for the English people (1536). Dr Luther Weigle, chair of the committee for the Revised Standard Version, received in the mail a small tin box filled with the ashes of the RSV, together with a scathing letter vilifying him for his part in its translation (c. 1957).[1] 'We have made at least some progress since the Middle Ages: nowadays we burn only the translation – in the old days they burned the translator.'[2]

Translation in the Making

I have not published a sustained translation of any part of the Bible,[3] nor have I served on a committee for the making of a version of the

---

[1] Metzger told the story at a special meeting in the convention of the Society of Biblical Literature in 1997, where he was honoured on his eightieth birthday for his untiring work in textual criticism, translation and interpretation of the New Testament. See also his *Reminiscences of an Octogenarian* (Hendrickson Publishers, 1997). The story of the burning of the RSV appears also in Bruce M. Metzger, 'Problems Confronting Translators of the Bible', *The Making of the New Revised Standard Version* (Grand Rapids: Eerdmans, 1991), 51.

[2] Eugene H. Glassman, *The Translation Debate: What Makes a Bible Translation Good?* (Downers Grove: InterVarsity Press, 1981), 15.

[3] Except as explanatory within books or articles.

Bible. But I do translate for myself, and I teach students how to translate the Greek New Testament into English. So I have some idea of what is involved in translating the ancient text of the Bible into modern English idiom.

Several factors are involved, most of them having to do with the person of the translator: (1) What am I doing when I am translating? This defines the process. (2) Why am I translating? This expresses motive. (3) How can I be faithful to the intended sense of the text? This keeps creative imagination within proper bounds. (4) To what extent can I suspend my personal biases in the process? This is where self-appropriation comes in.

Definition

Our English word 'translate' comes directly from the Latin, *translatus*, a past participle of *transferre*. Two words are combined in this one word: *trans* + *latus*. The first has to do with *change*, and the second with *movement* (or re-movement) of some sort, especially movement that involves carrying. For example, we speak of Enoch of Genesis being translated out of this earthly life into a heavenly realm (Gen. 5.24). Enoch's state of being in the new realm would be different from his state in his earthly life. The process of carrying (*latus*) him over out of this life into another involved change (*trans*). So it is also with carrying the meaning out of one language form into another. The form changes.

Change of language form begs a question: To what extent does the meaning change when the form changes? There is some truth in the adage, 'something is lost in translation'. The loss, however great or small, happens because form and function fit together like hand in glove. The shimmering feeling that comes over us in hearing a reading of a well-crafted poem in one language may not come over an audience listening to a translated version of the same poem. Of course, the translator may be at home in both languages and a skilled wordsmith. Such a person may craft the new form in a way that creates a similar shimmering feeling. Similar, yes, but not exactly the same as the effect the source language generates in the primary audience.

Let me illustrate from an experience in the faculty lounge where I eat lunch with some colleagues of Mennonite heritage. Sometimes when they reminisce about their early life in their Mennonite homes and churches they will use a so-called Low German saying, and all of them will laugh hilariously. Then they realize that some of the non-Mennonites in the group missed the sense, so they try to translate the saying out of Low German into modern English. None of the rest of us laughs. Then comes the explanation from the Mennonite group: 'It just isn't the same in English.'

The job of a translator involves building a bridge that will carry the sense from the source language into the receptor language with the same effect. If the bridge is not well built the intended sense will suffer damage in the transfer to the target language. The materials necessary for bridge building can be summed up in a word: *scholarship*.

Without good scholarship a good translation is impossible. Biblical scholarship means that the persons involved in translating the biblical text have spent years in research in several areas. They have studied at length the grammar, syntax and idiosyncrasies of the source language and the receptor language. They have examined the literature and cultural remains of the ancient culture in which the source language originated and in which also it found its first home. Biblical scholars have to become familiar with the customs of the world of the source text, and sensitive in carrying over the customs into the new language and culture where the same customs do not exist. Is it all right for a translator to transform the ancient, unfamiliar custom into a new custom that is more or less analogous to the one in the source text? Translators wrestle with this dilemma. Transformation of elements in a text does not constitute a translation of the text. The conventional elements in a text make up its fabric. When the textured fabric is transformed into a different texture, a new meaning is generated. Enough for definition.

Motive

Translators of the Bible have good reason for making a translation. Otherwise why would they tackle such an arduous task? Translators of the Bible believe that people should be able to read, or hear, the Bible in their own idiomatic language. When some of the people of Israel were dispersed into other parts of the Greek world, into Egypt in particular, they learned the new Greek language of their new location. Over time the families of the dispersed communities knew little or nothing of Hebrew, the original language of their Bible. A translation out of Hebrew into Greek, thereafter called the Septuagint, was made to solve the problem. That was about 200 BCE.

It happens also that a language changes over time in cultural development, and nowhere more so than in English. The late J. B. Phillips of London, for example, gathered a group of young people around him on Saturday evenings for instruction in religion. He discovered when he read the New Testament from the Authorized Version of 1611 that young people found the language foreign to their ears. Out of that experience Phillips began to translate the New Testament into modern idiomatic English, beginning with the Letters of Paul. Phillips' young students soon developed an appetite for his updated language of the New Testament.

Similar motives lie behind other retranslations of the Bible. The point of translation is communication. If a worthy body of literature – and what could be more worthy than Scripture – does not communicate its sense in the language of a cultural group of readers, that literature becomes dysfunctional. The central motive, therefore, for translating the Bible out of its original language into a new language is to make the intended sense of the biblical texts accessible to the people in the new culture.

Faithfulness

I remember Joel Nederhood, radio speaker on the Back to God Hour, giving a lecture in seminary in the late 1960s on the qualifications of a good preacher. One line, repeated several times in his lecture, has remained with me ever since: 'good preaching comes from a passion to communicate.'[4] The same is no less true for a translator of the Bible. Yet herein lies also the potential peril for a translator.

A translator has to keep one eye on the target audience and the other on the source text. Faithfulness to the task of communicating effectively cannot at the same time compromise the commitment to the meaning of the source text. Textured into the fabric of the biblical texts are all kinds of unfamiliar hues, designs, characters, events, institutions, ideologies. A translator has to be faithful to the text from which the new translation comes, and faithful also to 'the passion to communicate' in the new language. Herein lies the tension of translation.

Numerous examples of customs, figures, ideologies come to mind. Who are the Samaritans? Do we know any such people in our culture? How does a translator render the figure of the Samaritan in the parable Jesus told to his Jewish audience? Which despised figure in the new culture and language would carry the same punch as the Samaritan did

---

[4] Nederhood was quoting his mentor, Peter Eldersville.

in the first telling of that parable in a Palestinian Jewish setting? The problem with leaving the Samaritan untranslated is that the new readers imagine what they wish about the man thus designated. He shows compassion to the fullest, so we call him 'good' without a quiver in our voice. But Samaritans are not good in the minds of first-century Palestinian Jewish people, and they are certainly not better than the Jewish priests and Levites as the parable implies. How does a translator carry over into the new language and culture all the deep emotive connotation wrapped up in the figure of the Samaritan in the parable of Jesus?

A good translation is faithful to the intended sense of the source text. Replacing the text figures with new ones will lose something in the translation. Better to let the reader tease out the significance of the elements in the text, and to do so in the company of others, than to obliterate the formal elements of the source text. The teasing out may prove to be the very means of engaging the reader with the text. A translation cannot play the role of an exegete and interpreter. Let the reader discover and interpret. An interested reader will do just that and benefit greatly. Translations are not made for dolts, but for intelligent people. Intelligent people do not need to have the Bible made into the language of the comic strips, nor amplified well beyond the bounds of a reasonable paraphrase.

One wonders, for example, how a congregation of first readers was able to understand Paul's complex arguments and rich vocabulary in his letter to the Romans. Or how the first readers of Hebrews figured out the tightly textured language of this sermon-like epistle? Granted, the first audiences knew the Greek language first hand, but the Greek vocabulary and style in these biblical documents are not simple, nor are the arguments easy to grasp. By all accounts the authors of the New Testament considered their first audiences wistfully intelligent, able to understand complex thought patterns, big words, complex argumentation, etc. When translators try to reach the lowest denominator of contemporary readers by putting the biblical text in the simplest possible style they border on betrayal of the intended sense of the source text.

The biblical texts were written for mature audiences, not for novices or children. Faithfulness in translation calls for recognition of the distinctive style in each of the various books of the canon. When this factor in translation is ignored the result is sameness of style from one biblical document to the next.

Bias

No one is without bias. We come by our biases honestly: from home and school, from church and culture. Biases are not something we can take or leave, like eating ice cream or refraining from eating it. They are deep-seated beliefs that govern how we think and live. I live in a scientific environment and am biased in that direction. When I watched the movie, 'The Gods Must Be Crazy', my scientific bias made me smile as I tried to suspend my disbelief in the character who threw the Coke bottle off the edge of the world. My bias was showing as I smiled.

Translators, like preachers, live with bias. A Baptist preacher, for example, cannot be expected to find a hint of infant baptism in the New Testament. A Roman Catholic or Reformed preacher, however, might readily find some ground for infant baptism in the New Testament (e.g. Acts 16.33). A social gospel preacher would present a very different message from that of an evangelical charismatic preacher, each one claiming to be 'right'. Translators are equally prone to bias in their work of translating Scripture. The challenge of their job, however, is to suspend their own biases while they allow the bias of the text of Scripture to stand in the new language.

Not everyone agrees with this principle. Some would say that certain biases of the New Testament are offensive and should be softened, or removed altogether. For example, the Gospel of John appears to exhibit a certain bias against 'the Jews' as a people.[5] Repeatedly the term occurs in that Gospel, and often in a very negative light. In the post-holocaust world, however, any bias against the Jewish people is unconscionable. 'The Jews' means something in the present time that it did not mean in the first century, even in the Gospel of John. Given this reality of our time, some scholars argue for a retranslation of 'the Jews' (*hoi Ioudaioi*) that removes the present-day negative bias. 'The Judeans' is one suggestion,[6] although not an altogether satisfactory one. It designates a geographical area rather than a pattern of thought and life. 'Israelites' is a possible alternative, although not truly a translation of the culturally specific *Ioudaioi*.[7]

Keeping personal bias in proper check in the process of translation requires a high degree of self-appropriation. All of us operate out of our

[5] E.g. John 8.44, 'You are from your father the devil.'
[6] Adopted by the editors of the *Biblical Theology Bulletin.*
[7] Philip Esler adopts 'Israelites' in his book on Galatians, or simply leaves *Ioudaioi* untranslated, *Galatians* (London: Routledge, 1998), 3–5, 137, 139.

own horizon. It cannot be otherwise. We see just as far as our horizon permits. Genuine self-appropriation makes us highly conscious of our biases, and opens the way to self-correction, further investigation, and a sympathetic understanding of other horizons of thought and life. Disciplined self-appropriation is the mark of a good translator. Without it there is no safeguard against personal bias coming through in the translation of the biblical text.

Kinds of Translations

Essentially three kinds of translation exist: (1) a translation by a committee of scholars, (2) a translation of an individual scholar, sometimes called a private translation; and (3) a paraphrasitic trans-lation, generally referred to simply as a paraphrase. The first of these is judged to be most free from bias and most likely to render the strict meaning of the original text.

A Committee Translation

When a committee is struck for a new translation of the Bible, or a revision of an earlier translation, the idea is 'to safeguard the translation from sectarian bias',[8] or any other bias that may be present. For example, the New International Version boasts a cross-section of participants from the United States, Great Britain, Canada, Australia and New Zealand, representing a variety of denominations including Anglican, Assemblies of God, Baptist, Brethren, Christian Reformed, Church of Christ, Evangelical Free, Lutheran, Mennonite, Methodist, Nazarene, Presbyterian, Wesleyan, and others.[9] Noticeably missing from this transdenominational list in the preface of the New International Version are representatives from the Roman Catholic Church and the United Church of Canada. One wonders, for example, why a scholar from the largest Protestant denomination in Canada, the United Church of Canada, would not represent that country on the committee.

Even a committee, set up 'to safeguard the translation from sectarian bias', can itself be formed out of a bias, consciously or unconsciously. Why would a committee for an *international* translation of the Bible not have members from Africa, Latin America, or India? Even more

---

[8] From the Preface to the New International Version, 1984.
[9] These are the ones listed in the Preface to the NIV, 1984.

telling, why would such a committee not have someone from the Middle East on the committee? A Jewish scholar perhaps? A Syrian Christian?

Bias can occur at several levels, one being gender. Gender bias can be curbed by appropriate gender balance on the committee. What is the ratio of women to men on the committee? How were the particular women selected? Gender bias can be equally as subversive to a good translation as a sectarian bias. Similarly, having only parents serve on the translation committee creates yet another bias. Why not seek out a number of unmarried people to help with the translation?

Despite these blind spots, so difficult to overcome in forming a translation committee for the production of a version, the translation of the Bible that results from the work of a translation committee is much more useful for serious biblical study than the translation of an individual scholar.

An individual translation

Many individuals have tackled the task of translating Scripture throughout the ages. In the case of the English Bible, the names of Wycliffe, Tyndale, Coverdale, Weymouth, Moffatt, Phillips and Barclay are well known. Each of these in their own time and place and circumstance translated the Bible for the people of their day, and with significant effect. Each of these saw some nuance in the biblical texts that others had not seen. They thought their translation was an improvement over those that had gone before. The plethora of private translations of the Bible into English to date testifies both to the openness of language and insight and discovery, and also to the truth of Robert M. Grant's statement, 'there can never be an absolutely final translation'.[10]

Compared to working on a translation committee, the individual translator's task is relatively easy. The individual has the freedom to choose the words and turn of phrase that seem best, without the checks and balances of peer translators in a committee. This does not mean that the individual translation should be rejected out of hand. Far from it. More often than not the untrammelled insight and expertise of a well-qualified translator such as James Moffatt or J. B. Phillips shed

[10] Robert M. Grant, *Historical Introduction to the New Testament* (New York: Harper & Row, 1963), 55.

worthwhile light on the meaning of a text of Scripture that might otherwise be missed.

A paraphrase

As the etymology of the word implies, a paraphrase restates the core meaning of a text *alongside* and beyond the words customarily used to translate the same text. The aim of a paraphrase is to make the sentence structure flow easily in the contemporary culture without losing the kernel meaning of the text.

Some people have a low view of a paraphrase, believing that the one making the paraphrase takes liberty with the text in rendering the meaning in contemporary dress. This criticism is not always justified. The integrity of a paraphrase lies in its ability to keep the kernel meaning intact while rendering the sense of the text in an easy-flowing style.

The point of a paraphrase is to make the new idiom speak as forcefully as the original idiom did in the first language. To achieve that, the one making the paraphrase looks for *dynamic equivalence* in the new language, rather than a literal representation of the original form. A notable example of a paraphrase is the Living Bible, claimed by some to be 'a faithful, clear, idiomatic and expressive representation of the meaning of the original'.[11] Updated in 1996 under the title, *Holy Bible: New Living Translation*, this paraphrase is said to be 'easy to understand – relevant for today'.[12] Recall what I said about making every text in translation easy to understand. *There are some things in [Paul's letters] hard to understand*, as 2 Peter 3.16 attests.

By way of comparison it may be useful to set out examples of translated texts from a committee translation, the New Revised Standard Version, side by side with the same texts in the paraphrase of the New Living Translation. (See Table 9.1.)

Notice the freedom the paraphrase takes. Galatians 3.28 does not have the words 'for you are all Christians'. Paul does not use the term 'Christian' anywhere in his letters. The New Living Translation paraphrase of Romans 2.13 has those who obey the law *declared right in God's sight*, even though Paul used only one Greek word for the action of 'righting'. Is 'declared' appropriate before 'right'? Why not 'made

---

[11] Glassman, *Translation Debate*, 31, quoting Robert G. Bratcher, 'The Living New Testament Paraphrased', *The Bible Translator*, 20 (July 1969), 39, 131.
[12] Taken from the front cover.

Table 9.1

New Revised Standard Version (1989)	New Living Translation (1996)
Romans 2.13 For it is not the hearers of the law who are righteous in God's sight, but the doers of the law who will be justified.	Romans 2.13 For it is not merely knowing the law that brings God's approval. Those who obey the law will be declared right in God's sight.
Galatians 3.28 There is no longer Jew or Greek, there is no longer slave or free, there is no longer male and female; for all of you are one in Christ Jesus.	Galatians 3.28 There is no longer Jew or Gentile, slave or free, male or female. For you are all Christians – you are one in Christ Jesus.
Matthew 5.29 If your right eye causes you to sin, tear it out and throw it away.	Matthew 5.29 So if your eye – even if it is your good eye – causes you to lust, gouge it out and throw it away.
Matthew 5.3 Blessed are the poor in spirit, for theirs is the kingdom of heaven.	Matthew 5.3 God blesses those who realize their need for him, for the kingdom of heaven is given to them.
Psalm 23.1 The LORD is my shepherd, I shall not want.	Psalm 23.1 The LORD is my shepherd; I have everything I need.
Psalm 103.1 Bless the LORD, O my soul, and all that is within me, bless his holy name.	Psalm 103.1 Praise the LORD, I tell myself; with my whole heart I will praise his holy name.
Genesis 3.4–5 But the serpent said to the woman, 'You will not die; for God knows that when you eat of it your eyes will be opened, and you will be like God, knowing good and evil.'	Genesis 3.4–5 'You won't die'! the serpent hissed. 'God knows that your eyes will be opened when you eat it. You will become just like God, knowing everything, both good and evil.'

right'? 'Justified' of the NRSV may not be the best rendering in English, but it is an attempt not to add unduly to Paul's loaded term.[13]

Is *your right eye* in Matthew 5.29 *your good eye* as the New Living Translation has it? Did the serpent of Genesis 3.4 *hiss* the words to the woman in Eden? Did he tell her she would *know everything*?

The comparison at least illustrates the point that a version, such as the New Revised Standard Version, tends to adhere quite tightly to the texture of the original text. For this reason a reputable committee translation is indispensable for serious study of the biblical texts. Of course, the better path would be to learn the original languages for yourself, and be able to check the degree to which the translators have taken liberty with the primary text in their 'passion to communicate' in the second language.

This chapter on translation, written in English, would not be complete without at least a glance at the fortunes of the English Bible through the centuries. The lines of its pedigree are drawn for easy reference in the chart in Table 9.2.

Tracing the Steps of the English Bible

Three temporal stages in the story seem to present themselves. The first stage pre-dates the production of the Authorized Version of 1611; the second is the long, unchallenged tenure of the King James Version (KJV) up to the first major revision, and the third, the major revisions of the KJV in the twentieth century along with multiple new translations.

Before the Authorized Version of 1611

The translation of the Bible into English accompanies the development of the English language itself. Christianity arrived in England via the Roman occupation of the island before the beginning of English as a distinct language. With the invasion of the Angles and Saxons from Europe in the fifth century a new language and culture began to emerge, at the same time diminishing the presence and power of the Christian movement. Eventually, at about 600, the Church sent missionaries under the leadership of one Augustine (not the bishop of Hippo). The Bible the missionaries brought with them was the Latin

---

[13] E. P. Sanders coined the word 'righteoused' to translate Paul's passive of *dikaioō*.

Vulgate, useful only to the Roman Catholic missionaries who could read Latin.

The first signs of a translation appeared at about 670 when a young lad named *Caedmon*, connected in some way to the monastery at Whitby and able to understand some Latin, created poems in Old English based on passages of the Bible. The people remembered the poems and began to sing them. These poetic paraphrases could hardly be called a translation into Old English in the strict sense. That came from the mind and hand of Bishop Aldhelm of Sherborne at *c.* 700. Sources say he translated the Psalms out of the Vulgate into Old English.

In the 700s also, another man named *Bede*, of some repute as a scholar and monk at Yarrow, translated parts of the Scripture into the language of the people, Old English. He was in the middle of translating the Gospel of John when he died in 735 CE. After Bede nothing much in the way of translation appears in England until the ascendancy of *King Alfred the Great* (871–901). Alfred was interested in history, literature and culture, and sought to instil the same in his subjects. He translated some historical works into Old English, and also parts of Exodus and Acts for incorporation into his law code. Monks and priests of the period freely produced interlinear translations of the Latin Vulgate: the Latin on one line and the corresponding Old English below the Latin words.

The Normans arrived on the shores of England in 1066, and with them the French language. The Norman invasion marks the beginning of a transition from Old English to a more French-oriented Middle English, the language of Geoffrey Chaucer (1342–1400).

Evidence of any significant translation of any part of the Bible into Middle English is scant, and any that did come out served only the clerics in their ministry. The laity of England in the year 1300 did not have a single copy of the Bible in their own language. And even if they did, few of them could read it. Literacy was still very much limited to courtiers, clerics, and professionals.

That situation began to change under the influence, vision and scholarship of *John Wycliffe* (*c.* 1329–1384). Wycliffe was an Oxford scholar and churchman of sorts. He criticized the church hierarchy and struggled to make the gospel relevant to the everyday life of the people of England. He gathered followers around him, who together with Wycliffe travelled the length and breadth of the land preaching the gospel. These preachers were dubbed Lollards (from 'Low Landers') by the church authorities, a term of derision and heresy. Wycliffe was convinced that the whole Bible should be available to the people of England in their own language, and he set the wheels in motion for the project.

He may not have done much of the translating himself, but he inspired his Lollards to complete his vision. By 1380 the first version of the Wycliffe Bible was published, four years before Wycliffe's death. The second came out shortly after his death in 1384. Another retranslation of the second edition appeared in 1388, produced by John Purvey, a devotee of Wycliffe. In this latter edition Purvey rendered the earlier edition into a more idiomatic Middle English, using the best Latin manuscripts of the Vulgate he could find for the job. Many of the Wycliffe Bibles have survived, testimony to the widespread acceptance and use of the translation among the people of England at that time. Here is a sampling of Purvey's version of the Wycliffe Bible, taken from the introduction to the parable of the Good Samaritan (Luke 10.25–28).

> And lo, a wise man of the lawe ros vp, temptynge hymn, and seiynge, Maister, what thing schal Y do to haue euerlastynge lijf? And he seide to hym, What is writun in the lawe? How redist thou? He asnweride and seide, Thou schalt loue thi Lord God of al thin herte, and of al thi soule, and of alle thi strengthis, and of al thi mynde; and thi neighbore as thi silf. And Ihs seide to hym, Thou hast answered rightly; do this thing, and thou schalt lyue.[14]

Church authorities, however, tried desperately to suppress this English Bible, but without much success it seems. Purvey and friends were imprisoned. Some died at the stake with Wycliffe Bibles tied around their necks. Yet Wycliffe's Bible prevailed, some people paying handsomely to own even a small part of it. Following an order from the Council of Constance in 1415, Wycliffe's bones were exhumed and burned, and the ashes thrown into the River Swift.

If Wycliffe deserves credit for giving England the first translation of the Latin Vulgate in Middle English in manuscript form, as he must be, then *William Tyndale* (1494–1536) has the honour of giving the English people the first printed edition of the Bible, translated from the original languages of Hebrew and Greek into Modern English.

A scholar at Cambridge, Tyndale was a child of the Renaissance and Reformation spirit. His work had the double advantage of Gutenberg's

---

[14] Taken from F. F. Bruce, *The English Bible: A History of Translations* (London: Lutterworth Press, 1961), 13

invention of the printing press and the spreading flame of Reformation rhetoric. Much of Tyndale's work was carried out on the continent, including a time in the city of Wittenberg where Luther published his famous theses of church reform. Luther's publication of his German Bible in 1522 may have stimulated Tyndale to do the same for the English Bible.

By 1525 Tyndale had his New Testament ready for printing at Cologne, but when the authorities learned of the plan they banned the printing. Tyndale escaped to Worms, where he had the first printing of the New Testament made in 1526. Copies soon reached England, smuggled there in bales of cloth and in barrels of other goods. When the news of the Tyndale Bible reached the ears of Cardinal Wolsey among others, a bonfire of Tyndale Bibles was set alight in St Paul's Cathedral. Wolsey bought up all the Tyndale Bibles he could find, whether in England or on the Continent, in a feverish attempt to eradicate them. Even Thomas More, himself a target of political intrigue, criticized Tyndale's translation vehemently. Meanwhile Tyndale was carefully working on a revision of his earlier English Bible. By 1534 the revision was complete, and ready for printing at Antwerp, a city of relative safety for Tyndale. This new version was a landmark work, used freely by the later translators of the KJV, 1611.

Tyndale was eventually captured and imprisoned near Brussels. He was tried and found guilty of heresy in August 1536, and sentenced to death. The executioner strangled him and then burned his body at the stake. Tyndale's last reported words were: 'Lord, open the King of England's eyes.' Even as he spoke those words, his prayer was answered, for Henry VIII had already approved the circulation of the Bible in English.

With this approval of King Henry VIII came revisions of Tyndale's Bible in rapid succession. First, *Miles Coverdale* (1488–1569), a graduate of Cambridge and influenced by the Reformation, spent time on the Continent, some of it working with Tyndale. Coverdale devoted himself to giving the Bible to the people of England in a language he believed they could understand. He translated the entire Bible and published it in 1535, probably at Marburg, Germany. He dedicated his translation to Henry VIII, while denouncing the Pope, a ploy that pleased Henry well. The king had Cranmer and his bishops check the Bible for heresy. When they reported none, Henry said, 'Then in God's name let it go abroad among our people.' Coverdale had leaned heavily on the translations of others, including Tyndale's, Luther's German

Bible, and the Latin Vulgate for his own work. His Bible shows marks of this dependence.

Second, *Matthew's Bible* is the work of John Rogers who adopted the pen name Thomas Matthew. Rogers was a student of Tyndale, and completed the work of translating the Old Testament, which Tyndale had left unfinished. In 1537 Cromwell convinced the king to issue a royal license not only for the sale and distribution of Matthew's Bible, but also for the revised translation of the Coverdale Bible. Both English translations were circulating in England at the same time. Matthew's Bible was dedicated to the king and presented to him publicly. The king then gave permission for it to be read in public.

Third, *The Great Bible*, named thus because of the size of its pages (16½ x 11 inches), became the first Bible of the Church of England. The English Bible now officially licensed, Cromwell asked Coverdale to make a new revision using Matthew's Bible as a base. The printing was completed in 1539, and the clergy ordered to make a copy of the Great Bible accessible to every congregation. In short order, this Bible became favourite reading of the literate people of England. Altogether six editions of the Great Bible – sometimes called the Cranmer Bible because of Cranmer's endorsement of it in the preface – were made between 1540 and 1541. With the royal license granted to the English Bible and the wide acceptance accorded the Great Bible, the Bible in English had become an inexorable fact of life from then on.

Three more English versions of the Bible deserve brief mention before pressing on to account for the authorization of a single version by King James I.

The *Geneva Bible* came in the wake of Queen Elizabeth's accession to the throne in 1558. Why would an English translation be called the Geneva Bible? Because its translators took refuge in Geneva Switzerland, home of Reformers, Calvin and Beza, from the bloody persecution of Mary Tudor. Mary sought to reverse the reforms of her father, Henry VIII, and of her brother, Edward VI. The English Bibles that circulated freely in the short reign of Edward were confiscated and burned in the reign of Mary. Promoters of the English translations, such as John Rogers and Thomas Cranmer, were executed. Others fled for refuge in Geneva, among them scholars like William Whittingham.

Whittingham produced a revision of the entire Bible in Geneva in 1560 and dedicated it to the new Protestant Queen Elizabeth. This Geneva Bible includes the Apocrypha of the Old Testament in an Appendix. Two other interesting features appear in this version for the first time: verse divisions and words printed in italics that have no parallel in the original text. The translators of the version authorized by King James followed both of these features in 1611. The anti-Roman Catholic and pro-Calvinist bias of the Geneva Bible is evident in the marginal notes.

This version became popular throughout Britain, especially so in Scotland. Scottish reformer, John Knox, favoured the Geneva Bible, produced as it was in the city of his own exile by his own friends of the Reformed faith. The Geneva Bible was also the Bible of Shakespeare, the Puritans and the Pilgrims. This Bible went through 160 editions and, along with the Tyndale version, strongly influenced the translation of the KJV.

The growing popularity of the Geneva Bible put the Great Bible of the churches into virtual disuse. Yet the Geneva Bible did not sit well with the English church authorities because of its controversial marginal notes, many of them Calvinistic. The Archbishop of Canterbury, Matthew Parker, set in motion a project to revise the Great Bible in line with the more deft translation of the Geneva scholars, but without the controversial notes. The revision, published in 1568 and named the *Bishops Bible*, replaced the Great Bible to become the official English version of the Church of England. Even so, the Bishops Bible was unable to displace the other versions that had imprinted themselves on the hearts of the English people over many years.

The *Douai-Rheims Bible* gets its name from the two cities of Europe with which it is associated. This Bible is the counterpart of the Protestant translations of the time. Just as Protestant scholars were forced to leave England during the reign of the Roman Catholic Queen Mary, so Roman Catholic scholars had to leave England during the reign of the Protestant Queen Elizabeth. William Allen from Oxford was one of them. He established a college at Douai in France in 1568, moved its headquarters to Rheims in 1578 and back to Douai in 1593. While the college was at Rheims, another Roman Catholic scholar, Gregory Martin, translated the New Testament of the Latin Vulgate into English at Rheims and published it in 1582. The Old Testament part he translated when the college had moved back to Douai. The motive for the translation was to provide an alternative to the 'false translations' of the Protestants.

The Roman Catholic bias in the Douai-Rheims translation comes through frequently. For example, *give us this day our supersubstantial bread* (Matt. 6.11) reflects a current doctrine of the Catholic Church; so also the line in the parable of the Good Samaritan, 'whatever thou shalt supererogate, I, at my return will repay thee' (Luke 10.35). Often where 'repentance' appears in other translations, the Douai-Rheims Bible will use 'penance'. In this version the Apocrypha, as might be expected, is not in an Appendix, but in the order in which the books appear in the Vulgate. The Douai-Rheims Bible went through several revisions, the most radical of them done by Bishop Richard Challoner (1691–1781), convert from Protestantism and influenced by the KJV of 1611.

The tenure of the Authorized Version (KJV) of 1611 to the first major revision

In 1604, shortly after James VI of Scotland was crowned James I of England, a conference was called at Hampton Court to address the complaint of the Puritan party of the Church of England. Out of the conference came a critical resolution:

> That a translation be made of the whole Bible, as consonant as can be to the original Hebrew and Greek; and this to be set out and printed, without any marginal notes, and only to be used in all Churches of England in time of divine service.[15]

The new king was interested in a new translation in any case, one that would replace the Bishops Bible in the churches and also the Geneva Bible that had become popular. Moreover, the king played a major role in getting the new translation off the ground. Six sub-committees were given the task of translating the whole Bible, each sub-committee working on one set of documents. Three were assigned to the Old Testament, one to the Apocrypha, and two to the New Testament. When the work of these sub-groups was complete, all the parts were brought together to be reviewed by a panel of twelve, two from each sub-committee. From there the complete translation was sent to the leading church people for sanction.

King James did more than set up the administration of the trans-lation. He was involved in drafting the rules. The Bishops Bible was to be the primary reference for the new translation, but re-examined in light of the Hebrew Bible and the Greek New Testament. Other translations were to be consulted in the process, not only English translations but Latin, German, Italian, and Spanish as well. But the English words must flow with nuance consistent with the context of

---

[15] In Bruce, *English Bible*, 96.

the passage. That meant that the repeated word in the original language need not be repeated in the English translation. For example, in Psalm 1.2 the Hebrew word (*hagah*) translated 'meditate' is the same word translated 'imagine' in Psalm 2.1. The context in the first instance is positively ponderous whereas in the second it is strategically scheming. A New Testament example would be Matthew 5.13 compared to Luke 14.35. In Matthew the Greek words (*tes ges*) translated 'the earth' are translated 'the land' in Luke. The context appears to be the same in both cases, but in Luke the words occur alongside 'the dunghill', so 'the land' rather than 'the earth' made more sense to the translators.

Another rule, followed also in the Geneva Bible, stated that English words not represented in the original language were to be signalled by italics. The idea was to make the sentence make sense in English. An example is at Hebrews 1.2: *God ... hath in these last days spoken unto us by his Son.* The pronoun 'his' does not appear in the Greek text.[16] Again, following the Geneva Bible, the chapter and verse divisions remained. No marginal notes were allowed, but the editors did provide a summary heading to each chapter for convenience. In some cases the summaries were as much interpretations as summaries.

The translators approved by King James were first-rate scholars, although not all equally pious. They all worked for free, having only room and board as their material reward. The first printing of their new version of 1500 pages emerged from the press of Robert Barker, King's Printer, in 1611. It appeared with an elaborate dedication to King James and an explanatory preface. The title page of the first edition read: 'The Holy Bible, Contayning the Old Testament and the New: Newly Translated out of the Originall tongues; & with the former Translations diligently compared and revised by his Maiesties speciall Commandment. Appointed to be read in Churches.'[17]

In view of the important role King James played in the promotion, production and authorization of the new version, it was widely hailed as the King James Version. Eventually, though, it was designated the Authorized Version of the Church of England. As time went by, revisions were made, sometimes because of printer's errors and sometimes because of the need to refine the earlier translations. The

---

[16] I have been present in church meetings where the speaker has mistakenly treated the italics of the Authorized Version as emphatic!

[17] From Ira Maurice Price, *The Ancestry of Our English Bible,* third revised edition by William A. Irwin and Allen P Wikgren (New York: Harper & Brothers, 1956), 273.

most important of these revisions came in the eighteenth century. Thomas Paris made an extensive revision at Cambridge in 1762, while Benjamin Blayney made another at Oxford in 1769. The spelling was updated, and the antiquated terms modernized. Blayney's text is the current form of the Authorized Version of King James I.

Even though marginal notes were not allowed in the version authorized by King James, some of the later editions had notes. One edition in particular is noteworthy. In 1701 Bishop Lloyd incorporated a chronology into the translated text. Lloyd borrowed his chronology from Archbishop Ussher of Armagh, Ireland. Ussher fixed the date of creation at 4004 BC, and worked out dates for other major events in the biblical story. Biblical scholars thereafter followed his system down to the twentieth century. Discoveries since Ussher, however, have demonstrated conclusively that his system was flawed beyond redemption.

Without a doubt, the Authorized Version of King James made an indelible mark on the mind and heart of English-speaking people around the world. It held sway for almost three centuries.

> Its simple, majestic Anglo-Saxon tongue, its clear, sparkling style, its directness and force of utterance have made it the model in language, style and dignity of some of the choicest writers of the last two centuries ... It has endeared itself to the hearts and lives of millions of Christians and has molded the characters of leaders in every walk of life.[18]

Major revisions and new translations in the twentieth century

In the middle of the nineteenth century efforts were made to revise the KJV, beginning with parts of the New Testament. By 1870 a more formal decision came from the Upper House of the Convocation of Canterbury under the leadership of Bishop Wilberforce of Winchester to revise the entire Authorized Version (KJV) of the Bible. Both houses passed the resolution. Sixteen biblical scholars were appointed to a committee to carry out the resolution. This committee then invited forty more biblical scholars from various denominations onto the Revision Committee. Roman Catholic scholars were invited, but did not accept. The members totalled fifty-four, the same number as the committee appointed by King James.

The committee also invited American scholars to participate, and they did so under the chairmanship of Dr Philip Schaff. The

---

[18] Price, *Ancestry*, 276f.

committees on both sides of the Atlantic met regularly for several hours at a sitting to carry out their arduous task of revising. The American suggestions were considered seriously, but could be rejected by the English committee if they felt so inclined. If rejected, the suggestions were placed in an Appendix. The English committee asked their American counterparts to support the English Revised Version, and not to publish their own version for a period of fourteen years. On 17 May 1881 Bishop Ellicott presented the *English Revised Version* of the New Testament to the Convocation of Canterbury. It was published immediately in England and shortly thereafter in the United States. The reception of the Revised Version was phenomenal. By the end of the first year sales of the Revised Version of the New Testament had reached about three million.

The work of revising the Old Testament took longer. Altogether 792 working days were spent on it before it finally appeared in print bound together with the New Testament on 19 May 1885.

One reason for the revision arose from the emergence of a critical text of New Testament, rather than the *Textus Receptus* used for the translation of the KJV. Altogether, the Revised Version of the New Testament differs from the KJV in more than 36,000 places.[19] In the Old Testament there are proportionately fewer changes. Another reason for the revision was to update the language. Some words had become offensive for public reading, while others were simply antiquated. Examples of the changes are: 'Holy Spirit' for 'Holy Ghost'; 'strange' for 'outlandish'; 'smooth' for 'peeled'; 'condemnation' for 'damnation'. In addition to these kinds of changes, the English Revised Version arranged the English text in paragraphs, rather than only chapter and verse divisions. In this way, each document would read like a book, not a collection of verses.

The committee in England disbanded shortly after its work was finished. The American committee, however, remained together in hope of a revision that would more adequately represent the American scholars' insights and style of English language. The work of revision completed, American readers of the Bible welcomed the publication of the *American Standard Version* on 26 August 1901 by Thomas Nelson and Sons of New York. The translation was reliable and the language accessible. But like all translations of the ancient Bible into living languages, these two revisions of the KJV served their time and culture.

[19] Price, *Ancestry*, 285.

Both of them went through further revision in the second half of the twentieth century.

Before surveying that latter half of the century, however, we do well to cast a glance at some of the other translations that came out in the wake of the two major revisions of the KJV at the beginning of the century.

With the ongoing discovery of manuscripts from the Ancient Near East, including some of the Old and New Testaments, coupled with the growing desire to communicate the message of the Bible (or parts thereof) in contemporary English, more translations appeared on the scene. The *Twentieth-Century New Testament* is the product of a group of people, rather unsung heroes of translation, whose finished work was published in 1901, revised and published again in 1904. It attempted to put the New Testament in vernacular English, and with significant success. Interestingly, the committee arranged the books in chronological, rather than canonical order, and provided an introduction to each book. 'This English Twentieth Century New Testament was a pioneer in the movement to translate the Scriptures into current speech.'[20]

Richard *Weymouth* of England, scholar and teacher of the classics, decided to translate the Greek New Testament into easy English at the beginning of the century. He took on the project in retirement, not to supplant the other English versions, but to supplement them with his more down to earth language for lay people to read. The title of his translation is telling: The New Testament in Modern Speech. Five editions came out after Weymouth's death in 1902, the fifth in 1929. Another translator is James Moffatt (1870–1944) from Scotland, professor first at Glasgow then at Oxford and later at Union Theological Seminary in New York. He believed the KJV was no longer satisfactory on several counts: its archaic language, the new insights into Greek vocabulary and syntax, and new manuscript evidence.

He published his translation of the New Testament in Oxford in 1913, and his Old Testament in 1924 – a remarkable achievement. His aim, like that of Weymouth, was to put the Bible into modern speech. His translation gained in popularity, and also in prestige among the academic elite, so skilled was he at turning an English phrase with effect, yet without losing the kernel sense of the original text.

In the United States Edgar J. *Goodspeed* (1871–1962), a strong proponent of modern translations, criticized the existing ones in

---

[20] Ewert, *Ancient Tablets*, 214, and n. 3.

public. The response to him was that he publish his own. After some hesitation, he proceeded to do so. Giving his new version the title, 'An American Translation', Goodspeed's aim was to produce a version made in America for the American people. His translation, published in 1923 by the University of Chicago Press, received no small criticism. One such, appearing in the St Louis Globe Democrat, merits quoting: 'It is as much an anachronism to put the gospels in colloquial American terms today as it would be to put pants[21] on the twelve apostles.'[22]

Back to England, we note two more translations, one by a Roman Catholic, Ronald Knox, and the other by a canon of the Anglican Church, J. B. Phillips. The Catholic authorities granted permission to Knox to translate the Vulgate New Testament into modern English. An able scholar in the classics, *Knox* published his commissioned translation of the New Testament in 1945, and the Old Testament in 1949. His Bible reads like an original composition in English, which was his objective. The Knox Bible was widely received.

Phillips, as I mentioned already, found his youth group disenchanted when he read to them from Paul's letters in the KJV. Encouraged by C. S. Lewis to pursue his goal of making the New Testament easily intelligible to non-church people, Phillips published his translation of Paul's letters in 1947 under the title, 'Letters to Young Churches'. He published other parts of the New Testament incrementally, bringing all the published parts together under one cover in 1958, titled *The New Testament in Modern English*.

Phillips operated under similar principles as others had before him, with a 'passion to communicate' the message of the Bible in easy-to-understand English. Phillips believed the verse divisions hindered the flow of the language, so he set them off in the margin in his translation. The Phillips New Testament of 1958 was more paraphrase than translation, perhaps at points more Phillips than New Testament.

When his New Testament had won the confidence of a large share of Bible readers over the years, Phillips decided to revise his English and bring his translation more in line with the Greek text of the New Testament (using the critical text of the United Bible Societies). The revision came out in 1972. 'Perhaps it is not always as spicy as the first edition, but it is a bit more accurate.'[23]

---

[21] American for 'trousers'.
[22] Cited in Ewert, *Ancient Tablets*, 218.
[23] Ewert, *Ancient Tablets*, 222.

The second half of the twentieth century saw an increasing number of English versions and translations of the Bible, too many to mention in this chapter. I limit the discussion to those most widely read to the present time, beginning with the *Revised Standard Version* of the New Testament in 1946.

In 1937 the International Council of Religious Education, North America, set up a revision committee to update the language of the American Standard Version of 1901. In that earlier version the attempt was made to preserve as much of the flavour of the KJV of 1611 as possible. By 1937 other translations had appeared that had no such commitment, and could eclipse the dominant position of the American Standard Version. The committee consisting of some thirty-two members from most of the major Protestant denominations completed the New Testament in 1946. The version reflects their attempt to remove as many of the archaisms of the Authorized Version as possible. The second personal pronouns were modernized, except where the deity is addressed: 'thee', 'thou', 'thy', 'thine' and 'ye' (plural) become 'you' and 'your' where human persons are addressed.

The committee made other formal changes as well, such as direct quotations enclosed with quotation marks; poetical parts set out in poetical form to a greater extent; Jehovah changed to Lord. By 1952 the Old Testament was completed and the whole Bible published in one volume. While the work on the Old Testament was in progress, the Dead Sea Scrolls of Qumran had come to light, and the Isaiah scroll was made available to the members responsible for the Old Testament. The committee made thirteen revisions to Isaiah based on the Qumran Isaiah. Otherwise the committee relied heavily on the existing Masoretic text, making some emendations where the manuscripts were defective in some way. Publicized on national television networks, the Revised Standard Version enjoyed almost instant appeal in large segments of the religious world, including also the Roman Catholic Church in 1965. Here was the first truly ecumenical Bible of the Christian Church. In its first ten years it had sold over twelve million copies.

The committee for the Revised Standard Version was a standing committee. It remained in place for ongoing revisions that might be deemed expedient in light of new textual evidence, or language change. The committee was expanded to include more women, Roman Catholics, and some Jewish representation for the Old Testament. In 1974 the National Council of Churches, prompted by the social changes that had happened in the sixties and seventies, approved another revision of the Revised Standard Version. The Council expected the committee to produce the new version not later than the mid-eighties.

It was not until late in 1989 that the new edition was ready for press. It was named simply, *New Revised Standard Version*. Mostly what was 'new' about it was the move to a more contemporary language. The earlier compromise on the second personal pronoun was surrendered. Now God would be addressed using the same pronoun as for humans. 'After all, the KJV made no distinction between speech addressed to God and speech addressed to humans, and neither did the ancient languages in which the biblical books were originally written.'[24] But the New Revised Standard Version (NRSV) made another notable innovation. It removed all the gender-exclusive language relating to the human family. Where 'man' includes both men and women in the Revised Standard Version, the NRSV has 'humankind'; where 'brothers' implies both genders the NRSV has 'brothers and sisters'. The gender inclusive language of the NRSV may not be as smooth as we might like, but it does remove the offensiveness of a male-based language, and conforms commendably to the consciousness in the post-modern world.

Unlike the Revised Standard Version and the NRSV, whose genealogy reaches back to the KJV and beyond to Tyndale, the *New English Bible* claims to be a brand new translation for modern English speaking people. The initiative started in the Church of Scotland, from there to the Church of England, Methodist, Baptist and Congregational churches. Eventually a committee was formed to carry out the task. C. H. Dodd was the single director of the project from 1949 until 1965. In 1965 G. R. Driver was appointed as co-director with Dodd. The aim of this translation was to make the language 'timeless' yet timely – an impossible undertaking. In addition, the style had to be such that could be read in public. Further, the translation should be faithful to the original text, not in a word-for-word translation, but in a dynamic equivalent representation of the meaning. Like the Revised Standard Version, the New English Bible retains the archaic personal pronoun, 'thou', 'thee', etc., for addressing God. (So much for the 'timeless' language.) Otherwise, the style of the New English Bible

---

[24] Robert C. Dentan, 'The Story of the New Revised Standard Version' in Metzger, *Making*, 5.

has much to commend it, although the poet T. S. Eliot is reported as calling it the product of 'dignified mediocrity'.[25]

More and more English translations came to the fore in the two decades of the seventies and eighties. A few of the most notable are identified here.

The *Jerusalem Bible* in English, translated by Roman Catholic scholars based in Christ's College, Liverpool, is the counterpart to the French *La Bible de Jérusalem*, but not a translation from the French. The Jerusalem Bible is the first Catholic version to be translated from the original Hebrew and Greek. Others came from the Latin Vulgate. The Jerusalem Bible has the Apocrypha and comes with notes, many of which explain the text according to Roman Catholic doctrine. The translation itself, first published in 1966, is even-handed and very readable.

On the American side, another Catholic translation of the whole Bible appeared four years after the British-made Jerusalem Bible, in 1970, under the name, *New American Bible*. It too has explanatory notes, paragraphs with verse numbers in small print, and a variety of English words used to translate a single Hebrew or Greek word. For example, the Greek word, *basileia*, appears in the translation as 'kingdom', 'reign', 'kingship', 'dominion' and 'nation'. The New American Bible is a worthy companion to the Jerusalem Bible and the other versions of the same period.

The *New American Standard Bible* came out incrementally over eleven years. In 1971 the Lockman Foundation of California, who had first published the American Standard Version of 1901, published the whole Bible. The names of the revising committee remain unknown for some reason. Their objective, like that of many committees before them, was to be faithful to the original languages and to communicate in contemporary English-American style. The New American Standard Bible reverted to the verse divisions rather than paragraphs of other modern versions. It followed the Revised Standard Version compromise of using the archaic pronoun for addressing God, and the common pronoun for humans.

Among the observable characteristics of this translation are the conservatism and literalism of its translators, as exhibited in their marginal notes, as well as in the translation itself. Evidence of this is seen, for example, in their attempt to harmonize passages that bear

---

[25] Ewert, *Ancient Tablets*, 235.

some conflicting factors (2 Sam. 24.1;1 Chron. 24.1; Acts 9.7/22.9). And again, their bias appears in the capitalization of words in the Old Testament believed to refer to the Messiah of the New Testament. As Edward P. Blair remarks, 'The English style, as a whole, remains over-literal, stilted, and non-idiomatic, in spite of the revisers' announced intention to render the grammar and terminology in contemporary English.'[26] Evangelical Christians in the United States and Canada were drawn to the New American Standard Bible; that is, until the *New International Version* made its appeal to the same evangelical constituency.

Representatives from the Christian Reformed Church and the National Association of Evangelicals gave birth to the idea of a new translation of the Bible in 1965. More than a hundred scholars from about thirty-four evangelical denominations and groups bought into the plan to produce a translation that would do for the modern evangelical church what the Authorized King James Version did for the church of its time, except that the New International Version did not include the Apocrypha in an Appendix. Sponsored by the New York Bible Society, the New Testament came out with abundant advertising in 1973, with the Old Testament following in 1978.

What seems to have motivated the translation was the perceived 'liberalism' in the Revised Standard Version and other translations. All members of the translating committee were expected to hold to the view of Scripture prescribed in the Westminster Confession, the Belgic Confession, and the Statement of Faith of the National Association of Evangelicals. Zondervan published the version, stating that the translators view the Bible as 'inerrant in the autographs'.[27]

Claiming to be a new translation, not a revision of an earlier version, the strength of this Bible lies particularly in its adherence to the best available critical Hebrew, Aramaic and Greek texts. Where a passage is questionable it is set in square brackets with a note of explanation (e.g. Mark 16.9–20). Passages are clearly outlined for the convenience of the reader, and the style is contemporary for the most part. But like any other translation of its kind, this version is equally subject to bias, in this case a conservative bias. For example, in a number of places in the Old Testament where a term might refer to Messiah of the New Testament, the term is capitalized (e.g. Ps. 2.2, 6, 7, 12; 16.10; Dan.

---

[26] Edward P. Blair, *The Illustrated Bible Handbook* (Nashville: Abingdon Press, 1987), 46.
[27] Blair, *Illustrated*, 52.

9.25–26). Many of the old terms are kept in this new translation: 'sanctify', 'saints', 'justified', 'predestined', 'holiness', 'redemption', etc.

This New International Version has become the new Bible of very many conservative, evangelical churches in North America. Rumours of revision have circulated recently in North America, to update the language and remove the gender-exclusive terms, as the NRSV did for the Revised Standard Version.[28] To date, the revision is not forthcoming in North America.

The *Good News Bible* made its debut at about the same time as the New International Version. Headed by Robert G. Bratcher, an advisory committee of the American Bible Society produced a version of the New Testament in 1966, another in 1967, and another in 1971 under the title, *Good News for Modern Man: Today's English Version.* This version captured the attention of the younger generation of readers, and others as well. Both testaments appeared in one volume in 1976 as the Good News Bible. The basic principle of translating for the committee was that of dynamic equivalent phrasing. Others had done the same before the Good News Bible, but this version was thoroughly committed to the rule. As stated earlier, dynamic equivalence in translation aims at creating the same feeling in the readers of the new language as that created in the first readers of the source language. For this translation also, the translators worked from the best critical texts of the two testaments. The Good News Bible provides helpful notes, headings of passages, maps, chronologies, and line drawings.

The *Contemporary English Version* is a product of the last decade of the twentieth century. Published by Thomas Nelson and sponsored by the American Bible Society, the Contemporary English Version claims to be 'the Bible for Today's Family'. Its translators worked directly from the original languages of both testaments in an effort to make this new version as *reliable* as possible, yet *readable* as well. The language is at the level of fifth grade (age ten) with a view to reaching the largest number of people in the English-speaking world. The method of translating was dynamic equivalence, thought for thought rather than word for word.

Following the lead of the NRSV, and aware of the need to do so, the translators of this version adopted the policy of gender-inclusive language. For example, this version renders Luke 2.52 in this way: *Jesus became wise, and his body grew strong. God was pleased with him and so were the people.*

---

[28] I understand that the British wing of the New International Version committee voted to revise the gender-exclusive language, among other things, while the Americans voted against the revision. I have not seen a copy of the British New International Version on sale in Canada.

The Revised Standard Version has ... *in favour with God and man*. All the old religious words, such as 'justification', 'redemption', 'reconciliation', 'propitiation', etc. are replaced with more common words or phrases.

This version provides notes about manuscript variants in a text, about other translations of a word, and about Bible history and culture. The New Testament was published in 1991 and the whole Bible in 1995.

Other translations from the second half of the twentieth century include the *Authentic New Testament* translated by a Jewish scholar (1955), *The New Testament: A New Translation* by Scottish commentator William Barclay (1968–69, 1980), *The Living Bible Paraphrased* by Kenneth Taylor (1971), the *New World Translation of the Holy Scriptures* published by the Jehovah's Witnesses (1960), the *New Jewish Version* sponsored by the Jewish Publication Society (1955), and the *New King James Version*, a somewhat modernized version of the older English Authorized Version of 1611, disregarding manuscript evidence since then, and published by Thomas Nelson, Inc. (1979/1982).

By way of summarizing the trek of the Bible in English, the following chart, updated from an original draft by the United Bible Societies, outlines the directions and connections (Table 9.2).

As in the making of books, so also in the making of translations, there is no end. How does one choose between them in our time of such an overflow of English Bibles? Here are a few basic guidelines of a positive nature:

1. The faithfulness of the translators to the form and function of the original text in rendering the meaning in the new language is imperative.
2. A good translation relies on the best critical text of the original languages.
3. A serious student of the Bible will want a translation that fairly represents the vocabulary, grammar, and syntax of the first languages.
4. A translation coming from a committee made up of scholars from diverse backgrounds and both genders is preferred.
5. The more current the language the better, including gender-inclusive language.

In a less positive vein, be wary of:

1. modern translations that rely on the *Textus Receptus* of Erasmus, as the King James translators of 1611 did;

Table 9.2 Chart of the English Bible

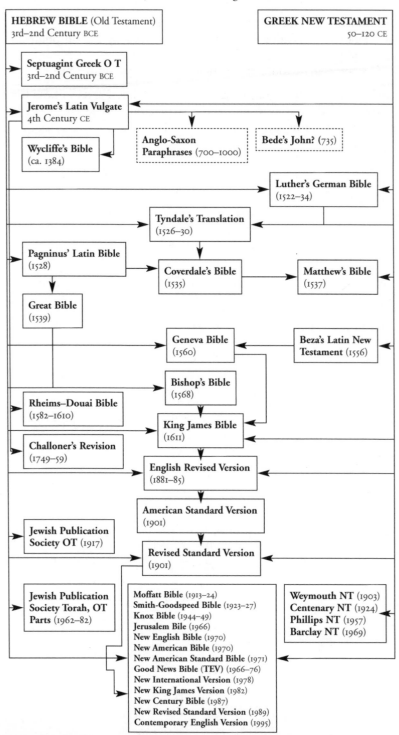

2. modern translations that refuse to update the language;
3. modern translations that amplify the meaning to the point of interpretation;
4. modern translations that deliberately translate from a bias.

However many translations there may be, the biblical texts still call for a *reading*. With reading comes also interpretation necessarily. That is the subject of our next section.

PART III

READING THE
SCRIPTURES
RESPONSIBLY

On Course . . .

Objective

To work out in experience the interactive operation we call 'reading' in an effort to enhance understanding of the biblical texts.

Lead Questions

1. *How do you understand reading as an interactive activity?*

2. *In what sense is the Bible both ancient and post-modern?*

3. *What is involved in 'interactive reading'?*

4. *What is meant by 'within the text', 'behind the text' and 'in front of the text'?*

5. *How important is 'insight' for reading the Bible, and how does one acquire it?*

6. *Look up the examples of texts cited for inquiry, and add your own questions to the ones listed.*

7. *What is one purpose of a 'reading community'?*

8. *How do you understand reading as 'decoding'?*

9. *What is the difference between 'decoding' and 'mediating' in the act of reading?*

10. *Describe the four 'broad stokes' mentioned as characteristic of the literature of the Bible.*

11. *In what way, or ways, is reading interpreting? And how is 'interpreting' also 'translating'?*

The Inter-Act of Reading

The mind and the object of sense are always practicing reciprocity of giving.

(Philo, Legum Allegoria, 29)

It may seem strange to write a chapter about *reading*. You can read, after all! You have learned the alphabet, how letters make words, words sentences, sentences paragraphs, and paragraphs essays. Since you know all that already, why should I expect you to peruse a chapter on the operation called 'reading'?

Those of us who have been reading for a long time have become very accustomed to the operation. It is second nature to us now – at least when we read in our own language (or languages). When we decide to read a book, including the Bible, we do not pause beforehand to remind ourselves of the steps in the operation. We simply have the operation in mind and proceed with confidence. At the same time, our decision to read a book or article usually means we select what to read. We may not, for example, decide to read a book on thoracic medicine. We would probably find the language difficult, the words unfamiliar and the explanation opaque, unless, of course, we are specialists in thoracic medicine. In short, reading requires that we bring something to the operation (competence) before receiving something from it (transformation).

Reading is an interactive operation, producing only as much meaning as the reader is capable of creating from the resident resources in the reader's mind and heart. For this reason alone it seems worth while to raise the question of the reading process in biblical studies: What makes for a competent reading of the biblical texts?

Another reason has to do with the Bible itself. The Bible is both ancient and post-modern[1] at the same time. It is ancient in that it was written in times and cultures far removed from ours; post-modern in

[1] As noted in Chapter 2 n.15, 'post-modern' is not a very helpful label for the current spirit of the age. The modern way of thinking has not disappeared; it runs alongside the new thinking. But 'post-modern' has currency now and will therefore be used throughout these chapters.

that it is held in high regard in religious congregations and in believers' minds in present time and cultures. In this regard also, then, we have reason for raising the matter of the reading operation: we read the ancient book with post-modern eyes and minds.[2]

For the sake of order I will set out four verbal images on which to hang the discussion of the *reading* of biblical texts: *interacting, decoding, mediating,* and *interpreting.* These images are verbal because reading is as much an activity as is digging the garden or painting the house.

Interacting

A text, any text, holds hands with two equally important partners. On one side stands the person who put the letters of the alphabet into words and the words into sentences and the sentences into a document. On the other side is the one who looks at the letters, words and document and recognizes order and purpose in them. At first glance, the partner who writes seems to have the upper hand in the production of meaning. The other partner merely has to 'read' what is there, as if reading were a simple, mechanical exercise. It is not. Where there WERE living, active, purposeful, intentional *writers* of the biblical texts, there ARE living, purposeful, intentional *readers* making sense out of the texts.

On the writers' side of the equation was a world full of ideas and habits of the heart that were characteristic of that world. Out of that fund of knowledge, much of it operating unconsciously in the writers' minds, came the ideas for the writing project, followed by the act of writing itself.

On the other side of the equation is the reader with a mind just as full of ideas, conventions, institutions and purposes from the twenty-first-century world, all of them simply present in consciousness informing the reader. Between the two, the one who puts the ink on the page in language form and the one who reads the linguistic marks, stands the inspired biblical text belonging neither to the writers nor to the readers.[3] The diagram following in Figure 10.1 illustrates the situation.

---

[2] On this point see John M. Court, *Reading the New Testament* (London: Routledge, 1997), 1–8.
[3] See further in R. M. Fowler, *Let the Reader Understand: Reader-Response Criticism and the Gospel of Mark* (Minneapolis: Fortress Press, 1991), 26. 'Saying that the reader is everything, the way some reader-response critics do, is misleading. Practically speaking, the text is important, the reader is important, and the interpretive community that provides the context in which text and reader interact is important.'

Figure 10.1

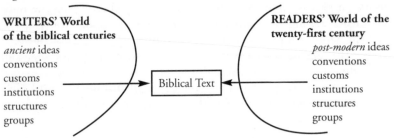

With this diagram before us we do well to mention three widely accepted aspects of reading a biblical text. They are: (1) reading what is scripted *within the text*, (2), reading with respect to what lies *behind the text*, and (3) reading from experience *in front of the text*. This order of reading is recommended by New Testament scholar Willard Swartley, among others. He proposes that the reader start with the text itself and move to the other two aspects of reading from that point. Here is how he plots the movement.

> The first important task in biblical interpretation is . . . *listening* carefully from *within* the text. . . . The second main task . . . is *learning* helpfully from *behind* the text. . . . Finally, the third important task . . . consists of *living* freely from *in front of* the text.[4]

Worthy as Swartley's respect for the centrality of the text may be in his three-part reading proposal, the act of reading as such occurs entirely 'in front of the text': in the conscious mind and heart of the reader. And that is where I propose to begin and end this discussion of interactive reading.

Readers start out to read from the world in which they live and move and have their being, from within the horizon of meaning that informs their life in society. It cannot be otherwise. Meaning encoded in texts does not pass mechanically through the eyes to the brain, as a train passes through the countryside to the station.[5] There is nothing mechanical about reading. Reading is a conscious operation in human imagination. It consists in experiencing the data of the text through the sense of sight. But that is only stage one. Spontaneously and dynamically the experience of the text moves to the level of understanding. At

---

[4] Willard M. Swartley, *Slavery, Sabbath, War and Women: Case Issues in Biblical Interpretation* (Scottdale: Herald Press, 1983), 224–5.

[5] Cf. Lonergan on 'the principle of the empty head', in *Method*, 157–8.

this level we try to order our experience of the text into a pattern that we can grasp. We find ourselves asking a web of interrelated questions about our experience of the text. Answers to the questions may come quickly or not so quickly. The ease and speed with which the answers come depends largely on the degree of insight we have garnered from tradition, from cross-cultural dialogue, and from research.[6]

Of course, having plenty of insight does not guarantee 'truth' in our understanding of a text. Insights have to be tested and proved to be useful in understanding the 'truth' from a text. The option is not less insight, but more valid insight. We may discover, for example, as we read a text that our insight is so lacking that we fail to understand what we experience from the data of the text. When that happens the only remedy is to gain more valid insight. Better to admit the lack of insight in reading a text than to pretend we understand. Pretence in whatever form is illusion. And who can be satisfied with illusion?

What follows are examples of texts from the New Testament that call for insight in the attempt to understand the sense of the text. At this point we move, as it were, from 'in front of the text' to 'within the text'. Yet in making this move we have not abandoned our reading position in front of the text. We are still alive and well there, bringing to bear on the text what we have in mind. Specifically we have questions in mind, as exemplified in my own reading of the texts below.

The texts themselves appear in *italics* followed by a question in regular type. Other questions will come as the text is pondered longer.

Mark 14.22: *[Jesus] took a loaf of bread, and after blessing it he broke it, gave it to [his disciples], and said, 'Take, eat: this is my body'.*

How would the first disciples have understood this statement in the context of their Passover meal with Jesus?

Luke 10.33: *A certain Samaritan ... had compassion on [the man who fell among robbers].*

What would have been the response of a Jewish audience at the time of Jesus to such a story about a Good Samaritan vis-à-vis their own Jewish Temple clerics?

---

[6] Investigations into reading the Bible through various cultural eyes, were presented in the International Meeting of the Society of Biblical Literature in Helsinki and are now available in print: Heikki Räisänen, Elisabeth Schüssler Fiorenza, R. S. Surirtharajah, Krister Stendahl, James Barr, *Reading the Bible in the Global Village: Helsinki* (Atlanta: Society of Biblical Literature, 2000).

Acts 19.11: *God did extraordinary miracles through Paul, so that when the handkerchiefs or aprons that had touched his skin were brought to the sick, their diseases left them.*

How could handkerchiefs and aprons carry the healing power from Paul's skin to the sick people?

1 Corinthians 11.14: *Does not nature itself teach you that if a man wears long hair, it is degrading to him?*

What in nature teaches us that long hair on a male is degrading?

2 Peter 3.16: *Paul wrote to you according to the wisdom given him, speaking of this as he does in all his letters. There are some things in them hard to understand, which the ignorant and unstable twist to their own destruction, as they do the other Scriptures.*

When were all of Paul's letters gathered together and regarded as equal to the older Scriptures?

Genesis 6.1: *... the sons of God saw that [women] were fair; and they took wives for themselves of all that they chose.*

Who are 'the sons of God'? Are they heavenly beings or earthly?

Ezekiel 3.1: *... eat this scroll, and go, speak to the house of Israel.*

What would be the point of ingesting a scroll before going to speak to the house of Israel? Is this text figurative language?

Questions of this sort draw us inside the texture of the text. The shape the questions take comes from the structure of the text and from the reader's current fund of insight. The operation is interactive. We sense the data of the text and seek to understand its various literary and historical hues. The questions, starting with one that leads to another and another, spring from our human way of coming to understand – our way of gaining appropriate insight. Sometimes the questions have to do with the grammar and syntax and imagery of the text itself, so we probe the structure and use the linguistic tools at our disposal to come to an understanding. But more often than not, the questions lead us inevitably into the world from which the text sprang into being, the world 'behind the text', a world unlike our own.

Samaritans do not live in our world. Long hair on males is not degrading in our world. The bread of Christ's body is to us the eucharistic bread of communion. In our world the medical profession frowns on the idea of the transfer of healing by means of pieces of cloth from a well person to a sick person. We generally do not refer to men who marry women as 'sons of God'. We have to gain insight from behind the text to figure out what is going on within the text. We have to understand.

In the end as in the beginning the person of the reader is the active subject 'in front of the text'. The living reader in front of the text drives the whole operation from beginning to end in a kind of interactive conversation.[7] The reader is first interested in reading the given text of Scripture, then becomes involved with the texture of the text, and then figures out what to make of it through gaining greater insight through research and further conversation within a community of readers.

The community of minds keeps a check on possible flights of fancy and false assumptions. Moreover, the conversation has wide range as well as depth. It starts with the text, continues in research, and culminates in the reading community. And the interactive conversation continues, always building on what we have already discovered in previous readings. Now we need to touch on the second peg on which this discussion hangs.

Decoding

In large measure reading is neither more nor less than decoding. I have set out below three literary codes to be broken for understanding. They are not Rorschach inkblots about which you can say anything that comes to mind. Each of the lines is truly a meaningful code. Probably not everyone will be competent to break all three. To do so the reader-decoder would have to study with someone who already knows the code and is willing to reveal its structure and meaning. As you glance over the three you are bound to notice one that you can decode without delay. You know the code has the same structure as this line you are reading at the moment. You don't need to translate it. You just know it. It is your code that you share in common with a reading community.[8] Take a minute to scan the three codes one at a time.

---

[7] See Gadamer, *Truth and Method*, 333, 352, and Chapter 5 above.

[8] This may sound akin to the theory of 'interpretive communities' put forward by Stanley Fish, *Is There a Text in This Class? The Authority of Interpretive Communities* (Cambridge, Mass.: Harvard University Press, 1980), 172. And it is in a sense, but I am employing the principle of 'interpretive community' much more broadly here than Fish envisions. A language is learned, as are patterns of thought and life in a cultural context. Out of that cultural fund the decoding and mediating are done. But I use the term community of readers in the narrow sense as well, to mean (1) a reading community of scholars, and/or (2) a reading community of faith. See also my discussion of 'common sense' in Chapter 4.

יְהוָה רֹעִי לֹא אֶחְסָר׃
κύριος ποιμαίνει με καὶ οὐδέν με ὑστερήσει
The LORD is my shepherd; I shall not want.

Clearly you can understand the bottom one. It is the opening line from the familiar twenty-third Psalm. As soon as your eyes reach that line you feel at home. You are master of the marks. But you must have noticed even in that line that one word appears in upper case, LORD. Why not Lord? Is the upper case structure merely to emphasize the importance of the being that the word LORD represents? If the answer is not forthcoming then research is needed. Remember, you cannot pretend to know, for pretence is the parent of illusion. As it happens, I have done the necessary research for this question.

This particular line of code is from the King James Version of the twenty-third Psalm, and I discovered from my research that the trans-lators wanted to signal to their English readers when they were translating the Hebrew name for the distinctive deity of the Israelite people (יְהוָה = YaWeH). There are several names for deity in the Hebrew Scriptures, but only one that is distinctively Israelite in origin and use. The name of that one appears in this version of the English code as LORD, not Lord.

We need to go back now to the first two codes. Were you able to decode both of them right away? If you were, then you have mastered the Hebrew and Greek codes. If not, you still may have guessed that the first two were simply different codes carrying the same meaning as the last one, the one you do know. But guessing does not make for good decoding of meaning. It happens that the three lines are all from the twenty-third Psalm, the first in Hebrew code, the second in Greek, and the third in English.

So much for knowing the data and rules of the code. That is the place to start, sure enough. But the decoding process in reading, as I said, is not mechanical. The process of decoding presents images to the reader's mind. The *word* 'shepherd' in this line of code, for example, is not an actual human figure that tends sheep. It is a word, and a word is only a series of signs on the page. But you know what that series symbolizes. So the series s-h-e-p-h-e-r-d triggers an image of a person caring for vulnerable animals that eat grass and bear wool.[9] Once that

---

[9] Imaging and imagining as I am presenting them here takes account of Derrida's program of the deconstruction of language, but does not devolve into an empty language that Derrida's program tends to do (e.g. Jacques Derrida, *Aporias* (Stanford: University Press, 1993), 3. What I am advancing is more in line with the metaphorical process espoused by Paul Ricoeur, 'Biblical Hermeneutics: The Metaphorical Process', *Semeia* 4, 75–106.

image is clear then the whole metaphor comes to life. The special deity of Israel is 'shepherd' to 'me'. Now imagination takes over.

The LORD is not exactly a human figure who tends sheep on a hillside. But your imagination tells you that the deity cares for you, leads you, sustains you, and on and on. Part of the decoding process in reading, a large part I would say, is in imaging and imagining. Picking up the image from the text code is just the beginning of the fuller stage of imagining. Imagining is not a matter of taking flight from the text code, but of engaging the code with a mind full of insight, of conversing freely within the field of vision and understanding operating between yourself and the text. That leads to my third hook for discussion.

Mediating

Reading is also mediating. This picks up on something I dealt with broadly in Chapter 4 about 'meaning'. Mediating is an adult activity, not an infant activity. The world of the infant is a world of immediacy. As the infant grows he/she begins to see and hear and feel and taste the world. They hear sounds in an open-ended pattern, and eventually learn to make their own meaningful sounds following the learned pattern. Parents rejoice when their children learn to speak as they do. Children's ability to speak means they are beginning to mediate the world for themselves. And their mediating powers continue to develop the more they discover about their world.[10]

Mediating the world is not simply a matter of managing our way around and through things. We mediate the things by meaning – meaning in the active sense. We mean something about trees and stones and potatoes and beets and birds and bandits. And we mean something from words that represent those things just listed. Reading is mediating in so far as the text code is valued for what it represents. What the text code represents, as in 'shepherd', is mediated not by the text code, but by the living, thinking, feeling reader interacting with the code. And that mediation process is called 'meaning'.

Of course, there has to be something there to mediate by meaning. When it comes to Scripture there is plenty represented therein, plenty of details but also broad strokes on the textual canvas around which the details are arranged. Four of those broad factors bear mention here as

---

[10] See further in Lonergan, *Method*, 28, 78–9.

context for the multi-textured fabric of the biblical texts that call for mediation.[11]

Literature

Many readers of the Bible consider it to be the Word of God written, and as such therefore not literature in the usual sense of the term. Holding this view of the Bible affects the way we read its texts, the way we mediate what the various texts represent. At the extreme, this view can block the mediating process by which we come to know what the text actually represents. The blocking occurs when we ignore the integrity of the texts we read. Plucking a small text from here and another from there and guessing at their meaning menaces the integrity of the plucked texts. The plucking comes easily when we think that each and every tiny text of the Bible is essentially and equally the same Word of God without difference, without context or history.

The alternative is to view the Bible as the Word of God *couched in literary forms.*[12] When we view the Bible thus we discover parables, psalms, narratives, oracles, arguments, apocalypses, and not merely a collection of verses or quotable quotes. Moreover, when I used the first line of the twenty-third Psalm I used it as belonging to that psalm, which in turn belongs in the Psalter of Israel. I need to have a whole order of tested insights in mind as I read that first line of Psalm 23, as with the other kinds of literature in the Bible.

Story/history

The Bible tells the stories of Israel's sojourn from slavery to freedom, from wilderness to Promised Land, from nomadic life to kingdom, from kingdom to exile, from exile to new commonwealth, from Jesus to Christianity. Behind and within each respective 'story' there is 'history': what was actually moving forward. An observant post-modern reader of the texts will pick up on the story and get a sense of the history at the same time, and will understand the intertwining of the two in the biblical texts. Some biblical scholars with a penchant for

[11] For a fuller discussion of the literary 'fabric' of texts see especially Vernon K. Robbins, *Exploring the Texture of Texts: A Guide to Socio-rhetorical Interpretation* (Valley Forge: Trinity Press International, 1996), 7–132.

[12] William A. Beardslee, *Literary Criticism of the New Testament. Guides to Biblical Scholarship* (Philadelphia: Fortress Press, 1970), 13. R. Alan Culpepper's approach to the Gospel of John is an example of taking the literary aspect of the Bible seriously, *Anatomy of the Fourth Gospel*, 3–11.

reconstructing the past find satisfaction in sifting out the verifiable facts and writing a critical history of what was actually moving forward.[13] Such a writing of the history serves the interest of the post-modern reader.

But the biblical writers were much more occupied with history as story. The story captures the heart of the people involved and creates a mirror image for the reading community. The telling and reading of the story opens up a world of meaning. For example, the single historical figure of Jesus stands encoded in the four Gospel stories of the New Testament. Each of the four stories carries the image of Jesus forward in lively fashion, free from the bounds and canons of modern historical critical writing. Historical critical writing has come from the modern penchant for scientific fact. The Gospel storytellers, by contrast, write the works and words of Jesus into lively narrative code for imagination and faith – quite a different agenda from the modern scientific one.

God

Not surprisingly, the biblical texts carry an abundance of sacred code. The only document of the sixty-six in the Christian canon that makes no mention of deity is the book of Esther. All the other writers were highly conscious of a being Other than themselves guiding their affairs and the affairs of their people. And the writers referred to the divine Other using various terms: God, Lord, Holy One, Christ, Son of God, Holy Spirit, etc. In addition to these markers for the sacred in the story the writers of the biblical texts employed imagery galore to communicate the sense of the sacred in the story. The deity is a rock, shepherd, warrior, strong tower, mother hen, lamb, lion, among others.

These images of the Other make the sense of the Other's nearness real and personal.[14] It is one thing to speak of God as Creator, but quite another to speak of the same God as Redeemer and friend. All these aspects of the sacred are present in biblical texts. More than that, the deity speaks directly in the texts, especially in the prophetic literature.

---

[13] An outstanding example of a scholar who has observed the intertwining of story and history in the texts of the Old Testament is John Bright, *A History of Israel*, fourth edition, edited by William P. Brown. (Westminster John Knox Press, 1999/2000). See also Martin Hengel, *Between Jesus and Paul* (Minneapolis: Fortress Press, 1983); and Ben F. Meyer, *The Early Christians: Their World Mission and Self-Discovery* (Wilmington: Michael Glazier, 1986).

[14] Some scholars recommend a theological reading of the Bible as the approach best suited to Scripture, e.g. Stephen E. Fowl, *Engaging Scripture: A Model for Theological Interpretation* (Oxford: Blackwell, 1998), 1–31.

Such sacred address is hailed as the Word of the Lord, and as such should be heeded by the readers.

People of God

Not only is there a sense of the divine Other in the texts of the Bible, but there is also a people belonging to the deity. They take on the name of the deity, and thus also the deity's life. They do this not so much by their own will, but by the will of God. The people are called together around a central covenant that all agree to adopt in their lives. By adopting the parameters of the covenant the people are marked off from the cultures around them. In the Old Testament the covenant is drawn up under the leadership of Moses and in the New Testament under the leadership of Jesus Christ. Around each of these two covenants a community gathers together in fellowship for the worship of their God who has claimed them for God's own (1 Pet. 2.9–10 NEB).

Covenant that creates community also creates what may be called a sub-culture, or counter-culture. The group gathered around the covenant-God stands within the larger culture, but bears its own unique name, expresses its own faith, and holds its own ideas and lives out its own habits of life.

I offer these four broad stokes of code as those that permeate the biblical canvas. The meaningful mediation of the variegated biblical world will have to take these four into account, I submit. Whatever else there is, and there is much else, these four are unavoidably present at almost every turn, pointing the way to an understanding of the rest.

Interpreting

Finally, reading is interpreting. Interpreting goes further than decoding or mediating. It aims at translating the intended sense of texts into conscious alternatives in the reader's life.[15] By 'translating' I mean more than the rendering of one text code into another text code. I mean the rendering of any biblical text code into non-text life. The New Testament word *hermeneuō* comes to mind. It has to do with making meaning present to the mind where it is otherwise not clear. From that word we derive our English word hermeneutics, the study of how the data of sense is appropriated into real-life alternatives.

[15] Cf. Richard L. Rohrbaugh, *The Biblical Interpreter: An Agrarian Bible in an Industrial Age* (Philadelphia: Fortress Press, 1978), 11–19; 103–14.

Appropriation, if it is to be authentic, takes the data of the Scripture texts beyond understanding to judgement and action. In short, appropriation takes the whole person into account. Proper understanding of the data passes over into the level of weighing, valuing, sizing up, before decisive action is reached. When decision is reached and action follows, the reader's life is transformed.

Reading in its fullest, richest sense does just that: *it transforms human life*. Reading is not repetitive, not even when the same text is read many times. With every reading comes fresh inquiry that bears fruit in transformed life and thought. But the reading has to be real reading, not imposed or habitual merely. The reader has to be attentive, intentional, insightful, and valuing. The texts do not have a 'life-message' of their own, which they send untrammelled to the human mind like a message over a telegraph wire. The texts come to life in the inter-act of reading.

On Course . . .

Objective

To illustrate how modern methodology, especially the historical critical model, works with biblical texts, and to indicate its limitation.

Lead Questions

1. *In what large Western movement is modern methodology said to have its beginning?*

2. *How might the Reformation of the sixteenth century be considered a precursor to modernity?*

3. *Define 'allegorical'.*

4. *In which main urban centre of the ancient Mediterranean basin was the allegorical way of interpreting practiced? Which Hellenistic Jewish philosopher practiced allegorization of the Jewish Scriptures in the first century?*

5. *Name at least one Christian thinker in Alexandria who wrote and taught using the allegorical approach?*

6. *What was Martin Luther's view of the allegorical approach?*

7. *What are the principal tenets of Modernity?*

8. *Describe 'historical criticism' as applied to the study of biblical literature.*

9. *How do you understand the practice of 'demythologizing'?*

10. *Who were some of the practitioners of the historical critical method on the Old and New Testaments in the eighteenth and nineteenth centuries?*

11. *What are source, form, and redaction analyses of biblical literature? Illustrate.*

12. *What is canon criticism? How does it differ from the historical criticism that preceded it? Compare the approach of Sanders and Childs.*

13. *Describe the break that Childs and Wink made with the longstanding historical critical approach to interpreting Scripture.*

II

Modern Ways of Reading the Ancient Scriptures

> It is common sense to take a method and try it. If it fails, admit it
> frankly and try another. But above all, try something.
>
> (Franklin D. Roosevelt)

Interpretation of Scripture has existed for as long as human beings
have been reading the Bible. Interpretation is a human activity. We
humans mediate meaning for ourselves, for our communities, and for
our world by this process called 'interpretation'. The models we use
vary depending on the culture and education in which we think and
live. To put the point more sharply: history provides the models to a
large extent. For those of us living in the modern/post-modern world
the reading models will necessarily conform to modern/post-modern
ways of thinking and living.

The test applicable to all of the specific models, although not always
deliberately observed, is that of general method, cited in Chapter 3: 'a
normative pattern of recurrent and related operations yielding
cumulative and progressive results.'[1] The present chapter will attempt
to account for *modern* models for reading the ancient Scriptures.

Before Modernity

Before proceeding with that agenda, however, we ought to be aware of
the path that has led to this modern place in biblical studies. If
modernity can be considered a mode of thinking and living then it
presupposes a way of thinking and living that is pre-modern. But the
time-line between the two cannot be clearly drawn, as it cannot
between modern and post-modern.

Modernity is usually associated with the tenets and products of the
Enlightenment movement of Europe in the seventeenth and eighteenth

---

[1] Lonergan, *Method*, 5.

centuries. Rationalism and sophistry of various kinds marked the period, and out of it came the age of science, which has been with us ever since. Modernity, as the term is now commonly understood, is the product of the Enlightenment.

But the Enlightenment had its forerunners, as every movement does. The Renaissance and Reformation of the sixteenth century were themselves enlightenment movements in their own right, capable of setting the spark that was to become the blaze of 'the modern age'. To the openness of the sixteenth century belongs the search for origins, the invention of the printing press, the development of literacy, the opening up of tradition, the thirst for learning, and a challenge to accepted ecclesiastical dogma and norms. We have in the sixteenth century, I submit, the early stages of what we commonly call 'modernity'.

To find out how the Scriptures were interpreted before modernity I shall go behind the Reformation, to a time rather less critical than our own, less reliant on empirical testing. Less critical, I say, but not non-critical or pre-critical. As long as the human family has occupied the planet its members have made history, and the only way to do that is to inquire, invent, explore, and develop. Even in the Church, where much of the theological thinking rested on tradition, there was still a conscious effort to interpret the Scriptures aright.

For at least fifteen hundred years of Church history the dominant method of reading Scripture texts in the Church was the *allegorical*. The roots of the allegorical method are not easy to trace. My own suspicion is that Plato's espousal of a dualistic order of the universe of being qualifies as a likely place to look. 'In the most famous passage in Plato ... he compares this world to a cave, in which we see only shadows of the realities in the bright world above.'[2] From that philosophical source in Athens, I submit, the allegorical method entered Hellenistic Judaism, as evidenced in the writings of Jewish philosopher Philo of Alexandria (*c.* 19 BCE–45 CE), contemporary of Jesus and Paul. Some of the principal features of the allegorical method deserve attention here, in so far as they have survived the rigour of the scientific method of modernity and have reappeared in new dress in post-modernity.

1. The allegorical method of reading Scripture rests on the assumption that the world consists of two realms of reality, matter and spirit. Texts in themselves are material.

[2] Bertrand Russell, *History of Western Philosophy* (London: George Allen & Unwin, 1961), 74.

2. Scripture was written to lift the reader out of the material world into the realm of the Spirit. In that realm true life and salvation are found, not in the mundane world of matter.

3. The literal sense of the text is the house in which the real meaning of the text resides. The astute reader has to open the door of the literal to find the inner meaning that sustains real life.

4. The historical context of a text is secondary. What matters above all is the spiritual element that connects with the living spirit of the interpreter.

5. The hidden, spiritual meaning can be discovered by competent minds attuned to the Spirit, and who have knowledge enough to open up the literal-historical sense.

Practiced largely at Alexandria and North Africa in the first four centuries of the Common Era, the allegorical method of reading Scripture captured the imagination of church leaders more broadly, and overshadowed the *literalist* reading propounded at Antioch of Syria. The Antioch school believed the truth of the revelation of God was found in history and in the literal record of saving history recorded in the Bible. By examining God's dealings with Israel as the text reveals it, so the Antioch school believed, the divine plan of salvation is appropriated. No special insight is necessary beyond the power of the mind to grasp what the text says plainly. But some texts in the Old Testament were hard to understand. And even the Antioch interpreters resorted to allegorization to make sense of them.

In other branches of the Church, particularly Alexandria of Egypt, the allegorical approach was readily adopted. Allegorical interpretation catered to the human longing for life beyond this mortal coil. Within the New Testament itself we find the allegorical mind-set at work. Paul in Galatians (4.21–31) admits using the allegorical method to read the story of Abraham's two sons, one by Hagar and the other by Sarah. His allegorical reading of the relevant texts (Gen. 16.15; 21.2–9) virtually transforms the literal meaning of those texts into a meaning suited to his situation and purpose at the time of writing his letter to the Galatians.

The same allegorical approach appears in the interpretation of the parable of the sower in Mark 4.13–20 (and par.). The soil, seed, thorns, path, etc. all mean something beyond the literal sense. One might argue, of course, that the parable of the sower/soils is really an allegory and should therefore be interpreted allegorically. The case is true only if it can be demonstrated that the story was told as an allegory and not as a parable. 'Parable' is a distinctive form of speech, more in line with riddle than allegory,[3] and calling for a way of reading suited to their form. Yet the parables of Jesus were prime targets for an allegorical interpretation in the Church for many centuries.

As I have mentioned Philo of Alexandria was a master allegorist of his Jewish Scriptures. A text that told of Abraham's wandering, Philo interpreted as a soul in search of the mind of God. With this thoroughly allegorical mind-set in place in Alexandria before the arrival of the Christians, the approach was ready-made for such a notable Christian thinker and writer as Origen (185–254 CE). He wrote many works including commentaries on Scripture texts, all of them exhibiting the allegorical paradigm.

The allegorical approach took hold in North Africa, especially in the interpretive practice of such a capable mind as St Augustine, Bishop of Hippo. Augustine developed his own rather complex approach to interpretation, but within it the allegorical approach remained. He identified a fourfold sense in Scripture: the literal, the moral, the allegorical, and the anagogical. Three of the four fall more or less into the sphere of the spiritual, which is clearly in keeping with St Augustine's Christian Neo-Platonic idea of the real world, which was for him the invisible world of the Spirit. 'The literal sense teaches what actually happened, the allegorical what you are to believe, the moral how you are to behave, the anagogical where you are going.'[4]

Gregory I (540–604 CE), architect of the medieval papacy, was also a notable theologian and moral reformer. In implementing his reforms, he did not hesitate to use the allegorical interpretation of Scripture texts in support of his programs. I mention these notable examples to illustrate the deep hold the allegorical method had on the Christian Church from the earliest time through the middle ages. With that I do not mean to say that a literal reading of the Bible had disappeared. Far from it. Antioch had made its mark, which would stay its course despite the popularity of the allegorical method. Outstanding among those who championed a more literal/historical reading of Scripture was Thomas Aquinas (c. 1224–1274 CE). Aquinas recognized a place for allegorical

---

[3] See my 'Engaging with the Parables', in *Jesus and his Parables*, 14ff.
[4] F. F. Bruce, 'The History of New Testament Study', in *New Testament Interpretation: Essays on Principles and Methods* (Grand Rapids: Eerdmans, 1977), 28.

interpretation, especially as Augustine had textured it into his schema, but Aquinas did not find it suitable for establishing doctrine.

Enter Modernity

With the dawning of the Renaissance and Reformation came an outright critique of the allegorical method of reading Scripture, beyond anything Aquinas or the Antioch school might have said. The Reformers, especially Martin Luther, broke with the authority of the Church and tradition. In councils and in publications Luther defended the principle of *sola scriptura* and the witness of his own Christian conscience. The authority of Scripture alone for life and thought made it necessary to develop valid methods of reading the sacred texts to derive their true meaning.

Luther derided the allegorical approach that found multiple meanings in Scripture texts. He believed the Bible contained one central message from beginning to end: justification by faith alone in Jesus Christ. All Scripture can be read in connection with this coherent centre. In place of the allegorical approach Luther applied historical and grammatical analysis in his reading of the original languages of Scripture. But in spite of his stated effort to eradicate the allegorical approach from his interpretation it continued to appear in his efforts to bring out a spiritual application. Perhaps some form of the allegorical will always be with us, as long as humans yearn for reality and life beyond the mundane.

The Reformation spirit, linked as it was with the rebirth of learning, modernity, as we know it now was not far away. Its features became more and more prominent from the seventeenth to the twentieth century. Its most striking feature, as I understand it, is the scientific method. Hypotheses have to be proved, not by some miracle or by mystical knowledge, but by the reasonable and responsible investigation of relevant data. Discoveries made in all areas of life and thought are deemed worthy to the extent that they measure up to the scrutiny of the empirical method of scientific research.

The scientific method observes the relevant data using the five senses, and evaluates the results using sufficient case studies to be able to make a final judgement on the viability of the matter in question. Scepticism marks the scientific method. Mere belief in constructs beyond the senses and beyond the laws of nature is called into question and subjected to the dictates of reason. As it developed from the sixteenth century onward the scientific method entered all fields of human endeavour: medicine, history, industry, politics, and not least biblical studies and theology. Nothing in modern society escaped the effects of the scientific method of investigation. The aim all along was the discovery of truth and the eradication of illusion and superstition.

Our job now is to set out the principal approaches to reading Scripture that emerged in the modern world. These approaches are still with us, modified and blended with new approaches to be sure, but remaining still in evidence in the discipline of biblical studies.

Historical Critical Method

The historical critical method of reading Scripture stands in contrast to the systematic-theological dogmatics. The latter is less concerned with the warp and woof of particular documents in the canon, and more with the construction of dogma drawn from everywhere and anywhere in the canon. Historical critical reading of texts takes the literary and historical parameters of individual documents deliberately into account.

Two scholars of the eighteenth century deserve recognition as pioneers in forging the historical critical template for future gener-ations of biblical interpreters. The first is Lutheran scholar, Johann Salomo Semler (1725–91), professor of theology at the University of Halle (1753–91). In his publications he defended the historical reading of biblical documents, which called into question the notion of divine inspiration of Scripture that guaranteed infallibility in all matters addressed therein. The second scholar of the same period, who pressed Semler's approach ahead, was Johann David Michaelis (1717–91). In the fourth edition of his *Einleitung in die göttlichen Schriften des Neuen Bundes* (*Introduction to the divine Scriptures of the New Covenant*) Michaelis advanced the historical character of the New Testament documents, using the earlier work of Semler.

In 1753 Robert Lowth, English bishop and lecturer, gave a series of lectures on the Psalms at Oxford University in which he expounded the nature of Hebrew parallelism evident in the Psalms. This literary critical approach had a profound impact on later interpretation of the poetry of the Psalms and other Hebrew poetry. His analysis placed the poetry of the Psalms in the historical context of Israelite life and thought. It was Hebrew poetry, not eighteenth-century English poetry.

The lectures were published in Latin as well as in English, *Lectures on the Sacred Poetry of the Hebrews*.[5]

Still with the Old Testament, German scholar, Julias Wellhausen (1844–1918), is best known for his analysis of the structure of the Pentateuch. His dating of the various layers of tradition in the five books marked the beginning of a long fascination with the forms and functions of the various types of material in the Pentateuch. His analysis was as much historical as it was literary. He asked about the time and place from which each of the parts of the Pentateuch came. Wellhausen's influence continues to exert itself in Old Testament scholarship to this day.[6]

Tübingen scholar, F. C. Baur (1792–1860), wrote extensively on the value of the historical critical understanding of the New Testament literature. His work marked a watershed in New Testament studies. From his reading of the Pauline letters and Acts he concluded that the Christian community in the early stages of development was sharply divided between the Jerusalem group and the Pauline mission churches. Peter was the key proponent of the Jerusalem branch and Paul the leader of the mission churches (see e.g. Gal. 2.11–14). Working with the Hegelian paradigm of *thesis, antithesis, synthesis*, Baur concluded the Jerusalem branch was the thesis, the Gentile mission churches the antithesis, and Catholic Christianity the synthesis.[7]

This observation led Baur to date Paul's letters and Acts much later than the traditional dating. He concluded that only Galatians, Corinthians and Romans were genuinely Pauline. The others were written later. Acts likewise for him was post-apostolic. It tends to gloss over the divisions in the Church, making Acts part of the developing catholic character of the Church in the second century. Baur's second-century date for Acts, however, was later revised in light of new evidence that put it back to the latter part of the first century.

Baur's influence reverberated throughout Europe and made its way in modulated form to Britain and the United States. The historical

---

[5] Lowth's major works, including his lectures on the Psalms, are available in an eight-volume set edited by David Reibel, *Robert Lowth 1710–1787: The Major Works* (New York: Routledge, 1995).

[6] The illustration from the Pentateuch in Chapter 6 owes a great deal to the original work of Wellhausen. Scholars Press has published a reprint of his analysis of the Pentateuch. Julius Wellhausen, *Prolegomena to the History of Israel* (Atlanta: Scholars Press, 1994).

[7] Baur's work on the history of early Christianity is accessible in Peter C. Hodgson's translation, with introduction and notes, Ferdinand Christian Baur, *Ferdinand Christian Baur on the Writing of Church History*, ed. and trans. Peter C. Hodgson (New York: Oxford University Press, 1968).

critical method of reading the biblical documents, like the scientific method generally, was solidly established before the end of the nineteenth century, and continued into the twentieth century unabated.

Six features of the method have remained more or less stable from its inception to the present time. They are as follows.

First, *the time of writing* a document plays into the meaning of the text. What was going on in the community of writers and first readers at the time of writing has to be taken into account for a proper understanding of the significance of the text.

Second, *the identity of the author* helps in figuring out the function of the texts within a particular document. The name of the author may be desirable but not necessary. The character of the author is more important. This can be learned from a careful reading of the document as a whole. From this attention to the author comes also an interest in *authorial intention* behind the text, an issue much debated in the present time. (See Chapter 4.)

Third, *the identity of the first readers* helps explain why texts manifest particularity. For example, the character of the Corinthian correspondence is quite different from that of Romans, yet both sets of documents come from the same authorial hand.

Fourth, *the occasion and purpose* of a document likewise facilitate the understanding of the texture of a document. This point applies to some documents more than others. For example, the prophetic oracles collected in the book of Isaiah were delivered on various occasions, and carry different purposes. At the time of publication of the collected oracles in one scroll the occasion would have changed, and the purpose of the document as a whole would be different from the purpose in any one of the oracles.

Fifth, *the social and religious context* of a document plays a part in the shaping of the thought and intention of the texts. The history-of-religions school would go on to say that religious thought develops in relation to other religious thought and practice in the religious scheme of things. In order to understand a particular religious and social pattern in biblical texts, the surrounding religions need to be studied as well to find the connections and developments. For example, Christian faith communities developed in the Hellenistic world. One should expect to find traces of the Hellenistic religious thought in Christian self-definition encoded in the New Testament texts. Likewise, Israel's faith formulations developed in the context of Ancient Near Eastern religions, and should be studied in that light.

Sixth, *biblical narrative material requires verification* by scientific investigation for historical veracity. Do the details of the biblical narrative find support in the historical facts? For example, Luke's narrative (2.1–2) about the census when Quirinius was governor of Syria in the reign of Augustus (Octavius) does 'not fit the history to which we have other access'.[8] By this rule of historical criticism supernatural elements in a narrative are dismissed as improbable, since such extraordinary occurrences are neither common to human experience nor compatible with the laws of nature. On this ground the miracles of the Bible, for example, are treated as stories of faith and have therefore no basis in historical fact.

The historical critical method of reading the ancient Scriptures was also quick to point out the mythic way of explaining reality. 'The myth is an expression of [human] understanding of reality', says Childs. 'It stems from a thought pattern which differs in decisive points from the modern critical one.'[9] The mythic way of understanding the world is more personal and concrete than the modern understanding. The mythic meaning of birth and death, sunrise and sunset, wet season and dry, seed time and harvest, is found not in empirical analysis or hypotheses, but *in illo tempore*, in that ideal time where perfect models of concrete reality were first conceived.[10]

In the Syriac Apocalypse of Baruch II, for example, the earthly city of Jerusalem has a celestial counterpart that pre-dates the earthly city and provides the paradigm for it. 'Doest thou think that this is that city of which I said, "On the palms of my hands have I graven thee"? This building now built in your midst is not that which is revealed with Me, that which was prepared beforehand here from the time when I took counsel to make Paradise, and showed it to Adam before he sinned' (4.2–7).[11]

This pre-philosophical, pre-modern way of viewing the world, much of which appears quite naturally in the literature of the Bible, became the object of historical critical scrutiny. 'The mythopoeic mind, tending toward the concrete'[12] was able to offer more than one

---

[8] Fred B. Craddock, *Luke: Interpretation* (Louisville: John Knox Press, 1990), 34. See also I. H. Marshall, *Luke: Historian and Theologian* (Grand Rapids: Zondervan, 1971), 69.

[9] Brevard S. Childs, *Myth and Reality in the Old Testament* (London: SCM Press, 1960), 17.

[10] See the discussion in Mircea Eliade, *The Myth of the Eternal Return, or Cosmos and History*, trans. Willard R. Trask (Princeton: Princeton University Press, 1954), 6–17.

[11] In R. H. Charles, ed., *The Apocrypha and Pseudepigrapha of the Old Testament in English* (Oxford: Clarendon Press, 1913).

[12] H. and H. A. Frankfort, *Before Philosophy: The Intellectual Adventure of Ancient Man* (Baltimore: Penguin Books, 1949), 29.

approach at the same time. The modern critical mind is uncomfortable with conflicting visions of reality.

The historical critical reading of the mythic parts of Scripture came to sharp expression in Rudolf Bultmann's program of demythologizing.[13] It was not that Bultmann had umbrage against the ancient way of thinking. The ancient view was simply not modern, so the proper thing to do was to find the existential truth inside the pre-scientific mythic form and reconstitute the truth in terms suitable to the modern way of thinking. The following (rather long and gender exclusive) citation illustrates Bultmann's notion that the mythological view of the world is simply obsolete.

> Can Christian preaching expect modern man *to accept the mythical view of the world as true?* To do so would be both senseless and impossible. It would be senseless, because there is nothing specifically Christian in the mythical view of the world as such. It is simply the cosmology of a pre-scientific age. Again, it would be impossible, because no man can adopt a view of the world by his own volition – it is already determined for him by his place in history. Of course such a view is not absolutely unalterable, and the individual may even contribute to its change. But he can do so only when he is faced by a new set of facts so compelling as to make his previous view of the world untenable.[14]

For example, we in our time have come to accept that our planet Earth is more or less spherical, that it rotates on its axis in a twenty-four-hour day, and that it orbits the sun in three hundred and sixty-five days. We accept also that our planet is one of many in our solar system, which in turn is one of many within the larger galaxy, and that myriad more galaxies exist beyond our comprehension. The idea of a flat, motionless earth and a tiered universe is alien to our modern understanding. Yet clearly a three-tiered universe is in view in such texts as Philippians 2.10: ... *at the name of Jesus every knee should bend,* **in heaven and on earth and under the earth**. Implicit in the bold words of this text is the view of a three-tiered universe, which modern minds can no longer accept. But the significance of the confession in the Philippians hymn is not lost by this incongruity between the two world-views. The confession acknowledges Jesus Christ as having won universal rule by his divine self-sacrifice, *even death on a cross* (2.8).

---

[13] See Bultmann's essay, 'The New Testament and Mythology' in *New Testament and Mythology*, ed. S.M. Ogden Philadelphia: Fortress Press, 1984, (German 1950), 1–43.

[14] Bultmann, 'New Testament and Mythology', 3.

In addition to this historical critical scrutiny of biblical texts, some scholars also developed ways of analysing the biblical documents as literary constructs. Four kinds of historical critical, literary analyses emerged from the end of the nineteenth to the middle of the twentieth century: source analysis, form analysis, tradition-history analysis, and redaction analysis. While an interrelationship exists between them each one may be conveniently discussed separately.

Detecting sources

The writers of Scripture did not compose their documents *ex nihilo*, as illustrated already in Chapter 6, 'Writing the Biblical Texts'. Other writings preceded the canonical form and doubtless influenced the shape of the final form. But unlike our modern practice of providing a bibliography or footnotes, the biblical writers and compilers simply incorporated selected texts into the texture of their literary production. What appear in our biblical documents, thus, are *clues* to sources used in the composition. Hence the detective work of source critics. Their aim is to identify types of sources embedded within biblical documents. Once identified, the sources can be labelled – as in the *JEDP* source hypothesis for the Pentateuch described above in Chapter 6 – and the social location and thought pattern of each source adjudicated.

The idea of incorporated sources is not altogether hypothetical. Some of the writers in both testaments actually point to documents behind (or beside) their own. The writer of Numbers (21.14–20), for example, explicitly cites the Wars of the Lord in his story of the sojourn of the Israelites. The cited document is not extant, but at least here is a direct reference to it. Similarly, the writer/compiler of Kings makes repeated reference to sources beside his own as carrying information in line with his story.[15] Even more striking in the New Testament, the preface to Luke–Acts points to *many [who] have undertaken to set down an orderly account of the events that have been fulfilled among us* (Luke 1.1–4). This recognition of other written sources means that the writer of this two-part document is familiar with written records about Jesus and his ministry that pre-date his own. The extent to which the 'orderly accounts' are textured into Luke–Acts is up to the source critic to determine.

For the most part the biblical writers do not reveal their sources explicitly. Direct citation occurs primarily where the writer wants to

---

[15] See e.g. 1 Kings 11.41; 15.7; 16.5; 2 Kings 8.23; 13.8.

signal fulfilment of prophetic Scripture. An author's reliance on unidentified sources is easier to detect where comparable materials exist, as in the case of Samuel–Kings and Chronicles in the Old Testament and Matthew, Mark and Luke in the New Testament. In the investigation of the three Synoptic Gospels, for example, it is now almost universally agreed that Mark was written before Matthew and Luke, and that both Matthew and Luke relied on Mark for a major part of their respective Gospels. In addition, Matthew and Luke share identical material not found in Mark. From this observation source critics conclude that a source (referred to as Q) is responsible for the 'sayings' type of material in these two Gospels. Not all biblical documents lend themselves to this kind of comparative analysis.

How then does a biblical scholar detect the multi-layered sources in a document? One of the clues is an unexpected change in vocabulary and style. In Genesis 1 and 2, for example, we find two different ways of recounting the story of creation. In Genesis 1 the name of the Creator is *Elohim* consistently, whereas the name of the creator in chapter 2 is *Yahweh Elohim*. Added to this change in vocabulary is a change in the style from chapter 1 to chapter 2. Not only are the vocabulary and style different from the first chapter to the second, but the story in the second is also a variant from the account in chapter 1. Variant stories is yet another clue to the presence of sources in the make-up of a biblical document. We saw already (Chapter 6) how two stories of the flood were wedded into one.

Interruptions in the flow of a passage is another clue to a source. Rudolf Bultmann observed significant disjuncture in John chapters 2 to 12, and detected a 'signs source' behind this section of the Fourth Gospel. For example, the narrator in John 2.11 states that the changing of water to wine was the first sign Jesus performed. In the next chapter Nicodemus notes that Jesus has performed a number of signs. Then in chapter 4 the narrator cites the sign of the healing of the centurion's son as the second sign. This kind of literary disjuncture appears throughout the whole section on the signs. The judgement of source criticism is that the writer's incorporation of written material into his document accounts for this condition in the literary end product.

Naming forms

Language has to be useful. To be useful in communication the language develops shape, or form. This is true in all ages of human relationship in society. A throne speech in Canada is not a newspaper editorial, much less a comic strip. It is a throne speech. When the throne speech is announced, as it was on CBC radio this morning on my way to work, I know essentially what to expect. The name itself communicates a great deal. A sermon is not a poem; neither is a newspaper advertisement a recipe for pound cake. We name the form of speech and thereby have an expectation of the function of everything inside that particular form.

The same is true of the Bible. Inside the Scriptures is a multiplicity of forms: psalm, parable, prophetic oracle, narrative, hymn, apocalypse, letter, etc. Any one of these could be a whole document, such as the letter addressed to Philemon and the church that meets in his house or the apocalypse under the name of Daniel in the Old Testament. But often the biblical documents contain smaller forms within them. The identification of the forms in documents facilitates the understanding of the sense communicated in the text. Moreover, form analysis seeks to classify units of text by the patterns the units exhibit (such as love poems, parables, sayings, elegies, legends). But more than that, form analysis attempts to trace the pattern back to period of oral transmission, and to the situation in life that would have given shape to the literary pattern.

Form criticism in biblical studies came into its own in the first half of the twentieth century.[16] The first biblical scholar to study forms in the Old Testament was Hermann Gunkel (1862–1932). He worked especially on Genesis, the Psalms, and the Prophets. His form-critical work on the Psalms is a classic, and continues to be a reference for ongoing study of that collection of Hebrew poetry. He identified types of Psalms, such as 'enthronement', 'thanksgiving', 'lament', etc.[17]

Gunkel's premise that Israel formed its expression of faith and life out of its experience provided one of the basic principles of form criticism for years to come in both Old Testament and New Testament studies: a situation in life shapes the oral form of speech that is remem-

---

[16] Gene Tucker, *Form Criticism of the Old Testament* (Philadelphia: Fortress Press, 1971), 5–6.
[17] Hermann Gunkel, *Introduction to Psalms: The Genres of the Religious Lyric of Israel*, completed Joachim Begrich, trans. James D. Nogalski (Macon: Mercer University Press, 1998).

bered and transmitted. In New Testament K. L. Schmidt, Martin Dibelius, and Rudolf Bultmann refined the method, applying it particularly to Gospel literature.[18]

People in communities of the ancient world *told* their experiences long before the oral form was committed to writing. In this oral state the material about life, belief and behaviour developed a linguistic mould suited to the kind of material and life experience representing in the language. A prophetic oracle is first proclaimed out of the spirit of the prophet, and remembered in the community. Eventually the oracle is written in an anthology of oracles, such as the anthology of Isaiah or Jeremiah. The same is true for a psalm or a proverb. The psalm is sung on a suitable occasion, such as that of a temple festival, and a proverb is uttered as wise instruction in a particular situation. By the same token the parables of Jesus were first spoken in a situation in the ministry of Jesus in Second Temple Palestine, and then moved into other situations in the life of the post-Easter Church, and thence into the written Gospels.

Stories are told in community life, songs are sung there, poems recited and prayers uttered there. The form itself tells a tale about the situation that gave rise to the form. 'The *Sitz im Leben* [situation in life] is not, however, an individual historical event, but a typical situation or occupation in the life of a community.'[19] For example, the hymn of Philippians 2.6–11 is in adoration of Christ. It is confessional and exalting. It probably came out of a worship setting in early Hellenistic-Jewish Christ-community. Or again, the royal psalms of the Psalter were doubtless sung at the coronation of the kings of Israel or Judah. And yet again, the 'handsomely sculpted kerygmatic formula'[20] in 1 Corinthians 15.3–5 came into Paul's written letter from an earlier life-situation in the emerging Church. It would have served well for instructing baptismal candidates.

Naming the form, and naming it as specifically as legitimately possible, is a goal of form criticism. By naming the form of speech the literature begins to take on a life setting in the community in which the form developed and functioned. This is particularly true for the

---

[18] See, for example, Rudolf Bultmann, 'The Study of the Synoptic Gospels' in *Form Criticism: Two Essays on New Testament Research*, trans. Frederick C. Grant (New York: Harper & Brothers, 1934/1962), 11–76.

[19] Rudolf Bultmann, *The History of the Synoptic Tradition*, trans. John Marsh (New York: Harper & Row, 1963), 4.

[20] Ben F. Meyer, *The Aims of Jesus* (London: SCM Press, 1979), 61.

years between Easter and the Pauline mission, 30–50 CE. From those years we have no extant literature from the Christ-communities around the Mediterranean. Analysis of forms within the Gospels, the Book of Acts and Paul's Letters opens a window onto the self-defining landscape of the fledgling Church. How were the *parables* shaped to fit the community's experience of Christ resurrected and coming again? What function did the *pronouncement stories* in the Gospels play in guiding the moral life of the community? How did the form match the mission experience of the faith community? What effect would the delay of the coming of Christ have had on the shaping of the Jesus tradition? In this respect form criticism has served a worthy purpose in biblical exegesis.

One of the outstanding forms in the Book of Acts is the 'speech' form. We find it in the mouth of key apostolic leaders in the development of the early Church. Peter's speech represents the Jerusalemite stage, Stephen's the Antiochan, and Paul's several speeches the Gentile mission stage.[21] In each case the texture of the respective speech bespeaks the character, time and situation of the speaker. Whether the speeches are drawn out of the oral tradition of the Church is debatable. They may be the artful creations of the writer of Acts, and are thus literary forms that bespeak as much the author's own theology and situation as they do the theology and situation of the earlier times of Peter, Stephen and Paul.

Tracing traditions

Closely related to the analysis of forms within the written texts of Scripture is the history of the several traditions in which the forms are employed from one community to another, from one time to another. The history of the traditional material is difficult to trace critically where the form appears in only one document. For this reason scholars interested in the development of traditional material are drawn to gospel literature of the New Testament and to Samuel–Kings and Chronicles literature of the Old Testament. In both cases forms can be compared and their history judged with some degree of probability.

Consider the well-known ransom saying of Mark 10.45. Jeremias traces the movement of this saying from its early Palestinian setting into the later Greek environment of the mission churches. In the earliest

---

[21] For this early stage of Christian self-definition see Martin Hengel, *Between Jesus and Paul,* 1–29; and Ben F. Meyer, *The Early Christians: Their World Mission and Self-Discovery* (Wilmington: Michael Glazier, 1986), 36–83.

Gospel of Mark the saying of Jesus reads: *the Son of Man came not to be served but to serve, and to give his life a ransom for many.* At Luke 22.27 the saying comes to the fore, but with quite different formulation: *For who is greater, the one who is at the table or the one who serves? Is it not the one at the table? But I am among you as one who serves.* Some scholars believe the Lukan version, although incorporated later than the one in Mark, is closer to the Jesus tradition. The serving in Luke is ethical, and less dogmatic. According to Jeremias, however, 'each of these two quite different illustrations of the way in which Jesus serves derives from *Palestinian tradition*'.[22]

The saying appears reformulated in 1 Timothy 2.6: *Christ Jesus, himself a man, who gave himself a ransom for all.* Jeremias contends that 1 Timothy 2.6 'has given Mark's Semitic wording a more pronounced Greek flavour in every word'.[23] Notice especially the change from 'Son of Man' (*ho huios tou anthropou*) in Mark to 'a man' (*anthropos*) in 1 Timothy. In short, as a form of speech moves from one community to another, from one setting to another, as in Palestinian (Mark) to Hellenistic (1 Timothy), the form is adapted to the new pattern of thought.

Each of Mark, Luke and 1 Timothy, incorporates the saying independently of the other. By comparing one with the other scholars are able to demonstrate how the form of a saying alters in its movement from one milieu to another. The form changes in keeping with the sociological environment and situation in which it is used. Tracing the history of formal traditional material is a mark of the historical critical way of interpreting texts of Scripture. But, like any one of the specific methods, tracing the history of traditional material does not stand alone.

Recognizing redaction

There is also the larger picture of how various traditional materials were combined and brought forward into one document. Whatever home the smaller discrete units of text (called *pericopae*) may have had prior to their incorporation into the biblical documents, their new place in a document serves the interests and intention of the redactor who brought them together. The study of the shape the sources and

---

[22] Joachim Jeremias, *New Testament Theology: Part One, The Proclamation of Jesus* (London: SCM Press, 1971), 293.

[23] Jeremias, *New Testament Theology*, 294.

traditions take within a document of Scripture is called *redaction criticism*.

This way of reading biblical literature came to the fore in post-war Germany.[24] 'Redaction criticism is an attempt to understand the theological viewpoint, the literary interests, and the life setting of the author, and how those might have shaped the author's presentation of the material.'[25] In the strict sense, though, a redactor is not an author. Authorship implies an original composition of a literary work. Redaction is more closely aligned with editorial activity, and is therefore more appropriately applied to documents dealing with traditional and historical material, such as the Pentateuch, the Historical Books of the Old Testament, the Gospels and Acts of the New Testament.

Beyond these kinds of documents, however, redaction was applied to prophets, Psalms and Proverbs. Isaiah, for example, was seen as a collection of oracles from the eighth-century prophet Isaiah (chapters 1–39), as well as oracles from a later period (chapters 40 to 66). The Psalms were viewed not as a random collection of poems, but a purposefully structured grouping of poems to form one overarching Psalter. The same holds for Proverbs.

Redaction criticism builds on source and form criticism. It asks how the earlier sources and forms were shaped by the redactor in the composition of the document as a whole. Redaction is more clearly detected where more than one document contains the same formal material. The Synoptic Gospels, for example, lend themselves well to redaction analysis. They share traditional material variously, whereas the Acts material has only minimal parallels elsewhere (at least within the canon). Yet even in Acts the redactor's hand can be detected, especially where narrative material corresponds to similar narrative in Paul's letters, as in the case of the narrative of the Jerusalem council meeting of Acts 15 and Galatians 2. Rather than pursue these two larger texts, I will illustrate the Acts redactor's touch from two smaller texts.

The story is about Paul being lowered down a wall in a basket to escape his persecutors. The story is unique and striking. Recorded in 2 Corinthians by Paul himself, this little story took hold in the Pauline tradition, and found its way eventually into Acts. The two versions are set out side by side in Table 11.1 for comparison.

---

[24] The names Günther Bornkamm, Hans Conzelmann and Willi Marxen were its chief proponents in New Testament studies.

[25] James R. Beasley et al., *An Introduction to the Bible* (Nashville: Abingdon Press, 1991), 42f.

Table 11.1

2 Corinthians 11.32–3	Acts 9.22–5
In Damascus, the governor under King Aretas guarded the city of Damascus in order to seize me, but I was let down in a basket through a window in the wall, and escaped from his hands	[Paul] became increasingly more powerful and confounded the Jews who lived in Damascus by proving that Jesus was the Messiah. After some time had passed, the Jews plotted to kill him, but their plot became known to [Paul]. They were watching the gates day and night so that they might kill him; but his disciples took him by night and let him down through an opening in the wall, lowering him in a basket

Paul's persecutor in 2 Corinthians is the Gentile governor of King Aretas, who ruled the Nabatean region from Petra. Whatever Paul was doing in that Gentile territory he evidently raised the ire of the King's governor against him. Then, in order for Paul to escape the governor's anger, someone lowered him in a basket from an open window. Paul's version of the story, recorded in the early fifties of the Common Era, comes through in the later book of Acts (*c.* 85–95 CE) quite differently.

Obviously the incident represented in both texts is the same one. The basic elements of the story are present in both versions: the city is Damascus, Paul is being pursued, and he was lowered down a wall in a basket through an opening. What has changed noticeably from Paul's narrative to that of Acts is the identity of the persecutors. In Paul's account a Gentile governor under orders from King Aretas[26] sought to capture him. In Acts the Jews are the culprits. This change in the narrative is almost certainly redactional. Throughout Acts the Jews consistently persecute Paul and challenge his mission. By contrast the Gentile powers are much less severe on Paul in Acts.

The redactor of Acts, himself a Gentile, lives at a time when the new Christian movement needs more positive recognition from the Roman authorities. The Acts redaction appears to defend the Christian community as freestanding, independent of Judaism, and non-threatening to Roman rule. In carrying out the defence the redactor casts the Jews in the role of persecutor of the new, and quite innocent, Christian movement. To accomplish this and other purposes of the

---

[26] Aretas' dominion extended from the Arabian Desert north through modern Jordan as far as Damascus of Syria. North of Damascus the governor had no jurisdiction.

document the redactor shapes traditional narratives to fit. In this sense, moreover, the redactor is also author. The reshaping and re-contextual-izing of sources and traditions constitutes nothing less than a new composition.

What is true for narrative material is equally so for sayings. One example from Matthew and Luke must suffice to illustrate the redaction of sayings. Both Matthew and Luke draw on the Q source for much of their sayings material, and they do so independently of each other. The well-known beatitude of Matthew 5.6 occurs also in Luke 6.21. The two versions are set out in Table 11.2.

The aim in this exercise is not to decide which of these is closer to the actual words of Jesus, but to illustrate the difference between the two redactional hands at work. Again, the similarity is clearly evident. The saying is a blessing on people who are hungry. The hungry can look forward to having their hunger satisfied. But Matthew adds a very significant word, 'righteousness'. For Matthew this word is schematic. In Matthew it defines the word-and-work of Jesus. From beginning to end Matthew highlights 'righteousness'. At the beginning Jesus' surrogate father, Joseph, is said to be a *righteous man* (1.19). At the end Pilate's wife warns her husband to *have nothing to do with that righteous man* (27.19). Matthew explains Jesus' baptism as an act *to fulfil all righteousness* (3.15). In short, Matthew presents Jesus as a teacher of righteousness, not unlike the teacher of righteousness in the Qumran scrolls, and pictures those who follow Jesus as disciples longing for the righteousness of God. Matthew's Jesus pronounces blessing on such, with a promise to satisfy their hunger for righteousness.

For Luke the matter is quite different. That Gospel favours the poor, the hungry, the lame; all who are socially disenfranchised. That Gospel presents Jesus as one anointed by the *Spirit of the Lord ... to bring good news to the poor ... to proclaim release to the captives and recovery of sight to the blind, to let the oppressed go free, to proclaim the year of the Lord's favour* (4.18–19). The hungry ones in Luke are hungry for bread to sustain physical life, in keeping with the general tenor of the whole Gospel of Luke.

Again in both of these examples the redactors are not merely collectors of material, not merely compilers pasting pieces of source material together at random. They do collect and they do compile, but they put their own distinctive stamp on the compilation by reshaping the collected materials and by dressing them in suitable narrative fabric. Their works are thus compositions, and they themselves authors in that sense.

237

Table 11.2

Matthew 5.6	Luke 6:21
Blessed are those who hunger and thirst for righteousness, for they will be filled.	Blessed are you who are hungry now, for you will be filled.

Considering canon

One step beyond redaction criticism, *canonical criticism* is a more recent approach, borderline between modern and post-modern interpretation. Two of its strongest proponents spring to mind immediately: James A. Sanders and Brevard S. Childs. According to Sanders, '1972 seems to mark its inception',[27] the year in which Sanders' first book on the subject appeared.[28]

Canonical criticism goes beyond the history of the canon to the *function* of canon in the communities that valued some books over others. Canonical criticism builds on the gains of the various historical critical approaches, but turns the searchlight on the shaping and receiving communities. Rather than ask about the origin of the book of Isaiah, for example, canonical criticism asks about the thought and life of the community that brought the disparate oracles together in one scroll. What were the values of that community? How was it able to celebrate the differences from one part of the book to another? Canonical criticism, especially that of Childs, is less interested in who wrote the script and more in who read it, and who reads it.

For Childs the authorship and integrity of a document is only one stage in the inquiry. Further inquiry is needed into the acceptance of the extant form of the book for the faith and life of the communities of readers along the way in history. 2 Corinthians, for example, has two very distinct parts: chapters 1 to 9 and chapters 10 to 13. The first part is conciliatory and invitational in tone, the second defensive and sarcastic. Historical critical scholarship ferrets out the history of composition of the two parts, whereas canonical criticism asks why a community would put the two parts together and value it for itself, the two-in-one. According to Childs, the canonical shape of 2 Corinthians illustrates a vision of the Church that considered the gospel of

[27] James A. Sanders, *Canon and Community: A Guide to Canonical Criticism* (Philadelphia: Fortress Press, 1984), 61.
[28] James A. Sanders, *Torah and Canon* (Philadelphia: Fortress Press, 1972), referenced in his *Canon and Community*, 18, n. 33.

reconciliation (chapters 1 to 9) balanced by gospel of judgement (chapters 10 to 13).

Childs' approach, as compared to that of Sanders is more synchronic. He considered the shape of the document as a whole as it was received by the Church, and canonized in that shape. Sanders' approach is more diachronic. He focuses on the history of the shape of the document that finally was accepted by the Church. Both of them, in the end, point to the need to study the canonical form of the documents as speaking to the needs of the communities that received them.

A canonical reading does not stop with the first readers merely, but asks about successive communities of readers, including the communities of the present time. Each of the successive communities, repeating the readings of the past, values the readings afresh in relation to their own situation in life. One might say each new community re-lives the canonical tradition as a hermeneutical community.

Canon critics, such as Sanders especially, do not attempt to harmonize the conflicting parts within books or between books. They celebrate the pluralism within the canon, as the communities of readers have done along the way. Sanders states the case for canonical pluralism this way:

> For almost every assertion one can find its contra-positive. The richness of the canon in this regard needs to be celebrated rather than ignored and denied as nearly all its adherents have tended to do. Conservatives deny it and liberals ignore it. Actually, it is one of the canon's most precious gifts that it contains its own self-corrective apparatus. No theological construct imposed on the Bible as canon escapes the scrutiny and critique of something else in it. Consistency is a mark of small minds. It can also be a manipulative tool in the hands of those who insist that the Bible is totally harmonious, and that they alone sing the tune![29]

For all its pluralism, or diversity, the canon signifies authority for the communities that read it. It judges their thought and life, and urges them toward the right, the good, and the true. Exploring the process and function of canon in communities thus opens up the biblical texts to new insights beyond the historical critical approach, and helps forge a link between scholars in the academy and clerics in the Church. Childs' approach in particular, so it seems to me, has helped in this

---

[29] Sanders, *Canon*, 46.

regard. Clergy and congregation ask not what they can do for the Bible, but ask rather what the Bible can do for them. Their interest is not in origin and authorship, in form and redaction. Their interest is in finding meaning here and now from texts that gained authority in communities past.[30]

Modern Paradigm Found Wanting

In the early 1970s, with the publication of the new canonical approaches to reading of Scriptures, the long-standing modern approaches were called into question. I will use one figure from the time to illustrate the movement. Childs and others had made similar pronouncements, perhaps with less fervour.

Walter Wink pronounced the historical critical paradigm 'bankrupt' under the title, *The Bible in Human Transformation: Toward a New Paradigm for Biblical Study* (1973).[31] In sharp polemical language Wink berated the modern paradigm of biblical studies for its inability to do what the biblical texts themselves intended: the transformation of the human spirit in social/communal relationships. Wink's strident attack on the guild of biblical scholars (to which he himself belonged) met with immediate recoil and/or rebuttal from colleagues with vested interest. Many had invested a lifetime plying their technical trade in opening up the biblical texts. To declare the product of their work 'bankrupt' was a hard pill to swallow. Here is a sampling of Wink's description of the bankruptcy.

> This detached, value-neutral, a-historical point of view is, of course, an illusion.... The historical critical method had a vested interest in undermining the Bible's authority.... The biblical scholar has removed himself from view, no shadow from the past can fall across his path. ... He examines the Bible, but he himself is not examined – except by his colleagues in the guild! ...The historical critical method has reduced the Bible to a dead letter. Our obeisance to technique has left the Bible sterile and ourselves empty. ... The outcome of biblical studies in the

---

[30] Sanders' diachronic approach to canon criticism continues to emphasize the importance of maintaining the focus on the parts that went into the make-up of the whole. 'Canonical criticism, using all the Enlightenment tools of exegesis at each layer of tradition, is especially concerned that resignifications of these canonical texts stay within permissible canonical limits of meaning', *Canon*, 78.

[31] Wink opens his book of some 83 pages with the provocative negative assertion, 'Historical biblical criticism is bankrupt', *The Bible in Human Transformation: Toward a New Paradigm for Biblical Study* (Philadelphia: Fortress Press, 1973), 1.

academy is a trained incapacity to deal with the real problems of actual persons in their daily lives. ... Biblical criticism has now, like revivalism, become bankrupt. ... It is based on an inadequate method, married to false objectivism, subjected to uncontrolled technologism, separated from a vital community, and has outlived its usefulness as presently practiced.[32]

Wink's pronouncement in 1973, stated with such zeal, was made on the cusp of a much larger paradigm shift in Western culture, daubed post-modernism. Wink's proposal 'toward a new paradigm for biblical study' was one of many such to follow in the next twenty-five years. His called for 'a dialectal hermeneutic' having three moments: fusion, distance and communion.

His working out of these three moments in his short essay is more confusing than it is helpful. Suffice it to say that Wink's drive was to carry out 'a de-construction of the assurances of modern [humankind]'.[33] His idea was to bring human existence as it is lived in the present in line with the biblical world-view.

> Thus [by fusion, distance and communion] there is achieved a communion of horizons, in which the encounter between the horizon of the transmitted text lights up one's own horizon and leads to self-disclosure and self-understanding, while at the same time one's own horizon lights up lost elements of the text and brings them forward with new relevance for life today.[34]

Wink's essay of 1973 exploded the persistent myth of objectivism in modern biblical investigation, and helped pave the way toward a more interactive reading of the biblical texts. After the initial shock of his provocative pronouncement of bankruptcy on the historical critical paradigm, one scholar after another put forward new ways of reading the ancient Scriptures.

To conclude, modern ways of reading the ancient Scriptures follow the lead of the Reformation and the dictates of the Enlightenment. Allegorical reading fell increasingly into disrepute with the emergence of the scientific method. Biblical scholars wrested the Bible from the Church in order to demystify it. A naïve reading of the texts was outlawed. The texts had to be read in the light of the history that gave them birth in the first place. That history was charged with myth-truth,

---

[32] Wink, *Bible in Human Transformation*, 3–15.
[33] Wink, *Bible in Human Transformation*, 32.
[34] Wink, *Bible in Human Transformation*, 66.

which in turn had to be demythologized to fit modern categories. More and more the texts were scrutinized for underlying sources, for embedded forms that grew out of settings in life, and for marks of redaction. Exegesis had to be objective, which meant objectifying every element of the text's history. The interpreter had to keep a safe distance from personal encounter with the text's meaning. Objective knowledge of the text's horizon was the goal. This is to state the case starkly. There were those church people who practiced historical critical reading of the biblical texts, and at the same time lived faithfully in relationship with God and the Church.

Cracks in the historical critical paradigm did not appear until the latter part of the twentieth century. Canonical criticism turned the spotlight once again on community consciousness of the text, but still warned against reckless departure from the tested and true results of historical criticism. Even Walter Wink, despite his declaration of 'bankruptcy' for the historical critical paradigm, fell back on the modern scientific paradigm for setting up his new 'fusion-distance-communion' dialectic paradigm.

On Course . . .

Objective

To engage in discussion of recent 'post-modern' methodology in the interpretation of biblical texts with understanding and discernment.

Lead Questions

1. How would you describe 'post-modernism'?

2. To what degree are modern historical critical methods still present in post-modern practice?

3. How would you answer the charge that post-modern interpreters are irresponsible?

4. What is a 'social-science approach' to biblical studies?

5. Who pioneered the social-science approach in the field of Old-Testament?

6. What are the names of two leading social-science interpreters in the field of New Testament studies?

7. Draw a chart of the difference between the agrarian world of the Bible and the industrial world of the present time.

8. What is a 'literary-narrative' interpretation? Name one practitioner who worked on the Gospel of John.

9. What is 'historical-rhetorical' interpretation? Name one practitioner who worked on Galatians.

10. How would you describe and illustrate 'intertextuality'? What facets might you look for in the biblical texts?

11. What way does Stanley Fish understand 'reader-response' criticism? How does Robert Fowler employ the approach to the Gospel of Mark?

12. What is meant by deconstruction, especially as Derrida works with language? How might the approach help with the understanding of a traditional interpretation of biblical texts such as 1 Timothy 2.11–15?

13. In what sense is a feminist interpretation a political reading of the biblical text? How does Schüssler Fiorenza make her appeal to her colleagues in biblical studies to deconstruct 'malestream' interpretation?

12

Other Ways of Reading the
Same Scriptures

There is no single way of reading that is correct or natural.
(Stanley Fish)

This chapter is about pushing the boundaries of reading biblical texts beyond the limits of traditional modernity.[1] This 'push' does not mean recoil from modern thought, nor a rejection of modernity in favour of a non-critical way of reading. It means, rather, the use of models for reading biblical texts not formerly adopted within the guild of modern biblical scholarship. The movement started in earnest in the decade of the 1970s.[2] As such, these newer ways of reading Scriptures fall under the current catchphrase, 'post-modern'.

I have divided the chapter into two principal parts. The first deals with reading models that expand the modern envelope considerably. The second identifies models that burst the bounds of modern reading, and thus are justly called 'post-modern'.

What is 'Post-modern'?

In the present time the terms 'post-modern' and 'post-modernity' are bandied about as commonplace, until someone asks what the phrases mean. At that point definitions are either not forthcoming, or are so varied when they do come forth that they render the terms inoperative. Yet that same non-definable quality is believed by some to be the very strength of the 'post-modern'. 'Postmodern thought is not one thing ... The name itself suggests that post-modernity defines itself over against "modernity",[3] or at least against the inhibiting aspects of modernity.

---

[1] By 'traditional modernity' I mean the canons of scientific method developed from the sixteenth century through the Enlightenment into the twentieth century.

[2] Exemplified in the writings of Childs, Maier, Wink, and others. E.g. Wink's pronouncement of bankruptcy on the historical critical method, discussed in Chapter 11.

[3] A. K. M. Adam, *What is Postmodern Biblical Criticism?* (Minneapolis: Fortress Press, 1995), 1.

At the heart of post-modern thinking, I believe, is a penchant for deconstructing anything foundational or absolute, including staid methodology of modernity. A generation ago the boom of post-modern thinking shattered universalist notions of unity and consistency. Universalist categories that would dare to impose themselves on particular communities were considered constructs devised by power brokers for the benefit of an elite class. Instead, 'the post-modern worldview operates with a community-based understanding of truth. It affirms that whatever we accept as truth and even the way we envision truth are dependent on the community in which we participate.'[4]

But post-modern approaches to biblical studies, as the term implies, carries forward much of the good enshrined in the historical critical method. To be sure, the post-modern explosion brought with it only the partial demise of hegemony of historical critical methods. The period is post-modern, not non-modern. New methods are welcome as long as they measure up to the claim the text places on them. Here again I elicit Lonergan's general method. The results of post-modern methodology in biblical studies are beneficial only in so far as they are cumulative and progressive. If the methods help us build on the achievements of the historical critical methods for the good, then they are to be welcomed.

According to Grenz, writing as recently as 1996, 'our society is in the throes of a cultural shift of immense proportions'.[5] The 'shift' in methodology in biblical studies has already happened, I would say. No longer is the discipline dominated by an Enlightenment world-view with historicism ruling methodology. There are now many 'methods', each one calling for espousal.

Since the 1970s post-modernism has become a cultural phenomenon. Its ethos has filtered into advertising, film, literature, philosophy, and no less biblical studies. The reading of the Scriptures is now under negotiation.[6] Traditional ways of interpreting the texts are exploded to make room for new imagination. Historical critical methods, though not displaced altogether, are being supplemented by multiple ways of reading texts. Noticeably, the 'author' and 'authorial intention' have been dethroned to make room for the 'reader', or 'reading community'.

---

[4] Stanley J. Grenz, *A Primer on Postmodernism* (Grand Rapids: Eerdmans, 1996), 8.
[5] Grenz, *Primer*, 11.
[6] Witness the title of Walter Brueggemann's book of the 1990s, *Texts Under Negotiation: The Bible and Postmodern Imagination* (Minneapolis: Fortress Press, 1993).

Post-modern biblical scholars do not work willy-nilly with texts, stringing together some far-out notions. The ones I know are scholars in the full sense of the term, but are simply not committed to working with one theory and practice, historical criticism, over against others. They work out of a thorough grasp of the discipline, its history and currency, but with an eye also to the fabric of community life. They aim at demystifying ideology and methodology to allow the human spirit freedom to encounter the texts authentically. From their place in both guild and community, post-modern biblical interpreters attempt to deconstruct established readings to allow new light to illuminate the text, to enjoy a fresh encounter with the Scripture, and also to challenge the structures of communal and societal life. In short, post-modern readers 'want to resist the bad habits we have fallen into under the influence of modernity'.[7]

Pushing the Envelope

In the last quarter-century, some interpreters of Scripture merely expanded the modern methodological envelope. That is, they still rely on historical information for their work, but move beyond it to uncover other facets of the texts not yet explored. Those who put each of these approaches to use do so as specialists. They discover a new way of reading, probe a host of relevant sources for insight, and then put the new insights into the service of reading Scripture texts. The results are often rewarding.

Some of the approaches tend to be limited by the specialized nature of the approach (as in the social-science model below). Little can be done about the limitation: specialization is necessary for precision and accuracy. At the same time, methodologies should not be construed as watertight compartments, the domain of the privileged few specialists. Each method contributes to understanding overall.

Social-Science reading

We begin with the social-science reading of the Scripture texts. In one sense, the social-science approaches belong to the newer method-ologies. On the other hand, they can be very modern, substituting sociology for history.

---

[7] Adam, *What is Postmodern?*, 1.

Historical critics recognized all along the impact of culture on the biblical authors, which in turn found its way into their texts. Usually the cultural components cited were micro factors. Such elements as creation stories in ancient near eastern texts were noted and compared to the biblical stories of creation. And form criticism did ask questions about the *Sitz im Leben* of the form under investigation. But a thoroughgoing exploration of the social fabric of a given culture of the times and places of biblical texts was not undertaken in breadth and depth until the latter part of the twentieth century.

Some biblical scholars began to recognize the gains accrued from sociology, anthropology, and psychology in studying contemporary institutions, peoples and cultures. Why not use the same tools of social science to investigate the ancient ones as well? The investigation could surely shed light on the texts created and read within particular social settings. A number of scholars accepted the challenge of probing the general social factors that made up Mediterranean cultures to gain insight into the socially textured nature of biblical texts.

A social-science reading of Scripture rests on the premise that human thought is socially located. Everything in the human person's repertoire is conditioned by the reality of the society in which the person lives. Language constitutes the most striking evidence of the social location of thought. A person learns a language by living in a group where the language is used. Language is laden with the social elements that make life what it is in that particular location. When the language moves from its own social location into another via text, the inside story ends up with numerous gaps. Readers in the second location of thought read the text, of course, but as they do so they are obliged to fill the gaps with material from their own social location of thought. Otherwise how could they understand the story at all?

Scholars in the social-science field call for a rereading of the biblical texts that fills the gaps as much as possible from insight gained from a study of the social setting of the ancient Mediterranean world. In 1978, for example, Richard Rohrbaugh published a telling monograph entitled, *The Biblical Interpreter: An Agrarian Bible in an Industrial Age*. In it he sought to instruct preachers on the art and skill of translating the socially conditioned texts of the Bible into modern alternatives. He urged preachers not to settle for broad abstract categories of thought, or general applications characteristic of our own time. Even the universal quest for individual meaning and personal fulfilment, espoused by such twentieth-century scholars as Rudolf Bultmann, was not sufficient for the task of translating the socially conditioned categories of biblical texts into contemporary life. Granted, there is existential concern in all human beings, ancient and modern, else how could we connect with each other at all. But the social categories of thought are different. Before the translation can take place the interpreter needs to grasp the social location of the texts. Only then can an adequate re-signification, or translation, occur.

At the heart of the difference between the ancient writers of the biblical texts and modern readers, according to Rohrbaugh, is an agrarian mind-set (biblical) versus an industrial mind-set (modern). 'The Scriptures were written by and for persons whose perceptions of reality were conditioned by an agrarian and preindustrial society, while it is being interpreted by and for hearers in an industrial world.'[8] With the industrial revolution a major shift happened. More and more people became urban, and the society, rural and urban, was enveloped in a massive technological advance. The difference between the two worlds, agrarian and industrial, and the two corresponding world-views, has to be taken into account in reading the Scriptures. To be sure, people in both worlds eat and drink and try to survive in the world, and generally have much in common as human beings. Yet the two socially conditioned world-views and the practices that accompany them are scarcely congruent.

Profiles of the two respective social structures are complex, and cannot be attempted in detail within the scope of this chapter. A comparative chart of the main features of both must suffice.[9]

Ancient agriculture, as it developed such tools as the iron plough, and domesticated animals for work, provided a surplus of produce and more settled life. Urban centres sprang up, and saw the specialization of skills and the advancement of military technology. Territorial boundaries broadened to eventually become empires. Increasingly urbanization happened, and increasingly the urban centres dominated the agrarian landscape politically, culturally and economically. Social inequality became more and more a fact of life in the agrarian world. Social class was inescapable. As Table 12.1 shows, the industrial world and world-view differ markedly from those of the agrarian. The biblical texts come from the agrarian. Analysis of the social structure of reality

---

[8] Richard L. Rohrbaugh, *The Biblical Interpreter: An Agrarian Bible in an Industrial Age* (Philadelphia: Fortress Press, 1978), 18.

[9] The percentages are based on demographics in North America.

Table 12.1

Agrarian Social Reality	Industrial Social Reality
• Beginning: the invention of agriculture (*c.* 6000 years ago)	• Beginning: the industrial revolution (*c.* 1760 CE)
• Pre-industrial urban centres	• Large industrial urban cities
• CORPORATE/COMMUNITY LIFE	• INDIVIDUALISM
• Honour/shame (group conscience)	• Innocence/guilt (individual conscience)
• Ruler in control	• More democratic control
• Elite governing class	• Manufacturing bosses
• Inequalities abound	• Move toward egalitarian mode
• Alliance between religion and state	• Separation of State and Religion
• 90% peasant farmers, working a subsistence plot	• About 4% of the population are industrial agriculturalists
• Women subservient	• Women upwardly mobile to equal status
• 90% of population rural	• Over 90% urban
• 90–95% in agriculture and raw materials	• 5% in agriculture and raw materials
• About 3% of the population literate	• About 97% of the population literate
• Life expectancy 20 years at birth in the first century	• Life expectancy 80 years at birth at the present time
• Limited specialization in occupations	• Highly specialized occupations
• Small bureaucracy	• Elaborate bureaucracy
• Numerous widows and orphans	• Relatively few widows and orphans
• No government sponsored income assistance	• Government sponsored income assistance available
• No industrial corporations	• Many industrial corporations
• Family is the unit of production	• Individual worker the unit of production

in which the texts were written creates 'distance' between the modern industrialist reader and the agrarian texts. Recognizing the 'distance' is necessary before appropriate transfer of significance can happen.

> Reading is always a social act. If both reader and writer share the same social system and the same experience, adequate communication is highly probable. But if either reader or writer comes from a different social system, then, as a rule, nonunderstanding – or at best misunderstanding – will be the result.[10]

The social order in agrarian societies was not egalitarian by any means. It was, rather, more pyramidal, with the vast majority of the

---

[10] Bruce J. Malina and Richard L. Rohrbaugh, *Social-Science Commentary on the Synoptic Gospels* (Minneapolis: Fortress Press, 1992), 14.

population barely subsisting off the land. Gerhard Lenski's diagram in Figure 12.2[11] illustrates the power and privilege of the small number of elite ruling class against the large poorer class of peasant farmers, always in danger of being pushed off their subsistence plot into the lowest strata of expendables.

A pioneering work in sociological methodology in Old Testament was that of Norman Gottwald in 1979. His investigation of the socio-cultural life of Israel upon The Israelites' arrival in Canaan, the land of promise, is unsurpassed in its probing into the social/cultic structures of the time, and how these shaped Israelite religion.[12] In New Testament, Bruce Malina joined forces with Richard Rohrbaugh for the writing of a social-science commentary on the Synoptic Gospels, and another on the Gospel of John. Every pericopé of the Gospels is read in those commentaries through the lens of the social location of first-century Mediterranean life. An excerpt from their commentary on the Synoptic Gospels will illustrate how the social-science approach works.

The text is Luke 3.23a, which reads: *Jesus was about thirty years old when he began his work.* Malina's and Rohrbaugh's 'Reading Scenario' for this text is as follows:

> For a person to reach the age of eighty-four would be highly unusual. In the cities of antiquity nearly a third of the live births were dead before age six. By the mid-teens 60 percent would have died, by the mid-twenties 75 percent, and 90 percent by the mid-forties. Perhaps 3 percent reached their sixties. Few low-status people lived out their thirties. The ancient glorification of youth and the veneration of the elderly (who in nonliterate societies are the only repository of community memory and knowledge) are thus easily understood. Moreover, we might note that at thirty (Luke 3.23) Jesus was not a young man, that much of his audience would have been younger than he, disease-ridden, and looking at a decade or less of life expectancy.[13]

Malina also teamed up with Jerome Neyrey to produce a social-science analysis of Paul in 1996, under the title, *Portraits of Paul: An Archaeology of Ancient Personality.* In that work also one finds the same characteristic features of agrarian social life as these scholars construe it. In a similar vein, Wayne Meeks wrote about *The First Urban Christians*

---

[11] I am indebted to Gerhard Lenski for this diagram of agrarian social stratification, in *Power and Privilege: A Theory of Social Stratification* (New York: McGraw-Hill, 1966), 284.

[12] Norman K. Gottwald, *The Tribes of Yahweh: A Sociology of the Religion of Liberated Israel, 1250–1050 B.C.E.* (Maryknoll: Orbis, 1979), 376–699 especially.

[13] Malina and Rohrbaugh, *Synoptic Gospels,* 305.

Figure 12.1

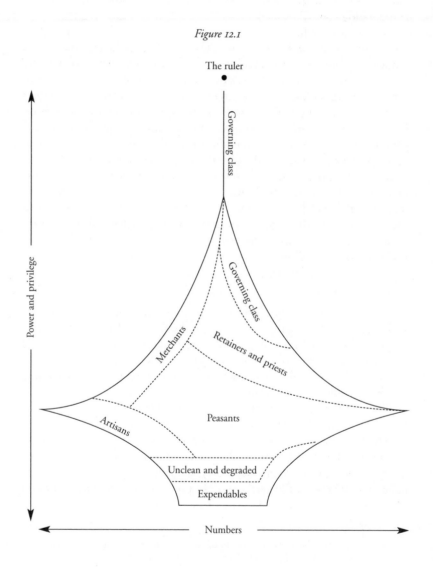

as people of the first-century agrarian society, with some variations on the themes highlighted by Malina, Rohrbaugh and Neyrey. These all have worked with models drawn from sociology and cultural anthropology.

Others have applied psychological analysis to biblical texts. Richard Q. Ford is a case in point. Ford is a psychotherapist. He applied the tools of his modern speciality to an analysis of some of the ancient narrative parables of Jesus.[14] He argued in his book that readers should develop 'the art of listening' to the various characters in the stories Jesus told by knowing their social setting, and by tuning in to their responses within the parable form. In reality, though, literal listening is not possible in the reading of the parables, as it would be in a psychotherapist's office. Ford may be 'hearing' more than the characters in the parables are actually 'telling' him.

More and more such social-science studies have appeared in the last quarter of the twentieth century.[15] While they do well in trying to recapture the social life and thought of the first writers and readers of the biblical texts they are not complete in themselves. Texts are new creations, each one having its own distinctive character. As such, they invite a literary reading.

Literary reading

A literary reading of biblical texts is not merely recognition of grammar and syntax. Nor is it a matter of parsing the figures of speech an author employs in the delivery of text-meaning. A literary reading also goes beyond source, form and redactional analysis discussed in the previous chapter. A literary reading of a whole text asks how the text as a whole achieves its effect on the reader/audience.

Not all texts lend themselves to a fully-fledged literary analysis. The book of Proverbs, for example, is a collection of wise sayings, any one of which could be extracted from the collection and used independently. The book of Psalms is likewise a collection of poems each one discrete and subject to literary analysis appropriate to itself. Yet the collection, whether of Proverbs or Psalm poems, is seen more and more

---

[14] Richard Q. Ford, *The Parables of Jesus: Recovering the Art of Listening* (Minneapolis: Fortress Press, 1997), 2. 'I use ways in which psychotherapists have been trained to listen.'

[15] For example, William R. Herzog II, *Parables as Subversive Speech: Jesus as Pedagogue of the Oppressed* (Louisville: Westminster/John Knox Press, 1994). This book analyses a number of the narrative parables of Jesus using social-science tools and the social and literary work of Paulo Freire in Brazil and Chile. See also Richard A. Horsley, *Archaeology, History, and Society in Galilee: The Social Context of Jesus and the Rabbis* (Valley Forge: Trinity Press International, 1996), 1–189.

as consciously structured, although not in the same way as a book such as Genesis. As a structured body of literary forms, moreover, the collection itself has literary design yielding effect.

A large part of the Old Testament, however, is narrative, written in a way that will evoke response from the audience in Israel. In the New Testament, the Letters of Paul are genuine letters to particular congregations, each letter consisting mostly of argument and subject therefore to rhetorical analysis. The Gospels, however, are stories about Jesus and lend themselves well to a narrative reading. Their design and purpose is not merely to chronicle the ministry of Jesus, but to 'tell' the story of it. As stories each of the Gospels has literary design, much like a modern novel: they evoke response in line with the design of the literary work.

We begin our review of a literary reading of the Bible with *rhetorical analysis* along historical lines. The letters of Paul are laced with rhetorical texture, as several scholars in recent times have observed. That is, the principal purpose of the letters is to persuade the audience to think and act in keeping with the convictions underlying the rhetoric. Would Paul have known the rules of rhetoric of his time? Dieter Betz says yes.

Betz explored Paul's letters in search of rhetorical form with which Paul might have been familiar, and found it in Galatians, and in 2 Corinthians 8 and 9. The form in these three bodies of text, says Betz, follows the rules of rhetoric taught by Cicero,[16] a skilled lawyer in Rome a century before Paul, and by Quintilian,[17] contemporary of Paul and teacher of oratory in Rome. The works of both men on oratory have survived. They, among others, provided Betz with a ready reference for his rhetorical analysis of Galatians and 2 Corinthians 8 and 9. I will use Betz's commentary on Galatians to illustrate his observation.

Published in 1979, the Galatians commentary still rests on the usual pillars of the historical critical reconstruction (authorship, addressees, opponents, date, etc.). But then Betz focuses on 'the literary composition and function of Galatians', and argues that 'Paul's letter to the Galatians can be analysed according to Greco-roman rhetoric and epistolography'. [18] Betz identified the surface structure of this

---

[16] Cicero, *Rhetorica ad Herennium, LCL,* trans. Harry Caplan (Cambridge, Mass.: Harvard University Press, 1954).

[17] M. F. Quintilian, *The Institutio Oratoria of Quintilian, LCL*, Vol. I, trans. H. E. Butler (New York: G. P. Putnam's Son, 1920).

[18] Dieter Betz, *Galatians: A Commentary on Paul's Letter to the Churches in Galatia* (Philadelphia: Fortress Press, 1979), 14.

'apologetic letter' genre using the Latin terms from the rhetorical schools of the day thus: Epistolary Prescript (1.1–5), Exordium (introduction, 1.6–11), Narratio (statement of facts, 1.12—2.14), Propositio (thesis, 2.15–21), Probatio (proofs, 3.1—4.31), Exhortatio (exhortation, 5.1—6.10); Conclusio (epistolary postscript, 6.11–18). Insightful as this identification is, it scarcely exploits the range of Paul's rhetorical nuance resonating throughout the letter. Betz's commentary still exhibits a strong tie to the historical critical method of interpretation.

Prophetic literature of the Old Testament also lends itself well to a rhetorical analysis. The prophetic speeches are persuasive in character. They expect the audience to think and live differently. Whether the form is prose or poetry, the effect is persuasive. Traditional rhetorical analysts usually identify three kinds of oratory: judicial (legal), deliberative (political) and epideictic (ceremonial). Much of prophetic literature falls under the rubric of deliberative (e.g. Isa. 1.2–20; Amos 3.1–15), but also epideictic Isa. 8.21—9.6).[19] The same rhetorical analysis could be applied to dramatic-poetic literature of Job. The aim of the dialogues is to persuade the audience to move toward an appropriate view of the suffering of the righteous.

In these few examples of traditional rhetorical criticism the focus was on the one doing the persuading, otherwise called 'the author': the letter-writer, the prophet, or poet. 'Because it plays a part in the author's ideology and the audience's condition, rhetoric is a study that impinges on the three dimensions of literature discourse: the literature itself, its readers, and its author.'[20] It remained for another group of analysts to push the envelope of rhetorical criticism away from the intention of the author to the receptivity and response of the audience.

In recent years a number of scholars have read the narrative parts of both Old and New Testaments using the tools of literary criticism. The assumption is that story-telling in the ancient world and novel-writing in the modern world follow the same pattern.

To illustrate how *narrative reading* operates I refer to Alan Culpepper's work of 1983 on the Gospel of John, *Anatomy of the Fourth Gospel: A Study in Literary Design.*[21] In that study Culpepper executed a

---

[19] See further on rhetoric in Old Testament literature in Yehoshua Gitay, 'Rhetorical Criticism', in Stephen R. Haynes and Steven L. McKenzie, eds., *To Each Its Own Meaning: An Introduction to Biblical Criticisms and Their Application* (Louisville: Westminister/John Knox Press, 1993), 135–49.

[20] Gitay, 'Rhetorical Criticism', 146.

[21] Culpepper, *Anatomy of the Fourth Gospel.*

reading strategy on the Fourth Gospel that had not till then been done. The work was well received and led to more studies along the same lines.[22]

Culpepper's model, based on those of modern literary critics, he crystallized in the diagram shown in Figure 12.3.[23]

In this way of reading John the 'real author' and 'real reader' are removed from the inner workings of the story. The Gospel as a whole is, of course, the creation of a real author but his identity and character cannot be directly associated with anything found within the dramatic narrative itself. Even the 'implied author' and 'implied reader' sit at the outer points of the design of the Gospel story. Thus also 'real time' is not intrinsic to the story. 'Narrative time' envelopes the story, and works into the structure via the narrator.

The narrator, created by the real author, is vital to the story. It is the narrator who sheds light on events and settings, who portrays characters and thickens plot, and generates action-dialogue. In John the narrator has a third-person point of view for the most part, and is omniscient. He knows the divine origin of Jesus, what is in the mind of Jesus, and the extent of Jesus' knowledge of the characters in the story. The narrator also knows what the characters think, especially the group-character of the disciples. This 'whispering wizard', the narrator, coaches the implied reader in grasping the significance of the situation. Narrative comments facilitate the reader's insight and point of view. The narrator will even translate terms, which is another way of inserting implicit commentary, and will explain direct quotation for the implied reader. These narrative insertions come up again and again throughout the plot of the story. The following is a sampling.[24]

6.6	This he said to test him, for he himself knew what he would do.
3.25	He himself knew what was in everyone.
1.42	'You are to be called Cephas' (which is translated Peter).
7.37–39	'Let anyone who is thirsty come to me, and let the one who believes in me drink.' Now he said this about the Spirit . . .
9.22	[The blind man's] parents said this because they were afraid of the Jews.

[22] Culpepper's student Paul D.Duke, for example, wrote a striking monograph on *Irony in the Fourth Gospel* (Atlanta: John Knox Press, 1985).

[23] Culpepper, *Anatomy*, 6.

[24] See the much larger selection in Culpepper, *Anatomy*, 22–5. Used by permission of Augsburg Fortress.

Figure 12.2

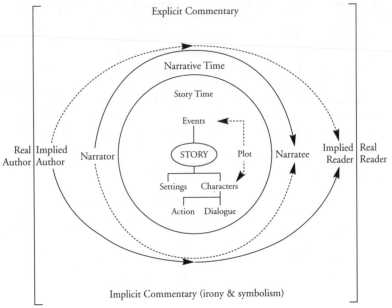

12.42   Many, even of the authorities, believed in him. But because of the Pharisees they did not confess it, for fear that they would be put out of the synagogue.

20.9   [Peter and the other disciple] did not understand the scripture, that he must rise from the dead.

Characters also occupy the narrative of the Fourth Gospel. Each of them is painted into the literary canvas in a way that generates response from the implied reader. Nicodemus is a 'night-time' inquirer, representing a group of Jewish leaders sympathetic to Jesus but not willing to leave their positions in Judaism to join the Christ-community. Nicodemus and his kind do not see. By contrast, the blind man who obeys Jesus' word sees clearly and can instruct the ones who say they see (9.24–34). Various other characters stand in contrast to each other. Not least among them are Peter and the other disciple whom Jesus loved.

The unnamed disciple is close to Jesus and mediates the mind of Jesus to Peter (13.24–26). He has influence with the high priest and negotiates Peter's entry into the courtyard (18.15–16). He outruns Peter and reaches the empty tomb first (20.4). These are characters enmeshed in the plot structure, not merely biographies of historical figures.

Implicit commentary abounds in John, present largely in the multi-faceted symbols. Water symbolism in particular runs throughout the Gospel. Not all the water is life-giving. The water in the Jewish water pots requires the word of Jesus to become life-giving at the wedding (2.7–8). The well of Jacob provides only temporary, physical sustenance (4.12–15). The five-porch pool of Bethesda lacks the power to give life to the paralysed man (5.2–7). Over against this kind of water is the life-giving water that Jesus gives, evidenced dramatically in the sign of Jesus weeping at the tomb of Lazarus. The tears of Jesus are the only sign of water in the whole scene (11.35). Life comes out of death in that scene, and even more so when the blood and water pour from Jesus' side at his death (19.34).

Culpepper's analysis of literary design in John, while relevant and instructive, still leaves his reader wondering: Is that all there is? What is the eye-opener in the story? Where is the engagement with the drama of the story with a view to transformation? Literary analysis of biblical texts, whether of Hebrew poetry or Johannine narrative structure, must surely include the theological and the transformational. The biblical narrative, as John Court says of Luke 24, carries 'a potential to become interactive, to engage the reader with dramatic intensity, and to lift a story from the past into an inspiration for the present and the future'.[25]

Literary analysis extends beyond the explicitly narrative texts. Prophet literature of the Old Testament, for example, has poetic/oracular interspersed with narrative elements. The letters of Paul are largely argument, but they have narrative elements and poetic elements.

Norman Petersen, for example, reads the letter to Philemon through 'the sociology of Paul's narrative world'.[26] He argues that in 'some sense letters "have" stories and ... these stories provide us with the narrative worlds we will explore'.[27] The story of Onesimus in the letter to Philemon begs reconstructing, according to Petersen, out of the fund of text extant in the short letter to Philemon. The fund on the surface is a short letter containing an argument, but that fund is underwritten with narrative elements including point of view, characterization, plot, irony, and symbolism.

---

[25] John M. Court, *Reading the New Testament* (London: Routledge, 1997), 39.
[26] Norman R. Petersen, *Rediscovering Paul: Philemon and the Sociology of Paul's Narrative World* (Philadelphia: Fortress Press, 1985).
[27] Petersen, *Rediscovering*, 2.

Breaking the Boundaries

Perhaps the bounds of the modern paradigm are already broken by literary-narrative analysis discussed above. In that model, 'real author' and 'real reader', so important to the historical critical method, are little more than parentheses beside the literary form of the text. But they are still in view nonetheless. The bounds are broken when the focus falls exclusively on text-and-reader – any reader – and the production of meaning that issues from the reading activity itself.

Intertextuality

Brueggemann uses a highly evocative phrase to describe the postmodern reading of Scripture. He calls it 'the practice of texts'.[28] By that phrase he does not mean the author's practice at writing the texts, but the reader's practice at reading them. Texts are rich in texture, not plain and unilateral. Nor is their texture completely original, even though the composition may be quite different from any other. Galatians is different from Romans, despite the similarity of terms and subject matter. Samuel–Kings is different from Chronicles, even though many of the stories in both bodies are parallel. The difference acknowledged, none of the texts appears out of nowhere. Every text has *intertexture*. And a growing number of biblical scholars have exposed the phenomenon in their reading of the texts, and have produced some fascinating results.

To illustrate the notion of intertextuality from our own lives I refer again to Lonergan. Recall his two-way knowing circuit. The human being does not merely start fresh every day in *experiencing, understanding, judging* and *deciding* about the world. That is the upward movement, to be sure. But the downward movement has already happened. Insights are already gained. They are the stuff we take with us as we enter every new day of *experiencing, understanding, judging* and *deciding*. Those insights gained come from a huge variety of encounters with reality.

When we build a house in a particular part of the world insights are present to help us decide on the style of the building. How much more when we create a poem or write a novel! All of the texts residing in our consciousness are textured into the new text. The text is new and different from any other, yet it has within it texts already received.

---

[28] Brueggemann, *Negotiation*, 62.

When the new text emerges the old texts are written into the new in a way befitting the new. It may be even better to say the old texts under-write the new. They live between the lines, as it were.

The other day I was asked to give two seminars on 'prejudice'. The host asked for a title for each of them. I called the first, 'Prejudice Disclosed: Everybody Has Some?' After dashing the title off to my host I thought more about it. Suddenly I realized I had drawn a phrase from a song I heard long ago, a blues song I had not heard for a long time. Neil Diamond sang it and I enjoyed listening to it. The song title, I believe, was, 'Songs Sung Blue'. From listening to that song I picked up the phrase, 'Everybody has some'. Maybe Neil Diamond sang, 'one', not 'some'. But my text in consciousness reads 'some'. Now, many years later, the words spring to life again in a different context, yet not unrelated to the blues, to form a new text structure. That is part of intertextuality. Of course, there can be conscious dialogue between a text remembered and the new text coming into being. Both constitute intertextuality. And the biblical texts abound with it, which, when it is discovered, enriches the reader's experience of the text.

But there is more to intertextuality. The reader intersects with the text by bringing other texts to the reading operation. This intersection of text before the eyes and texts behind the eyes, in the reader's mind, is dynamic intertextuality. It is dynamic in that texts read once are not finished. Rereading brings to light a new intersection, because with each new round of reading other texts come to the fore out of the fund of texts in mind already.

Clearly, 'text' implies more than the printed words on paper, or the digital words on screen. Bradley Chance and Milton Horne have labelled three kinds of text that operate in intertextual reading.[29] The first is the *literary text*. Written texts refer to other texts to validate the claim of the new text. Or the new text may simply echo the other text. Numerous examples from modern texts illustrate the point. Martin Luther King Jr echoed Lincoln's address in the opening line of his speech: 'Five score years ago ...' Why not say simply one hundred years ago? Lincoln's phrasing was, 'Four score and seven years ago ...' Lincoln's speech lies between the lines in King's speech. Those who hear the intertextuality in King's text feel the power of the new text, under-written as it is by the famous address of Lincoln.

---

[29] J. Bradley Chance and Milton P. Horne, *Rereading the Bible: An Introduction to the Biblical Story* (Upper Saddle River, N.J.: Prentice Hall, 2000), 12–23.

Pierre Elliott Trudeau, former Prime Minister of Canada, in his acceptance speech following the last election of his long political career, thanked the people for their support over many years, and then spoke of promises he had made during the campaign. Into that part of his address he incorporated a line from Robert Frost's poem, without any reference to Frost: 'I have promises to keep, and miles to go before I sleep.' Anyone who appreciated that great Frost poem, and then heard it textured into Trudeau's speech that night, were led thereby to feel akin with Trudeau. This way of interweaving one text into another, where there is verbal correspondence, is called 'micro-level intertextuality'.[30]

Richard B. Hays traversed the letters of Paul looking for micro-level intertextuality, and published his findings in *Echoes of Scripture in the Letters of Paul*. Hays' principal concern was with Paul's way of re-texturing the texts of the Old Covenant Scriptures into the new texts of his letters. For Hays this exercise was one way of resolving the 'puzzle of Pauline hermeneutics'.[31] Often Paul cites the text he incorporates (e.g. Rom 8.36; 10.15; 1 Cor. 1.31; 2 Cor. 8.15), sometimes he *alludes* to a text (1 Cor. 5:1, 7), and sometimes *echoes* a text (1 Cor. 5.5[32]). This re-texturing of an old text is an act of interpretation.

> As we move farther away from overt citation, the source recedes into the discursive distance, the intertextual relations become less determinate, and the demand placed on the reader's listening powers grows greater. As we near the vanishing point of the echo, it inevitably becomes difficult to decide whether we are really hearing an echo at all, or whether we are only conjuring things out of the murmurings of our own imaginations.[33]

Macro-intertextuality occurs when an author alludes to an event, institution, or important figure from the shared literary tradition. This level of intertextuality is also called typology.[34] In this case the words of the old text do not necessarily correspond to the words in the new text, but the larger schema underwrites the new text. Adam is, of course, in

---

[30] Chance and Horne, *Rereading*, 13.

[31] Richard B. Hays, *Echoes of Scripture in the Letters of Paul* (New Haven: Yale University Press, 1989), 1ff.

[32] See my 'Atonement Texture in 1 Corinthians 5:5', *JSNT* 71 (1998), 29–50.

[33] Hays, *Echoes*, 23.

[34] See Leonhard Goppelt, *Typos: The Typological Interpretation of the Old Testament in the New*, trans. Donald H. Madvig (Grand Rapids: Eerdmans, 1982); also my *The Figure of Jesus in the Typological Thought of Paul* (Dissertation, Hamilton: McMaster University, 1985).

Genesis, but he is also in the Jewish tradition. Adam is written into the text of 1 Corinthians 15 and Romans 5 beyond the wording of the original account of the figure. Adam figures into the new texts of 1 Corinthians and Romans as representative head of the human race caught in the grip of sin and of death. By contrast, Abraham is a positive type of the Gentiles who come to faith in Christ apart from works of Torah (Rom. 4.1ff.; Gal. 3.6ff.).

But the phenomenon of intertextuality goes well beyond the retexturing of an older literary text in a newer one. There is also the *social text*, or the culture text. Chance and Horne see the social text as 'that web of interrelated texts that one may identify minimally as language, ideology, theology, and history'.[35] Each of these deserves brief description for use in reading the biblical texts.

Language is a social phenomenon in that it is a learned pattern of communication. In Chapter 5 I discussed language as a capacity of the human mind. Here it means the particular pattern of sounds and signs that communicate. A language pattern carries in it the social fund of ideas and practices. For example, some cultures believe in the evil eye. How that social construct enters language is something that has to be discerned sensitively. How much of the evil eye lies within the fabric of the text of Matthew 6.22–3 is open for discussion. In the NRSV it reads: *The eye is the lamp of the body. So, if your eye is healthy, your whole body will be full of light; but if your eye is unhealthy, your whole body will be full of darkness.* But in the KJV it reads quite differently: *The light of the body is the eye: if therefore thine eye be single, thy whole body shall be full of light. But if thine eye be evil, thy whole body shall be full of darkness.* What is interesting is that the KJV of 1611 is less queasy about calling a person's eye 'evil' than the NRSV of 1989, where the word is rendered 'unhealthy'. The Greek word is *poneros*, which means 'bad', 'wicked', 'sinful', 'evil'. It is used of the devil: 'the evil one'. The point is that language carries the social nuance in its pattern and the nuance is not necessarily our own. The NRSV mutes the harshness of the notion of 'the evil eye' with the word 'unhealthy'. 'Unhealthy' works well for our culture, based as it is on the Enlightenment.

Language is also ritualistic. The form and function of the ritual dictates the pattern of the language. Listen to a wedding ceremony and you will hear a pattern quite different from the language of a sportscaster giving the latest scores. Besides the pattern of words as text, there

---

[35] Chance and Horne, *Rereading*, 21.

is also body text, or body language as it is sometimes called. I have already alluded to the meaning of a smile (Chapter 4). Similarly a wink means something in some societies, our own included. The shrugging of the shoulders, the frown, all of these are social language. When a narrator in a novel notes, 'the man shrugged and walked away', what is the nuance? Was the man approving? Disapproving? Angry? Indifferent? It is not easy to read social text, even in our own society. How much more so with a text many centuries removed from ours.

Ideology is a shared set of values and world-views. Ours in Europe and North America is very much the product of the Enlightenment. We value individual rights and freedoms, free enterprise, technology, democracy, science, education. Our texts will have our ideology textured into them invariably, because we are social beings. Even if we react to some of the ideology, the reaction will be in response to the ideology. I will say more on ideology later. For now the point is that the ideological grid that works for us in our social life figures into our text. So also the biblical texts.

Theology, or religion, is also part of the social text. People ask big questions, life and death questions, and the answers come in the form of theology. By that I mean people posit a transcendent power respon-sible for the unfolding of the universe. The way we posit and argue and conclude in religious exchange will differ, to be sure. But the religious dimension is ever present in one form or another, and enters the written text. Believers might assume that their views of God are identical with the biblical views. But when we press the issue we wonder how that could be. For example, how would we describe God's way of speaking to individuals? Would we say that the heavens opened and a voice was heard from heaven? We have our own imagination of the divine, and we express it in keeping with our social network. The Bible does the same. Reading the biblical texts demands a lively encounter with the theological-social text within the new text.

History is yet another social text. People like to tell their stories. Someone may tell the story of a whole era and a whole nation. The story is important for welding a people together. It is retold and rewritten, and as such becomes part of the fabric of the social text, which in turn finds its way variously into the new text. For example, when Paul informs the Corinthians, *Do you not know that you are God's temple and that God's Spirit dwells in you? If anyone destroys God's temple, God will destroy that person. For God's temple is holy, and you are that temple,* he has in mind the long and tortured story of the Temple in

Jerusalem. When modern believers read the same text they are scarcely thinking of the history of the Temple. The temple story is not our story, but it was Paul's story. It is textured into the Corinthians text.

Finally, the *interpretive text* also enters the fabric of the text being read. This is the text of the conscious self of the reader, full of inherited values and systems of thought. As soon as the reader begins to engage the text of Scripture the self-text intersects with the written text to produce meaning. Reading is participation with the text, with no less dynamism than that which produced the text in the first place. The interested reader has aspirations, struggles, insights, traditions, all of which are present in the reading operation. The biblical writers themselves were readers that produced a new text with meaning beyond the original meaning. The prophets of the Old Testament read the story of Israel and produced a new text out of their intersection with the various texts they read. The Gospel writers intersected with the stories of Jesus and produced their texts accordingly. Paul read the story of the emerging Church together with the story of Israel and produced new texts for his new communities of faith in Christ. And we do the same when we read the Prophets, Gospels and Paul. We participate in the texts to produce a new text in life and thought and perhaps also in a literary text.

Intertextuality, considered in this comprehensive way, marks a further move away from the supremacy of the author. Reading the social text within the text is not equal to the search for the world of the real author. The social text is the one woven into the fabric of the literary text. The last layer, the interpretive text, is equally interwoven into the reading of the text, and must, therefore, be taken into account in any consideration of intertextuality. This latter leads directly into the next section.

Reader-response

As the term implies, reader-response criticism places the interpretive accent on the process of reading a text. What matters most in reader-response is the present reader, alive and active in the production of meaning in relation to a text, not the absent author. In the new reading-scenario the text affects the reader in ways quite different from the affective force in another time and place.

Reader-response analysis is not of one piece. Radical critics occupy one side of the spectrum and more moderate ones the other side.

Stanley Fish represents the more radical side. He argues that a text is never independent of interpretation, but always subject to the reader's interaction with it. The text does not contain meaning for the reader, but does something to the reader in the process of reading. Text-being-read is a speech-act. The text affects the reader's imagination to produce meaning in the reader's mind. Fish qualifies his argument with the idea of a reading community.

On this point, however, I find Fish not altogether clear. Presumably the community from which the reading takes place sets the limits to reader-response. Each reading community is a temporal entity, able to respond at the level of the community consciousness. An extended quotation may help clarify Fish's reader-response criticism.

> The reader's response is not *to* the meaning; it is the meaning, or at least the medium in which what I wanted to call the meaning comes into being, and therefore to ignore or discount it is, or so I claimed, to risk missing a great deal of what is going on. ...[36] In my model the reader was freed from the tyranny of the text and given the central role in the production of meaning. ...[37] Language does not have a shape independent of context, but since language is only encountered in contexts and never in the abstract, it always has shape, although it is not always the same one. ...[38] I want to argue that there always is a text ... but that what is in it can change, and therefore at no level is it independent of and prior to interpretation. ... [39] How is it that a text so demonstrably unstable can be stabilized to such a degree that a large number of people know immediately what it means?[40] ... A sentence is never not in a context. We are never not in a situation. ... A set of interpretive assumptions is always in force. A sentence that seems to need no interpretation is already the product of one.[41]

The 'large number of people' who knows immediately what a text means represents the community consciousness. Accordingly, different reading communities will interpret the same text differently and legitimately. The issue concerns the locus of meaning. Fish locates it not in unstable texts but in the responsive act of reading the texts.

Fish did not apply his reading theory directly to biblical literature. Robert Fowler did. He interpreted the Gospel of Mark along reader-

---

[36] Fish, *Is There a Text in This Class?*, 3.

[37] Fish, *Is There a Text?*, 7.

[38] Fish, *Is There a Text?*, 268.

[39] Fish, *Is There a Text?*, 272.

[40] Fish, *Is There a Text?*, 275.

[41] Fish, *Is There a Text?*, 284.

response lines. Characteristic of reader-response generally, Fowler did not regard Mark as containing information, or even referring to some stable history outside itself. The text of the Gospel is itself the entity open to ever-new encounter. 'No longer can the language of the Gospel be regarded as primarily referential or informative; it has become rhetorical, affective, and powerful.'[42]

Yet the reader should be informed; competent in matters related to a close reading of the texture of the text. Fowler's reading of Mark depends not on the author's ability to produce the text, but on Fowler's ability to produce meaning from a reading of the text of Mark. 'A text must be self-authenticating, able to entangle the reader in its own network.'[43]

Again, the reading of Mark must affect the reader. The language acts upon the reader. Imagination is triggered, and the dance begins. Fowler imagines a responsive reading of Mark as a creative dance.

> The capability acquired by dancing Mark's dance is a response-ability, in two senses. First, indirection gives us a multitude of opportunities to respond to incongruous and uncertain stimuli. ... Second, indirection frequently places on the shoulders of the reader the heavy burden to take up the challenge of indirection and deal with it as best she can.[44]

Reader-response critics value their work as a liberating enterprise. The approach frees the biblical text from the control of disciplines such as history, sociology, and anthropology. 'This method allows readers to interact with the text in light of their own context, linguistic and literary competence, and need, as well as in light of the potentialities of the text.'[45]

An example of a reader-response interpretation may help clarify the approach. The text is Galatians 2.11–14, which reads as follows:

> *But when Cephas came to Antioch, I opposed him to his face, because he stood self-condemned; for until certain people came from James, he used to eat with the Gentiles. But after they came, he drew back and kept himself separate for fear of the circumcision faction. And the other Jews joined him in this hypocrisy, so that even Barnabas was led astray by their hypocrisy. But when I saw that they were not acting consistently with the truth of the gospel,*

---

[42] R. M. Fowler, *Let the Reader Understand: Reader-Response Criticism and the Gospel of Mark* (Minneapolis: Fortress Press, 1991), 3.

[43] Fowler, *Reader*, 62.

[44] Fowler, *Reader*, 226.

[45] Haynes and McKenzie, *To Each*, 207.

I said to Cephas before them all, 'If you, though a Jew, live like a Gentile and not like a Jew, how can you compel the Gentiles to live like Jews?'

I see characters and places in this text. I have their names, of course, and I could look around the immediate context of this pericopé (unit of text) to find out more about them, but I scarcely need to do so. I already have the characterization of the three named figures, one (Cephas) is explicit, and that of the other two (James and Barnabas) is implicit. And then there is the character of the first-person narrator. What does this text do to my imagination? I have an image of these characters inter-acting with each other at a place called Antioch. And I sense party politics involved. Contention arose between the narrator and Cephas. This character, Cephas, has been eating with the group called Gentiles, and then draws back when some people come from the other character, James. Accordingly, James must be (1) an authority figure feared by Cephas, and (2) he must not favour eating with Gentiles, and (3) his party is labelled 'circumcision'. The narrator is not afraid of this authority figure, James. Apparently the narrator thought Barnabas would stand with him, but 'even Barnabas' sided with Cephas. I imagine the narrator continues to eat with Gentiles and opposes Cephas for withdrawing. Do I side with this character, Cephas? No. Or Barnabas? No again. The story moves me to side with the narrator. I know how I would feel if someone refused to eat with me. I am left wondering how James could have generated such fear in these two characters.

Do I feel a holy anger here? Indeed I do. I feel it because the narrator has drawn me into the texture of the text. Something serious is happening in the scene to make the narrator oppose Cephas to his face. The scene comes to a climax with the telling question put to Cephas at the end: *How can you compel the Gentiles to live like Jews?* I leave the text wondering what is here to make Gentiles live like Jews? Does it have something to do with eating regulation? Or is Cephas' 'withdrawal' from Gentiles because they are not circumcised? Wondering itself is an act that happens in the imaginative reading of the texture of this text.

I have deliberately accented a limitation in this version of reader-response. I could reread this text with more insight into the characters of Cephas, James, Barnabas and the narrator, and more also into their situations. The insight gained is still mine, not bits of data collected from outside my conscious self. With every new acquisition of insight, and with every rereading of this pericopé, imagination expands. The text continues to affect the reader in the process of rereading.

Deconstruction: rereading

Deconstruction defies definition, by definition. Once a 'thing' is defined, or otherwise identified in language structure, it is arbitrary and artificial. Structuralists, who have sought to discover deep structure inherent in language patterns, are summarily disqualified by 'dissemination', as Derrida calls it.

> Dissemination endlessly opens up a *snag* in writing that can no longer be mended, a spot where neither meaning, however plural, nor *any form of presence* can pin/pen down [*agrapher*] the trace. Dissemination treats – doctors – that *point* where the movement of signification would regularly come to *tie down* the play of the trace, thus producing (a) history.[46]

Observe that this sentence has italics, and three kinds of brackets. These signs force the reader to pause, reconsider, reread. What is '(a) history', for example? It is, as Herbert Schneidau puts it, 'the word against the word'.[47] Structure is imposed, construed, adopted, manufactured, and that in language form. There is nothing inherent in things, nor in persons, nor in linguistic signs, that can be defined finally and completely. Language signifies the presence of the absent. That is all language is: a signifier of something not present. Derrida used the signature to illustrate the point. A signature is unique. Otherwise there would be confusion. The signature stands in for the person, but is not identical with the person. Identity is not possible in any case, since everything is in flux – or play. Human persons are not the same from one day to the next. The moment a person is characterized, identified, inscribed, at that very moment the person is not the same.

Deconstruction displaces foundations, all foundations. There is no undergirding *logos* that holds all things together. 'Deconstruction decentres that which has been constructed to be central.'[48] There is difference between opposites, of course. But the structure of the difference is construed, adopted, and authoritative. Here are some well-known opposites: light/darkness, male/female, good/evil, true/false, Mr/Mrs, professor/student. The first in the paired opposites is the privileged one. The first is dependent on the second for its 'meaning' and authority. The presence of the structured pair is arbitrary.

[46] Jacques Derrida, *Dissemination*, trans. Barbara Johnson (Chicago: University of Chicago Press, 1981), 26.

[47] Herbert N. Schneidau, 'The Word Against the Word', *Semeia* 23 (1982), 5.

[48] Adam, *Postmodern*, 28.

Preferences are arbitrary, not authoritative. They are built into the structure of social reality and mystified into absolute status. But the structures are not absolute, and because they are not they should be demystified.

Deconstruction enters biblical studies expecting structures and finding them in plentiful supply. If we ask what method the deconstructors use in rereading the biblical texts, we are asking the wrong question. Method, like identity, manifests foundation of some sort and is therefore consciously deconstructed. 'Deconstruction is congenitally suspicious of the concept of method itself.'[49] The same is true of meaning. Meaning does not exist in text. Like everything else meaning is forever in flux. Meaning is derived in play with the text. When we read the texts of Scripture, deconstructors say, we manufacture meaning. 'Meaning is what we make of texts, not an ingredient in texts.'[50]

Yet deconstructors do use method. They must do so, else how could they be understood. Here I return to Lonergan's cognitional theory. For example, when Derrida puts pen to paper he does not close his eyes and push the pen across the page at random. He writes with eyes open and mind working, and working in a way that other human beings will be able to follow. The general pattern in his writing matches mine. Otherwise I could not understand his deconstruction, nor make a judgement on his theory, nor act on my judgement about the validity of deconstruction.

Deconstruction notes also that interpreters are specialists, an elite group by virtue of education or profession. A professor of religion, or a minister in a church, is the acknowledged interpreter. Deconstruction challenges that structure. 'We are now free to, and obliged to, recognize that our Grandma may produce a sounder interpretation of a psalm than does a Reverend Professor.'[51] The problem with this illustration is that it assumes Grandmas are naïve realists, that naïve realist reading is more reliable than a critical realist reading. In this illustration also Grandmas are *structurally* not Reverend Professors. But they must at least be able to read. In that case they too will bring their interpretive text to *play* in the act of rereading. On what ground would they lay

[49] Stephen D. Moore, *Post Structuralism and the New Testament: Derrida and Foucault at the Foot of the Cross* (Minneapolis: Fortress Press, 1994), 6.
[50] Adam, *Postmodern*, 35.
[51] Adam, *Postmodern*, 35.

claim to their interpretation? What makes their rereading 'a sounder interpretation'?

Just as the text of this (Grandma) illustration is politically charged, so are the texts of Scripture. Deconstruction critics paved the way for political readings of Scripture, such as those of Robert and Mary Coote – or rather Mary and Robert Coote: *Power, Politics, and the Making of the Bible*. 'The Bible was produced by demands for legitimacy following changes in rule.'[52] These interpreters, among others, see a political agenda involved in the structure of the texts. Interpretation demands the deconstruction of the signifier, the text, to allow meaning to explode anew.

A deconstructive mode of reading can pry loose a sense of the text that would otherwise lie buried beneath the structure of traditional interpretation. I refer again to the text of 1 Timothy 2.11–15. This text has suffered for many centuries from the dominant male readings of the Church. Church authorities have muffled the liberating word for women in this text under the traditionally amplified 'submission/silent' structures. The liberating 'learn' needs room to move into the foreground, and play into the rereading of this text.

If you found this (rather long) section on deconstruction not as lucid as you would like, it goes with the territory. You should read Derrida for a real taste of a deconstructionist at work!

Political reading

In some measure, all reading, as all writing, is political. That is, both projects have an agenda beyond mere human interest in a subject. And the two agendas, that of writer and reader, need not, and often do not, correspond. That is especially so if the time and situation of writing is far removed from the time and situation of reading. Reading the Bible two thousand years after its first appearance on the world stage is a challenge to say the least. Not only does the Bible have its own political agenda textured into it, but the centuries of interpretation also have new agendas at work in the reading process.

A Marxist reading of the Bible, for example, will bring out elements that accommodate a Marxist political agenda, such as the community of goods practiced in the primitive Christ-community (Acts 2.44; 4.32). Where a text of the Bible fails to support the agenda then the text is

---

[52] Robert B. Coote and Mary P. Coote, *Power, Politics, and the Making of the Bible* (Minneapolis: Fortress Press, 1990), 162.

subject to critique, or rejection. Positive theism, for example, runs throughout the Bible, but is thoroughly suspect in the Marxist world-view. One might ask, then, how could a Marxist reading of the biblical texts understand them sympathetically? A Christian reader, however, may not find certain texts easy to understand, but the attitude towards them will be quite different. A Christian is a committed theist, and will continue the search with patience, not with the suspicion of a critical a-theist.

Deconstruction tackles the political elements both in the texts of Scripture and in the interpretations of those texts. A number of studies have appeared in the wake of post-modern, deconstructive reading of the texts that seek to dismantle the political structures that tend to dominate and oppress one group to the advantage of the other. I will point to two reading strategies to illustrate how deconstructive, political reading functions.

The first is the work of Neil Elliott in his masterful study of the Pauline corpus, *Liberating Paul: The Justice of God and the Politics of the Apostle* (1994). Elliott argues convincingly that 'Paul has been made an agent of oppression in our age'.[53] He highlights oppressive patterns of thought, institutionalized in the modern world, and anchored in the interpreted Paul: anti-Semitism in Nazi Germany, slavery of African Americans, oppression of women, tyrannizing of gays and lesbians, and the incestuous abuse of children, state sanctioned waging of war (to mention some).

The *ideological tyranny* in all of these situations has found support in the legacy of Paul. The text of Ephesians 5.22—6.9 has been used to relegate women into a subservient position, to force children into inces-tuous relationships, to endorse the slavery of African Americans in the southern United States. Similar appeal has been made to the Pastoral Epistles (e.g. 1 Tim. 2.8–15; 5.3–8). Likewise in waging war, appeal is made to Romans 13.1–7. In so many cases of oppression and victim-ization '[t]he canonical Paul's voice has been close, persistent, enduring'.[54] In all of the appeals the voice of the historical Paul has been silenced, says Elliott. The Apostle has become enslaved to the powers of his interpreters down to the present time. 'Paul himself has been made the prisoner of the power of Death ... Paul is in chains today, a slave

[53] Neil Elliott, *Liberating Paul: The Justice of God and the Politics of the Apostle* (Maryknoll: Orbis Books, 1994), 9.
[54] Elliott, *Liberating Paul*, 17.

of Death.'[55] Two questions arise: (1) How did Paul become 'an instrument in the legitimation of oppression'? (2) How can he be released from his chains?

Elliott cites three dynamics at work in the enslavement of Paul to the powers of his interpreters. First, many of the Pauline texts that have served to legitimate injustice are in pseudonymous letters (not written by the historical Paul). These writings from a later time call in Paul, as though he were still alive and writing, to legitimate accommodation to Roman society, especially in domestic and ecclesiastical settings. Second, Paul was seen, not as a political revolutionary in the way of Jesus of Palestinian society, but as a conservative constructor of house churches in urban environments. 'On this view, Paul's letters serve to protect privilege today ... [since] he found no reason to challenge the conventions of privilege from which he and his network of upper-class household-citizens so clearly benefited.'[56] And third, the tradition of the centuries has mystified Paul's theology as a-political, a-typical and in competition with other religions, especially Judaism. These concerns are, for the most part, imposed on Paul, so Elliott believes.

Elliott's goal in his work, he says, is to demystify Paul, to hear his voice again, 'a voice stifled and obscured through long centuries of interpretation'.[57] One wonders, though, who is reading politically. Are Paul's 'captors' the only ones who have put him in a political straight-jacket? Or are Paul's 'liberators', such as Elliott, just as political in their reading of his letters?

For a more specific political reading of Scripture texts, I turn to *feminist interpretations*, in particular that of Elisabeth Schüssler Fiorenza in her *Rhetoric and Ethic: The Politics of Biblical Studies* (1999). I intend here merely to identify some of the concerns feminist readers of Scripture voice, and something of their reading strategy.

Feminist interpretations do not all follow the same reading strategy. Basically, however, 'feminist criticism concentrates on the political, social, and economic rights of women'.[58] First and foremost in feminist reading of Scripture – and classical Western texts generally – the texts carry ideological gender. They cannot be otherwise. Nor is it that women's texts are gendered and men's texts neutral. All texts are

---

[55] Elliott, *Liberating Paul*, 20–1.
[56] Elliott, *Liberating Paul*, 22.
[57] Elliott, *Liberating Paul*, 24.
[58] Danna Nolan Fewell, 'Reading the Bible Ideologically: Feminist Criticism', in McKenzie and Haynes, *To Each*, 238.

gendered ideologically. Gender is not an inherent quality that differentiates one half of humankind from the other half. Gender is socially conditioned and therefore ideological. As Schüssler Fiorenza points out,' "woman" is not a unitary category but is ambiguous and ideologically typed. The category "woman-wo/men," like those of gender, race, or class is rhetorically-politically produced in the interest of relations of domination and subordination.'[59] Thus feminist interpretation goes beyond the ideology of gender to embrace all categories of domination. Feminism thus is 'a theory and practice of justice that seeks not just to understand but to change relations of marginalization and domination'.[60]

Biblical studies especially have been the domain of masculine-gendered scholarship, whose interpretations have by definition marginalized women. Schüssler Fiorenza calls on the discipline of biblical studies 'to return to its scholarly roots and to remember that it began as biblical criticism'.[61] By 'criticism' Schüssler Fiorenza means the weighing and judging of texts and their contexts. With such a reading strategy at work biblical texts are viewed with *suspicion*, as well they should. The biblical texts were written by men in a highly patriarchal system, and interpreted by an elite male readership for generations to the present time. Their ideology needs to be exposed, their structures deconstructed, and the interpretation reconstituted in liberating ways. The silenced women, and other marginalized non-persons in the public forum, are discovering their voice, and are calling for equal right to speech and life in society and church. 'Wo/men are not beasts of burden, sex objects, temptresses or "babies", but wo/men and other nonpersons – to use and expression of Gustavo Gutiérrez – who throughout the centuries were, and still are, marginalized and silenced in academy and church, are theological subjects and agents.'[62]

Part of Schüssler Fiorenza's deconstruction of malestream (cf. mainstream) interpretation aims at language, the language of the Bible itself and also the language of contemporary discourse. Marginalizing political ideology lives in language, is perpetuated in language, and through language can become demonic. No wonder she deconstructs language forms that tend towards oppressive attitudes. Consequently

---

[59] Elisabeth Schüssler Fiorenza, *Rhetoric and Ethic: The Politics of Biblical Studies* (Minneapolis: Fortress Press, 1999), 4.

[60] Schüssler Fiorenza, *Rhetoric*, 7.

[61] Schüssler Fiorenza, *Rhetoric*, 9.

[62] Schüssler Fiorenza, *Rhetoric*, 7.

she breaks 'second-place' words to reconstitute their meaning. Wo/men in Schüssler Fiorenza's discourse means people. S/he includes he, and fe/male includes male. As noted above, the structured way of thinking of the pairs is male and female, with male occupying the privileged position. Schüssler Fiorenza likewise rewrites God as G*d to challenge the andocentric connotation implicit in the traditional spelling of that English word. 'Such a form of writing . . . seeks to contravene the effects of androcentric "generic" language.'[63]

At heart the political feminist approach in biblical studies is *emancipatory*. Feminist interpreters, like all liberationist theologians, start from where they are, from the context in which they feel marginalized. Since all knowledge is perspectival and contextual, biblical and theological reading is avowedly the same. The starting point is not some abstract theory, but the praxis of experience. Rereading from the current context will of necessity challenge the stability of the traditional texts. Stable readings of Genesis 1 to 3 that cast women (as opposed to men) in a secondary and/or negative role will be exploded in a feminist reading strategy. The fixed status of silenced women in the texts of 1 Timothy 2.11–15 and 1 Corinthians 14.34–36 will burst open in the practice of feminist reading. Sacred texts whose source is said to be in a liberating, creating, loving God will not bind and restrict and marginalize. They will tend to liberate, heal and equalize the human family.

Conclusion

To conclude this chapter, the parade of reading strategies practiced today leaves us somewhat breathless in the effort to capture a strategy for ourselves. Maybe we should not try. The call of post-modern thinking is to plunge into the stream of reading strategies and read, or rather *reread*. Each of us will probably find that the strategies are not watertight compartments. We will find ourselves at some point calling upon the social sciences to help us out, at another literary criticism, at another intertexture, at another reader-response, and at another a political reading of some sort. The reading strategy has to be brokered, or negotiated, in terms of the text under consideration. Negotiated reading, as I have chosen to call it, will be the topic of the next chapter.

Beyond the strategies, however, is the heartbeat of the living thinking reader of the texts. Who the readers are will make a difference

---

[63] Schüssler Fiorenza, *Rhetoric*, 6.

in how they interpret what they read. Believers will be more likely to lay hold of the truth claims of the biblical texts than non-believers. Both can read the texts, to be sure, but the faithful seekers after divine truth will be more likely to find it in the texts that lay claim to it.

On Course . . .

Objective

To know how to negotiate a reading strategy for the interpretation of biblical texts.

Lead Questions

1. *What is the hyphenated term Vernon Robbins gives to his interpretive strategy? How do you understand to two parts of the term?*

2. *Name and describe the five 'textures' Robbins proposes for a socio-rhetorical interpretation of texts.*

3. *What model does Stephen Fowl propose for 'engaging Scripture'?*

4. *What basis does Fowl present in support of his model for interpretation?*

5. *What does Fowl mean when he says that interpretation of Scripture 'shapes and is shaped by' the faith community?*

6. *How does Lonergan's general method figure into a negotiated reading of biblical texts?*

7. *What are five questions that help in negotiating a reading of a text such as I Corinthians 5.1–13?*

8. *How authentic is the 'theological significance' section in the interpretation of I Corinthians 5? How far did it measure up to the claim of the text and the concern of the faith community?*

9. *Select a pericopé from the Old Testament or New Testament and attempt a negotiated interpretation.*

13

Negotiated Reading

Authenticity is the heart of the matter.
(Ben F. Meyer)

The rich harvest of reading strategies, from the historical critical paradigm through the multiple models of the last thirty years, puts us in the happy situation of having many alternatives from which to choose. The harvest is plentiful, to be sure, but the appropriation requires a degree of labour. Decisions have to be reached, and decisions take time and effort. They come from a clear understanding of the matter at hand and from sound judgement between alternatives. Understanding and judgement do not come as a matter of course. But come they must, because we do have alternative reading strategies before us now. Which one is more appropriate than the other? Do all of them apply equally to every biblical text? Is there a better way yet for reading the ancient Scriptures from this distance?

In response to this kind of inquiry, some biblical interpreters have combined several approaches from the modern and post-modern repertoire. Others have found all of the methods lacking the theological thrust characteristic of the texts themselves. I have singled out two representatives from both schools of thought to help point the way to what I am calling 'negotiated reading'. Vernon K. Robbins represents the first, combining the best of the modern and post-modern, and Stephen E. Fowl the second, a theological interpretation. For the negotiated reading that I propose in the end I call again upon the magisterial work of Bernard Lonergan, described in Chapters 2 and 3 above. I will argue that Lonergan's general method facilitates the navigation and negotiation between the alternative reading strategies. Successful appropriation of one or another of them will depend on how well attuned we are to the interpretive pattern within us, the pattern already there before the reading models appeared.

But first we need an overview and brief evaluation of the work of the two representatives, in hope that the exercise will point the way toward a negotiated reading of the biblical texts.

Vernon K. Robbins

In 1984 Vernon K. Robbins published his interpretation of the Gospel of Mark under the title, *Jesus the Teacher: A Socio-Rhetorical Interpretation of Mark*.[1] That work launched the socio-rhetorical approach to reading biblical literature. Since then Robbins has published helpful guides to the socio-rhetorical reading of the biblical texts.[2]

As the name implies, socio-rhetorical interpretation captures both the social-science approach and the literary/rhetorical approach. To make his reading strategy even more comprehensive Robbins adds other dimensions, including theological, historical, and deconstruction criticisms. By bringing together all of these features Robbins lays claim to 'an integrated approach to interpretation'.[3] The jury has still not reached a verdict on the viability of the 'integrated approach'. Do we use all possible approaches for every kind of text every time we read for understanding and transformation? I will argue below that a particular text will elicit the approach, or approaches, proper to its form and texture.

Robbins is fond of this word, *texture*, and rightly so. 'Socio-rhetorical criticism approaches the text as though it were a thickly textured tapestry. . . . Like an intricately woven tapestry, a text contains complex patterns and images.'[4] The job of the interpreter is to highlight the textures, to figure out their design and significance, to state the findings, and so to reach an interpretation of the text. Robbins cites five complex textures that one should expect to find in biblical texts. No more than a brief outline of each of them can be attempted here.

Inner texture gets inside the text to discover the literary design that catches the physical eye and the imagination. Repeated words and their progression in a pericopé call for attention and analysis. Inside the marked boundary of a text – opening and closing forms of address – the words are presented in story or argument or other 'speech' to create an effect in the mind and heart of the reader. Analysis of inner texture plots the course of the various terms of reference, looks for the sensory-

---

1 Vernon K. Robbins, *Jesus the Teacher: A Socio-Rhetorical Interpretation of Mark* (Philadelphia: Fortress Press, 1984).

2 Robbins, *Exploring the Texture of Texts: A Guide to Socio-Rhetorical Interpretation* (Valley Forge: Trinity Press International, 1996); idem., *The Tapestry of Early Christian Discourse: Rhetoric, Society and Ideology* (London: Routledge, 1996).

3 Robbins, *Exploring*, 2.

4 Robbins, *Exploring*, 2.

aesthetic texture, and seeks to discover premise, thesis, and conclusion. The point is that the text itself displays its texture for the attentive eye. The reader merely captures the impression the text makes on the mind by virtue its inner texture.

Intertexture, as noted in the previous chapter, deals with material incorporated from outside the text into the texture of the text under review. Robbins sees a variety of phenomena entering the text from different sources. *Oral-scribal* intertexture notices language forms from other texts and from people's everyday use of language coming into the text under investigation. *Social* intertexture also appears, from clothing to political arrangements. Likewise also *cultural* and *historical* intertexture appears in the literary weave of the text. 1 Corinthians 15.3–5 is an instance of cultural intertexture in so far as the text cites a Christ-faith tradition, not a written source, which is then textured into the weave of the argument that follows in the chapter. Robbins does not take into account the interpretive text, noted in Chapter 12, the complex text of the reader's life, which is no less involved in the exploration of the texture of texts.[5]

Social and cultural texture, to be distinguished from social and cultural intertexture, is that quality of a text that embodies a challenge to the existing social and cultural order. The text as text puts a question to the reader, according to Robbins: 'What kind of a social and cultural person would anyone be who lives in the "world" of a particular text?'[6] Specific and common social and cultural topics can be expected in the texture of biblical texts. To understand the topics one needs to know something of sociological and anthropological theory. 'Specific topics' calls the reader to ponder particular ways of responding to world-views in a given text. One text, or document, might respond in a different way from another text. It is up to the reader to discover the specific response. Common topics include honour–shame, patron–client contract, challenge–response, exchange systems, peasants, labourers, artisans, limited goods/abundant goods, purity codes, etc.

Ideological texture takes account of the differences in opinions and beliefs between groups of people. The differences exist in the social location of the biblical texts and in the social location of the readers of the biblical texts. '[I]deological texture concerns the biases, opinions,

---

[5] It could be argued, presumably, that Robbins' ideological texture covers the interpretive text. But there is more to the interpretive text, the self-text, than 'ideology'.

[6] Robbins, *Exploring*, 71.

preferences, and stereotypes of a particular writer and a particular reader.[7] For example, the texture of the Gospel of John represents a different ideology from the texture of Luke. Of John the Baptist Luke has no hesitation in saying, *among those that are born of women there is not a greater prophet than John the Baptist* (7.28). Scarcely would this opinion come through in the Fourth Gospel. The emphasis in that Gospel is more on what the Baptist is NOT: He is not the light (1.8); he is not the Christ (1.20); he is not Elijah (1.21); he is not worthy to untie the sandal-strap of the one coming after him (1.27). On the reading side, the same is true. My reading of texts comes from the convictions and discoveries I have espoused as a Christian educator and church leader, and is different from those of another reader from a different ideological context.

Sacred texture takes note of the divine in a text. God sometimes 'speaks' in texts, certainly in prophetic texts. More directly still God's voice is heard in the Gospel of Mark at the baptism of Jesus and at the transfiguration, but not at the crucifixion when Jesus cries out to God, as one forsaken. The presence and absence of deity in a text is noteworthy. Other aspects of the sacred in a biblical text include a holy person, divine Sprit, salvation-history, human redemption, human commitment, religious community, and ethical instruction.

The sacred texture of biblical texts seems rather obvious. The texts are from a religious community and for a religious community. A reader should expect to find sacred texture in biblical texts. Robbins cautions, however, that some readers tend to find the sacred in biblical texts to the exclusion of other textures. They end up with a single weave, not very appealing, and barely related to the tapestry of the life-situation embodied in the texts. 'As an interpreter works carefully with the nature of language itself in a text, with the relation of a text to other texts, and with the material, social, cultural, and ideological nature of life, a thick description of the sacred texture of a text emerges.'[8]

Robbins sets out in his *Exploring the Texture of Texts* to broker 'theological criticism (Schneiders 1991) together [with other approaches] into an integrated approach to interpretation',[9] but falls rather short of the mark in the end. Neither his discussion of the ideological texture, nor that of the sacred texture, lives up to the

---

[7] Robbins, *Exploring*, 95.
[8] Robbins, *Exploring*, 130.
[9] Robbins, *Exploring*, 2.

challenge of a theological reading of the texts. In the conclusion of his book Robbins makes no concerted effort to show how a socio-rhetorical interpretation of biblical texts yields fruit in human transformation. A socio-rhetorical reading 'does mean that phenomena reside in texts in a manner that makes them programmatically and systematically analysable, even though all the time the interpreters are deeply invested ideologically'.[10]

Despite this shortcoming in Robbins' socio-rhetorical approach, his proposal for a comprehensive analysis of the complex texture of texts is welcome and deserving of careful attention and appropriation. Complemented by theological interpretation the socio-rhetorical approach has potential of yielding valuable and cumulative results.[11]

Stephen E. Fowl

Stephen Fowl focused on a theological interpretation of Scripture in his 1998 publication, *Engaging Scripture: A Model for Theological Interpretation*. His starting point for a theological interpretation is not the text as text. Nor is his premise the reading ability of a human being. Rather, Fowl acknowledges the priority of the community of faith in Christ, a community formed by the reading of Scriptures, and therefore qualified to interpret the texts that formed it. Fowl distinguishes a theological interpretation from biblical theology. Theological interpretation is always work in progress. Biblical theology states the findings, and then uses them as a grid for viewing the texts in successive rounds of reading. A theological interpretation grows out of Christian experience and aims at enhancing Christian life and thought. A theological interpretation is, for Fowl, a Christian interpretation. 'Christian interpretation of scripture needs to involve a complex inter-action in which Christian convictions, practices, and concerns are brought to bear on scriptural interpretation in ways that both shape that interpretation and are shaped by it.'[12]

Fowl admits that his approach is not altogether new. He reaches back to pre-modern ways of reading that have fallen into disrepute. His attempt to re-establish a pre-modern reading strategy does not discount the gains made throughout the modern and post-modern periods. But

[10] Robbins, *Exploring*, 132.
[11] Lonergan, *Method*, 5.
[12] Stephen E. Fowl, *Engaging Scripture: A Model for Theological Interpretation* (Oxford: Blackwell, 1998), 8.

he does elicit an earlier model that took seriously the convictions, practices and concerns that grew out of reading the Scriptures, and were, in turn, present in the rereading of Scriptures.

The novelty of Fowl's approach comes from his idea of 'underdetermined interpretation',[13] over against determinate and anti-determinate models of interpretation. A determinate interpretation 'will stress that biblical texts have a meaning'.[14] The task of the reader in this model is to uncover the meaning of the text through the skilled mastery of certain disciplines. Once the meaning is mastered it can be formulated into doctrine and practice, and the texts thereafter read from the fixed understanding of meaning. One of the problems with a determinate reading of biblical texts is that errors of judgement have been made in the history of the Church. 'The use of biblical texts to underwrite the kidnapping of Africans and their enslavement in the United States and the Dutch Reformed Church's use of the Bible to support apartheid come immediately to mind.'[15]

An anti-determinate interpretation is not one that merely makes interpretation relative to the interpreter. Anti-determinate interpretation, in Fowl's purposes, operates on the theory of deconstruction, discussed earlier. As we have seen, deconstruction dismantles the dominant view by noticing something *other*. The process is an ongoing affair, always suspicious of stable constructs, especially texts. Moreover, Fowl moves beyond both determinate and anti-determinate models of interpretation to underdetermined interpretation.

Underdetermined interpretation, as I understand Fowl's argument, is a middle ground between the two extremes of determinate and anti-determinate modes of interpretation. 'The central interpretive claim here is that our discussions, debates, and arguments about texts will be better served by eliminating claims about textual meaning in favour of more precise accounts of our interpretive aims, interests, and practices.'[16] Part of the program of underdetermined interpretation thus involves couching the practice of reading the biblical texts in terms other than 'meaning'. Underdetermined interpretation asks all kinds of questions about the text's context, its aims and social location. All of this can be done without recourse to the determinate notion of

---

[13] Fowl, *Engaging*, 56ff.
[14] Fowl, *Engaging*, 33.
[15] Fowl, *Engaging*, 36.
[16] Fowl, *Engaging*, 56.

'meaning',[17] and with full acknowledgement of the interpretive aims, interests and practices.

For Fowl the point to an underdetermined reading of biblical texts is that 'theological convictions, ecclesial practices, and communal and social concerns should *shape and be shaped by* biblical interpretation'.[18] At issue in shaping and being shaped by interpretation is a complex interaction between the texture of the biblical text and the texture of 'theological, moral, material, political, and ecclesial concerns that are part of the day-to-day lives of Christians struggling to live faithfully before God in the contexts in which they find themselves'.[19]

The theological interpretation that Fowl proposes, based on an underdetermined reading strategy, emerges out of vigilant and virtuous communities. This qualifier is intended to defuse the charge that Christian communities have read (and still read) the texts in ways that support oppressive and evil practices. Texts do not have ideologies, Fowl argues, any more than they possess meaning.[20] A theological interpretation springs, Fowl assumes, from lives delivered from the tyranny of sin, in communities vigilant in faithfulness to God the deliverer. Theological readers engaged in underdetermined interpretation of Scripture have experienced forgiveness and reconciliation. These are the ones best qualified to interpret the biblical texts. These are the ones competent in charity, having received the same freely from their charitable God in Christ. Issues can be argued and debated in the process of interpretation, but the practice will be consonant with a Christian mind attuned to the Spirit of Christ, exemplified in the hymn to Christ:

> *who, being in the form of God,*
> *did not regard equality with God as something to be exploited,*
> *but emptied himself, taking the form of a slave,*
> *being born in human likeness.*
> *And being found in human form,*
> *he humbled himself and became obedient to the point of death*
> *– even death on a cross.* (Phil. 2.6–8)[21]

I consider Fowl's proposed theological interpretation a valuable complement to the sweep of Robbins' socio-rhetorical interpretation.

---

[17] Meyer refers to 'the intended sense of texts' rather than the 'meaning' in texts, in *Critical Realism*, 17ff.

[18] Fowl, *Engaging*, 60.

[19] Fowl, *Engaging*, 60.

[20] Fowl, *Engaging*, 60.

[21] See the discussion in Fowl, *Engaging*, 190–206.

While Robbins pays close attention to the complex texture of the texts, he has little to say about the faith communities born and nurtured out of interpreting the texts for their life of faith in the world. Fowl attends to this latter aspect. He does so, not to the exclusion of the disciplined work of biblical scholars, for he himself is a notable biblical scholar. His plea for a theological interpretation that *shapes and is shaped* by the convictions, practices and concerns of the Christian community is a value added to the scholarly contribution to the task of biblical interpretation. Fowl invites the engagement of scholars in the project, 'Christian biblical scholars in particular'.[22]

I would add, with respect, that Christians can benefit greatly from listening to a Jewish reading of the Old Testament, and equally also from a Jewish reading of the New Testament. More broadly still, reading the Bible across cultures might help some of us in my part of the world to rethink our practices of justice, of virtue and vigilance, adopted in the privileged, Western-Northern Christian churches.

Towards a Negotiated Reading

A move towards a negotiated reading of Scripture will take a great deal of diligence from the readers. What I mean by a negotiated reading of biblical texts is this: *making value judgements and decisions about the viability of one or another reading strategy in the act of executing an interpretation of particular texts of Scripture.* The judgements are made not in isolation from the proposed text, but in the act of engaging with the text authentically. Authentic engagement is what counts above all. This puts the onus on the person of the interpreter, because ultimately that is where it belongs. Texts do not interpret themselves, any more than facts speak for themselves. Interpreters decide how to proceed after paying careful attention to what lies before them.

Approaching the data

Recall Lonergan's dynamic levels of consciousness, from which we discover general method: *experiencing, understanding, judging and deciding.* This is how we come to know an unknown. The first level, *experiencing,* leads to *understanding,* understanding to *judging,* and

---

[22] Fowl, *Engaging,* 206.

judging to *deciding* in dynamic, spontaneous sequence until the circuit is complete.[23]

We really do have to *attend* to the data at hand, level one. Careful, self-conscious attention to the data of the text paves the way to an understanding of how to proceed. To use an analogy, if I want to cut down a tree whose trunk is eighteen inches in diameter and whose height is thirty feet, I pay attention to every feature, especially the tree's thickness and height. And I will check which way the wind is blowing. How do I proceed with the operation of cutting down such a tree? This object before me is not a cabbage plant. It is not a tomato plant. It is a tree. My observation leads me to understand something of the possible methods for cutting down such a tree.

I would not use a bread knife, or a pair of scissors. These instruments might cut through the stem of a cabbage or a tomato, but they would not fulfil the task of cutting down this particular tree. There are viable alternatives: a chain saw, a heavy axe, and a crosscut saw. These are all the viable alternatives I can think of for this particular operation. And I will need to take up an appropriate position in relation to the way the wind is blowing. I would not want the tree to fall on me!

Similar negotiation is needed for interpreting texts of Scripture. Not all of them require exactly the same approach, and not all of them require the application of all the possible reading strategies. But all of the texts do require an attentive, intelligent, rational, responsible, person self-consciously engaged in the execution of authentic interpretation.

Dialogue with others is bound to help the negotiation. As a white male living in North America I need to take seriously the reading strategy of feminist interpreters. And I will need to listen and learn from the interpretive text of readers living in oppressed societies. My own place is one of privilege and freedom. If I do not listen sensitively to the voices from other places, from other social locations than my own, I risk having the interpretation fall painfully on my head. I need to feel which way the wind is blowing, so to speak. As Fowl puts it, there are convictions, practices and concerns alive and active in my community, and in other communities. I need to hear them.

The negotiation also calls for earnest dialogue between the academy and the faith community. The faith community has the concerns of their everyday lives in mind. Their interest is in finding answers to the

---

[23] Lonergan, *Method*, 5ff.

life issues that face the people of the congregation at work, home, and in corporate and private worship. Individuals in an academic community also face similar issues of life. But within the academic departments related to biblical studies scholars work in their discipline with a view to new information, new ways of working. They pursue their studies without any constraints of confessions of faith.

I submit that the two groups need each other. The Church needs to do its theological and ethical duty with the best information and insight available. Scholars need to hear from the faith communities to give value to their diligence. They need to know what their work has to do with the lives of people struggling with hard issues of life and death.

A case study

For the remainder of the chapter I will attempt to demonstrate how a negotiated reading of a text would proceed, using various strategies brokered interactively in relation to the character of the text under review. The text is 1 Corinthians 5.1–13, presented here with line numbers, rather than verse divisions, for specific reference in the interpretation[24]

Several fundamental questions guide my reading of the selected text. Answers to them in relation to 1 Corinthians 5 should result in a relevant approach to understanding and appropriating this text. The same can be done for any text of Scripture. This is what I mean by a negotiated reading.

1. What is my social location as reader of this text? This question helps keep my self-text active in the interpretive action.
2. What *kind* of text is this? This pushes me to pay attention to the boundaries and structure of this particular text, to name the form, all in an effort to find an appropriate reading strategy.
3. What is the *texture* of the text? In answer to this question I focus on details of grammar, style, cultural reference, intertexture, rhetoric, etc.
4. What is the *literary location* of this text? This question reminds me to look on both sides of this pericopé for clues to its intended sense.
5. What is the *theological significance* of the text? Here I am challenged to think about issues of life and thought and behaviour encoded in the text in relation to my own.

---

[24] I have presented a more extensive analysis of this text elsewhere, V. George Shillington, 'Atonement Texture in 1 Cor. 5:5', *JSNT* 71 (1998), 29–50.

Table 13.1

I Corinthians 5.1–13

1 IT IS ACTUALLY REPORTED THAT THERE IS SEXUAL IMMORALITY AMONG
2 YOU, AND OF A KIND THAT IS NOT FOUND EVEN AMONG PAGANS; FOR A
3 MAN IS LIVING WITH HIS FATHER'S WIFE. AND YOU ARE ARROGANT!
4 SHOULD YOU NOT RATHER HAVE MOURNED, SO THAT HE WHO HAS
5 DONE THIS WOULD HAVE BEEN REMOVED FROM AMONG YOU?
6 FOR THOUGH ABSENT IN BODY, I AM PRESENT IN SPIRIT; AND AS IF
7 PRESENT

8 I HAVE ALREADY PRONOUNCED JUDGMENT IN THE NAME OF THE LORD
9 JESUS ON THE MAN WHO HAS DONE SUCH A THING. WHEN YOU ARE
10 ASSEMBLED, AND MY SPIRIT IS PRESENT WITH THE POWER OF OUR LORD
11 JESUS, YOU ARE TO HAND THIS MAN OVER TO SATAN FOR THE
12 DESTRUCTION OF THE FLESH, SO THAT HIS SPIRIT MAY BE SAVED IN THE
13 DAY OF THE LORD.

14 YOUR BOASTING IS NOT A GOOD THING. DO YOU NOT KNOW THAT A
15 LITTLE YEAST LEAVENS THE WHOLE BATCH OF DOUGH? CLEAN OUT THE
16 OLD YEAST SO THAT YOU MAY BE A NEW BATCH, AS YOU REALLY ARE
17 UNLEAVENED. FOR OUR PASCHAL LAMB, CHRIST, HAS BEEN
18 SACRIFICED. THEREFORE, LET US CELEBRATE THE FESTIVAL, NOT WITH
19 THE OLD YEAST, THE YEAST OF MALICE AND EVIL, BUT WITH THE
20 UNLEAVENED BREAD OF SINCERITY AND TRUTH.

21 I WROTE TO YOU IN MY LETTER NOT TO ASSOCIATE WITH SEXUALLY
22 IMMORAL PERSONS – NOT AT ALL MEANING THE IMMORAL OF THIS
23 WORLD, OR THE GREEDY AND ROBBERS, OR IDOLATERS, SINCE YOU
24 WOULD THEN NEED TO GO OUT OF THE WORLD. BUT NOW I AM WRITING
25 TO YOU NOT TO ASSOCIATE WITH ANYONE WHO BEARS THE NAME OF
26 BROTHER OR SISTER WHO IS SEXUALLY IMMORAL OR GREEDY, OR IS AN
27 IDOLATER, REVILER, DRUNKARD, OR ROBBER. DO NOT EVEN EAT WITH
28 SUCH A ONE. FOR WHAT HAVE I TO DO WITH JUDGING THOSE OUTSIDE?
29 IS IT NOT THOSE WHO ARE INSIDE THAT YOU ARE TO JUDGE? GOD WILL
30 JUDGE THOSE OUTSIDE. 'DRIVE OUT THE WICKED PERSON FROM AMONG
31 YOU.'

First, who I am affects my understanding and judgement of what I read in this text. I am an educated white male, born and nurtured in a strict family in Presbyterian tradition in Northern Ireland, currently an ordained minister in a believers' church in Canada, and concurrently a professor of New Testament studies and theology in a Canadian university. All of this and more constitute my interpretive text, which comes into play as I experience, understand, judge, and respond to the texture of this text. I view my interpretive task to be one of bridging the current concerns of my faith community with my academic discipline as a biblical scholar. The challenge will be to measure up to the standard set in the academic discipline, while speaking authentically to the issues of life and thought at work in the faith community.

Second, I observe the form of the text to be 'argument' with all the attending features of argumentative rhetoric. This text is not a parable, proverb, psalm, miracle story, or law code. It is an *argument that passes sentence*, with a conclusion that calls for action on the part of the group towards one member of the group. Recognizing the form of the text as 'argument' prompts me to distinguish the conclusion from the rhetorical texture that leads to the conclusion.

Third, this argument has thick literary texture, the uncovering of which will help in understanding the severity of the sentence executed on the one by the many. The *inner texture* of the text is bounded by *the opening* comment about a report and *the closing* injunction to the group. Between these two boundary markers are internal elements that pinpoint the problem and pave the path toward a solution. The problem is *sexual immorality* (*porneia*), repeated five times altogether, twice in the opening paragraph (1–7) and three times in the concluding paragraph (21–31). With its reoccurrence at the end of the argument this problem term (*porneia*) joins up with a cognate term, *evil/wicked* [person] (19, 30). Both terms signal the intolerable nature of the problem.

But the problem is specified promptly in the opening 'reporting on the report': *a man is living with his* father's *wife* (3), an incestuous relationship. But that is not the sum and substance of the problem within the texture of the argument. Another term shifts the focus from the individual to the group-life. *Among you* (plural) comes up immediately following the lead problem-term (1–2), and then it appears again as the problem is further specified (5), and again in the final injunction (30–31). The group-problem is further illustrated by the visual image of the pervasive action of leavening a lump of dough in the rhetorical question: *Do you not know that a little yeast leavens the whole batch of dough?* (14–15). At issue in the problem-texture is the spread of sexual immorality, specified as incest, to the group-members all.

The woman involved is strangely out of focus, except that she is *his father's wife* (3), probably stepmother. Was she complicit in the 'sexual immorality'? Did the man force her into the immoral situation, and thus make her victim? Was the woman a member of the believing group along with the man? Was she – as we would say today – 'a consenting adult'? I am simply left wondering about the role and status of the woman in the problem of 'sexual immorality'. The texture of the text code does not permit further extrapolation beyond wondering along these lines.

The texture of the solution is carried in terms of authority: *judgement/judging* (8, 28, 29, 30), *my spirit is present with the power of our Lord Jesus* (10–11), *pronounce* (8), *hand over* (11), *drive out* (30). These power words, and imperative action words, are directed to the group-mind, not to the *wicked person* (30). As a whole, the group acts to purge itself of the problem.

The *intertexture* woven supportively into the inner texture of the argument is at points subtle and at points not so subtle. When the problem is identified as *a man living with his father's wife* (2–3) the Levitical code forbidding the sin of incest springs to light (Lev. 18.8; 20.11).[25] And when the yeast-in-dough analogy comes up, the feast of Passover comes into focus, with Christ becoming the paschal lamb of the celebration (17–18).

But there appears also a more subtle piece of intertexture at the point of the first pronouncement of judgement (11–13), rendered literally: *you* (pl.) *are to hand such a person over to Satan for the destruction of the flesh, so that the spirit may be saved in the day of the Lord.* 'Satan' is the Lord's archrival, drawn in here out of a long tradition of evil activity and personality under various names. The figure of Azazel in Leviticus 16 comes to mind immediately. The priests of Israel sacrificed one of two goats on the Day of Atonement to this enigmatic figure, Azazel. The tradition held (variously) that this desert dwelling demon destroyed the flesh of the goat, and thus took away the sins of community on the Day of Atonement. The act of handing over the goat to Azazel saved the life of the community for the Lord. I hear an echo in this pronouncement of judgement to the atonement ritual of ridding the community of sin over which the people of Israel mourn (4). Balancing this echo to the atonement scapegoat, and following the pronouncement, is the allusion to the joyous festival of salvation, the Passover.

If I am hearing correctly the echo of the Jewish atonement ritual in the injunction to the group (11–13), then the texture of the injunction implies the expulsion of the sexually immoral man from the

---

[25] See the incisive, and very helpful, treatment of the Priestly sections of the Pentateuch with respect to sexual misconduct in the holy community in Waldemar Janzen, *Old Testament Ethics: A Paradigmatic Approach* (Louisville: Westminster/John Knox Press, 1994), 57–68; 106–18.

community into the domain of Satan will result in the loss of physical life (*flesh*) for the sake of the spirit-life of the End-time group from which he is expelled. (The Greek text of line 12 reads '*the* spirit' (*to pneuma*), not *his* spirit (*autou pneuma*).)

An unusual piece of intertexture appears in the last paragraph (lines 21–27). Reference is made to a previous letter on the same general topic of sexual immorality. In this new texture a finer point is put on the subject: persons who practice vices of this sort are not permitted in the fictive kinship of the virtuous community of Christ (24–26). *Do not even eat with such a person* (27–28), a possible reference to the Eucharist.

The final injunction (30–31) is unmistakably an intertexture from another part of the Torah, Deuteronomy 17.7: *Drive out the wicked person from among you.* The Greek wording of the LXX text of Deuteronomy 17.7 is almost identical to this injunction in I Corinthians 5. The context of the Deuteronomy text, however, instructs the community on how to execute the death penalty on an accused person, and so *to purge the evil [one] from your midst*. This intertexture may imply that the *wicked person* will meet his death by his own deviance once he is expelled from the protection of the community.

The weave of *social, cultural, ideological, and sacred texture* is clearly evident in this text of I Corinthians 5. The Jewish socio-cultural life as the Israel of God comes through in the atonement and Passover allusions. Noteworthy also is the sociological remark that the kind of immorality specified is not even practiced among Gentiles. The new community, however, belongs neither to an exclusive Jewish culture nor to an otherwise Gentile culture, but to the 'culture' of Jesus Christ. The power and provenance of the injunction flows from the same Lord Jesus. Thus far the texture of the argument.

Fourth, the text is situated in the midst of instructions about the nature of communal life in Christ. After citing the 'report' about factions in the community (I Cor. 1.11), the text proceeds to issue a warning not to jeopardize the sacred life of the community. The members' life together is imaged as *God's temple*, an institution not to be destroyed by anyone, for *if anyone destroys God's temple, God will destroy that person. For God's temple is holy, and you are that temple* (3.16–17).

When the 'report' about incest going on within the fictive family, the church, comes up for execution in chapter 5, it comes as no surprise to find atonement texture and Passover texture, both temple images, woven into the judgement-argument. Then following that argument the temple image reappears in chapter 6, where other sexual matters are scrutinized and adjudicated (6.19). Moreover, the argument judging incest in the community falls inside a larger concern for the sacred character of communal life in Christ.

Fifth, the theological currency of this text is unmistakable. To use Fowl's phrase, the reading of this text 'shapes and is shaped by' the convictions, practices and concerns of the faith community.

I have not had the occasion to observe what my church today would say about the marriage of a stepson to his stepmother, following the death of his biological father. The church may frown on it, but I doubt if it would 'hand the man or woman over to Satan', where the two are willing participants in the union.

But there are moral concerns on which the faith community does need to act more readily and spontaneously than it does. United as they are in the love of Christ, members and leaders sometimes need to make judgement and decision on wrongdoing *in the power of our Lord Jesus* (10).

Recently I heard a woman interviewed on a local radio station where I live. The woman told of her joy as a young Christian woman at finding a husband who shared her faith, who belonged to her church, asked her to be his wife. Not long after she was married she was subjected to abuse from her husband. As their children were growing up the woman also discovered that her husband was sexually molesting her two-year-old daughter. When she had verified her daughter's statement by eliciting a confession from her husband, she called Child and Family Services. She handed the man over to the authorities. He was charged, found guilty and sentenced to fifteen months in gaol. After serving the time in gaol, the incestuous man was released. He returned to church life and worship.

As I interact with this story from the woman on radio, and with the text of 1 Corinthians 5 at the same time, I am struck that the woman did not go directly to the church where she and the man were members. She reported the problem to the social and legal authorities first. Only later when the man was arrested did she report the matter to the pastor of her church. The church did not act in judgement on the man, who claimed to have the right to behave as he did within his own family. The church did not hand him over to the authorities, nor expel him from the community of Christ.

Nor is this an isolated case of violence within Christian families. Documented cases of sexual abuse, totalling 19.8 per cent of a random sampling of church members in one local area of one denomination in Canada according to one authority,[26] indicate either the church's insensitivity to the problem among its members, or the church's inability to do anything about the problem.

This theological-ethical negotiation between reading the text and listening to a report of incest among church members affects my judgement and action. If the community of Christ truly is virtuous and vigilant, as Fowl asks us to assume, then my interactive reading leads me to plead for church judgement on the sexual abuser in keeping with the church's character as temple of God, sanctuary for victims, and witness to the surrounding culture. Abusers have no place in God's holy temple.

Conclusion

With the help of Vernon Robbins and Stephen Fowl, I have tried to set forth an approach in this chapter that takes into account the many possible exigencies of a text that present themselves to an attentive reader. The two terms, 'text' and 'reader', provide the key to authentic interpretation of biblical texts. In the act of reading the texts, the reader brings to the operation a living presence that the text does not possess. The living reader feels the pain of sexual violence, illustrated in the case of the woman interviewed on radio, and reads texts such as 1 Corinthians 5 out of concern for the action of God on her behalf. Other readers in community with the woman share her concern, because they read the same text with the same conviction and concern.

I have also approached the text as a self-conscious Christian human being, holding myself accountable to my community and to a normative pattern of coming to know. How successful I have been in doing so I leave to the judgement of fellow readers similarly involved in knowing and doing.

---

[26] Isaac Block, *Assault on God's image: Domestic Abuse* (Winnipeg: Windflower Communications, 1991).

14

Conclusion

'A place to start' in biblical studies is also a place to end, with the person of the reader of Scripture in communion with those of like mind. I have worked through the foregoing chapters on the premise that a self-appropriating reader, aware of the God-given human capacity for making an unknown known, is by that token competent to enter into biblical studies.

Normative pattern

Lonergan referred to the pattern by which we come to know as *normative*.[1] That is, all humans share the operation in common. Becoming self-aware of the normative pattern provides the generative matrix for studying any and all aspects related to the field of biblical studies and theology.

The pattern is not something we humans construct, as in manufacturing suitable tools for accomplishing a task. The pattern is present in our human consciousness, waiting to be discovered. But the discovery cannot be made by someone else observing us. Others may notice our brown eyes or our distinctive way of walking. How we humans come to know an unknown, however, emerges through a process of self-discovery. It is a dynamic process, so we cannot stop what we are doing and reflect on the subject. The pattern becomes evident as we are actively engaged in knowing and doing: *experiencing, understanding, judging and deciding.*[2]

But learning these words in this order is not equal to self-discovery. The challenge is to test the validity of the pattern of operations in the act of knowing and doing. Whether we use Lonergan's terms for the pattern makes little difference. At issue is whether the pattern is present. I have found that it is, and have invited the reader to discover its presence while they 'make sense' of what I have written. Awareness

---

[1] Lonergan, *Method*, 6.
[2] Lonergan, *Method*, 13–20.

of the pattern, shared among our fellow human travelers, provides a valuable and viable check on inappropriate reading of the biblical texts.

Reconstituting traditions

I have suggested also in Part II that the traditions about the Bible need to be explored and exploited for their current value. What the traditions did beneficially for communities past may not serve present communities with the same benefit. At the same time the traditions about the Bible need to be respected, and then reconstituted in light of what we know and cherish in current life.[3]

Stories of the origins and development of the Bible need to be retold in ways that invite interaction with the traditions. Did Moses really write all five books of the Pentateuch? Did Paul actually write everything that appears under his name? What can we learn from the Churches' action of listing certain documents as 'a rule of faith' while excluding others? What is the benefit of a critical text of Scripture, as compared to a 'received text'? Do new translations detract from faith or enhance it?

Questions such as these arise out of a concern for truth, not factual truth merely, but 'truth' as lived authentically. Traditions, to be of value, must speak reasonably into the situation in life here and now. Their currency five hundred years ago must give way to a new currency five hundred years later. In this updating, this exploiting that we do, the normative pattern of operations is still at work yielding cumulative and progressive results.

Responsible reading

The same is true for the reading strategies discussed in Part III. How are we to decide which ones are more appropriate than others? What makes Walter Wink's pronouncement of bankruptcy on the historical critical paradigm of modernity valid or invalid? What makes Shillington's appeal for a negotiated reading of Scripture texts valid or invalid? We have no other court of appeal than the dynamic pattern of recurrent and related operations present in ourselves to address these questions.[4]

---

[3] Walter Brueggemann writes and preaches toward 'the liberation of the biblical text for the church in a new situation', in *Texts Under Negotiation*, vii.
[4] Lonergan, *Method*, 19–20.

With that pattern we are able to hold each other accountable for the product of our work. Where self-correction is called for, as it often is, the call must come in terms of the same pattern. If I have missed the mark in my representation of Robbins or Fowl, for example, someone will need to draw the problem to my attention, help me understand where I missed the mark and how far, call on me to evaluate the viability of their claim, and expect me to act accordingly.

Doing theology

In the final analysis, doing biblical studies responsibly should lead to doing theology charitably.[5] I have not entered into an extended discussion of theology, but I hope I have pointed the way to authentic outworking of biblical studies. The process is ongoing. Issues and concerns in Church and society call for a word-and-act of compassion, correction, and change. Believing communities reading the texts of Scripture in relation to their corporate and individual lives do so expecting the Word to transform their conventional existence into radical renewal of mind and heart.

But the same communities need resources within and beyond themselves. They do, of course, need the mutual respect of each other in calling attention to the need for renewal. In Chapter 13 I cited a case of abuse and incest in a church. Here was a case where victims went undetected in a Christian community, and their plight unresolved in that context. Here was a case of an immoral man going unchecked. Doing theology requires diligence in caring for the life-situation of members of the community, on the one hand, and speaking out against violence and injustice in society on the other.

Meeting of minds

In addition to the resources resident in the faith community, the community can use profitably the resources of biblical scholars who spend their days in research and teaching and writing. Church people – but not all – have long since tended to be suspicious of biblical scholarship.[6] Scholars unravel the fabric of faith, so it is assumed, and erode

---

[5] A reference to the thesis of Stephen E. Fowl, *Engaging Scripture*, where he calls for theological interpretation, not biblical theology. Doing theology, as I call it, is the dynamic outworking of theological interpretation.

[6] See the discussion of the history of the tension between the Church and the academy in Mark A. Noll, *Between Faith and Criticism: Evangelicals, Scholarship, and the Bible in America* (San Francisco: Harper & Row, 1986), 11–185.

relationship to God and Christ. Scholars, in this perception, can offer little for doing theology in a church setting. Where this perception is true of biblical scholars, I agree that churches are just as well without their contribution.

But not all biblical scholars are destructive to faith and faithfulness, any more than all churches ignore the plight of victims in their midst. Faith communities can use the insights and discoveries of concerned scholars. The goal of good scholarship is truth. Church people should not fear truth, for *the truth will make you free* (John 8.32). More to the point, both church people and scholars engage each other using the same fundamental pattern of operations for the mutual benefit of all concerned. One can call the other to account for inadequacy of insights and errors in judgement, but always with charity.

The sermon

When it comes to the sermon, still a focal part of the worship service, preachers carry a weighty responsibility. They have to be true to the claims of their sermons. A preacher cannot afford the stance, 'do what I say, not what I do'. The interpreted Word must first take hold in the life of the communicator and thence reach the heart and mind of the audience through the spoken word. Nor is it enough to have a passion to communicate. The sermon serves up a word on target, emerging out of authentic interaction with the text of Scripture in connection with the lives of the people gathered.

Moving from text to sermon is not an easy matter.[7] I have heard sermons that explain the details of a text from the pulpit, and when that lengthy part is finished the preacher tacks on the 'application'. Often the 'application' is only remotely related to the explanation of the text.

The preacher's interaction with the biblical text in the delivery of the sermon should draw the congregation in on the act. The preacher is merely a catalyst toward the engagement of the audience in the enterprise. It is this authentic engagement with Scripture that transforms the mind *so that you may discern what is the will of God – what is good and acceptable and perfect* (Rom. 12.2).

The texture of the sermon, to be effective, captures the imagination of the audience, drawing them into its weave. Sermons create

---

[7] See the helpful study done by Ernest Best, *From Text to Sermon: Responsible Use of the New Testament in Preaching* (Atlanta: John Knox Press, 1978), 113, 'The purpose of all understanding of Scripture is to make Christ appear in his church so that he shapes that church to be like himself.'

memories, and memories have a way of keeping transformation going. Who could forget the famous sermon of Martin Luther King Jr, 'I have a dream'? Every time I remember that sermon I imagine again the inequities of marginalized peoples, and wonder what to do about it. Doing theology in the sermon is a weighty responsibility.

There may be alternatives to the sermonic monologue. The congregation could be given opportunity to interact with the preacher and the sermon. Dialogue connects the life of the people with the substance of the sermon in creative ways. Another move that some congregations have made is to discuss the sermon in small groups. Whatever the model, the goal is to bring the Word of Scripture to life authentically in the lives of people. We need each other in the life-giving enterprise, bringing with us our cultural differences and mutual concerns.

The Scriptures invite honest inquiry from the reader, but they also expect the reading to produce cumulative results in moral, communal, socio-political, life and thought. To the degree that this book has advanced this cause effectively, its mission is accomplished and I am satisfied.

Bibliography

Abraham, W. J., *The Divine Inspiration of Holy Scripture*, Oxford: University Press, 1981.

Achtemeier, E., "The Impossible Possibility: Evaluating the Feminist Approach to the Bible and Theology," *Int.* 42 (1988): 45–57.

Adam, A. K. M. *What is Postmodern Biblical Criticism?* Minneapolis: Fortress Press, 1995.

Alonso, Schökel, L. "Hermeneutics in the Light of Language and Literature," *CBQ* 25 (1963): 371–86.

Anderson, B. W. "Tradition and Scripture in the Community of Faith." *JBL* 100 (1981): 5–21.

Archer, Gleason L, Jr., *A Survey of Old Testament Introduction*, Chicago: Moody Press, 1964.

Arndt, William F., and Gingrich, F. Wilbur, *A Greek-English Lexicon of the New Testament and Other Early Christian Literature*, Chicago: University of Chicago Press, 1957.

Asgough, R. S., *Voluntary Associations and Community Formation: Paul's Macedonian Christian Communities in Context* (Dissertation), Toronto: Wycliffe College, 1997.

Baker, T. G. A., " 'This is the Word of the Lord,' " *Theology* 93 (1990): 266–73.

Barclay, William, *Introducing the Bible,* Nashville: Abingdon Press, 1972.

Barfield, Owen, *Saving the Appearances: A Study of Idolatry*, New York: Harcourt Brace Jovanovich, N.D.

Barr, J., "The Literal, the Allegorical and Modern Biblical Scholarship," *JSOT* 44 (1989): 3–17.

Barr, J., "The Old Testament and the New Crisis of Biblical Authority," in *Int.* 25 (1971): 24–40.

Barton, J., "Reading the Bible as Literature: Two Questions for Biblical Critics," *LT* 1 (1987): 135–53.

Barton, J., "The Place of the Bible in Moral Debate," *Theology* 88 (1985): 204–9.

Barton, John, "Source Criticism", *ABD*, 6 (1992): 164.

Baur, Ferdinand Christian, *Ferdinand Christian Baur on the Writing of Church History,* ed. and trans. Peter C. Hodgson. New York: Oxford University Press, 1968.

Beardslee, William A., *Literary Criticism of the New Testament. Guides to Biblical Scholarship*, Philadelphia: Fortress Press, 1970.

Beasley, James R. *et al.*, eds. *An Introduction to the Bible*, Nashville: Abingdon Press, 1991.

Beasley-Murray, G. R., *Gospel of Light: theology in the Fourth Gospel*, Peabody: Hendrickson, 1991.

Best, E., "Scripture, Tradition and the Canon of the New Testament," *BJRL* 61 (1979): 258–89.

Betz, Hans Dieter, "The Sermon on the Mount and Q", in *Gospel Origins & Christian Beginnings: In Honor of James M. Robinson*, Sonoma CA: Polebridge Press, 1990: 19–34.

Betz, Hans Dieter, *Galatians: A Commentary on Paul's Letter to the Churches in Galatia*,. Philadelphia: Fortress Press, 1979.

Beyer, Hermann Wolfgang, "biblioj, biblion", *TDNT* I: 615–25.

Blair, Edward P., *The Illustrated Bible Handbook*, Nashville: Abingdon Press, 1987.

Block, Isaac, *Assault on God's Image: Domestic Abuse*, Winnipeg: Windflower Communications, 1991.

Bock, Philip K., *Modern Cultural Anthropology: An Introduction*, second edition, New York: Alfred A. Knopf, 1974.

Boorer, S., "The Importance of a Diachronic Approach," *CBQ* 51 (1989): 195–208.

Booth, Wayne C., *Critical Understanding: The Powers and Limits of Pluralism*, Chicago: University Press, 1979.

Bray, G., *Biblical Interpretation Past and Present*, Leicester: Apollos, 1996.

Bright, John, *A History of Israel*, fourth edition, ed. William P. Brown, Westminster John Knox Press, 1999 (2000).

Bright, John, "Modern Study of Old Testament Literature", in *The Bible and the Ancient Near East: Essays in Honour of William Foxwell Albright*, Edited by G. Ernest Wright, Garden City NY: Doubleday, 1961.

Brown, Raymond E., "The *Sensus Plenior* in the Last Ten Years." *CBQ* 25 (1963): 262–85.

Brown, Raymond E., Fitzmeyer, Joseph A. and Murphy, Roland E., *The New Jerome Biblical Commentary*. Upper Saddle River, NJ: Prentice Hall, 1990.

Brown, Raymond E., *The Community of the Beloved Disciple*, New York: Paulist Press, 1979.

Bruce, F. F., *The Books and the Parchments: How We Got our English Bible*, Old Tappen NJ: Fleming H. Revell, 1984.

Bruce, F. F., *The Canon of Scripture*, Downers Grove: InterVarsity Press, 1988.

Bruce, F. F., *The English Bible: A History of Translations*, London: Lutterworth Press, 1961.

Bruce, F. F., *The Gospel of John*, Grand Rapids: Eerdmans, 1983.

Brueggemann, W., "Imagination as a Mode of Fidelity," in Buller, J. S. et al, eds., *Understanding the Word* (B. W. Anderson Festschrift), Sheffield: JSOT Press, 1985: 21–31.

Brueggemann, W., *Interpretation and Obedience: From Faithful Reading to Faithful Living*, Minneapolis: Fortress Press, 1991.

Brueggemann, Walter, *Texts Under Negotiation: The Bible and Postmodern Imagination*, Minneapolis: Fortress Press, 1993.

Brueggemann, Walter. *The Creative Word: Canon as a Model for Biblical Education*. Philadelphia: Fortress Press, 1982.

Bultmann, R., "Is Exegesis Without Presuppositions Possible?" in *New Testament and Mythology*, ed. Ogden, S. M., Philadelphia: Fortress Press, 1984 (German, 1950): 145–53.

Bultmann, R., "The New Testament and Mythology" in *New Testament and Mythology*, ed. Ogden, S. M. Philadelphia: Fortress Press, 1984 (German 1950): 1–43.

Bultmann, R., "The Problem of Hermeneutics," in *New Testament and Mythology*, ed. Ogden, S. M. Philadelphia: Fortress Press, 1984 (German, 1950): 69–93.

Bultmann, R., Ernst Lohmeyer, *et al. Kerygma and Myth: A Theological Debate*. New York: Harper & Row, 1966.

Bultmann, R., *Form Criticism: Two Essays on New Testament Research*, Translated by Frederick C. Grant, New York: Harper, 1962.

Bultmann, R., *Jesus Christ and Mythology*, New York: Charles Scribner's Sons, 1958.

Bultmann, R., *The History of the Synoptic Tradition*, New York: Harper & Row, 1963.

Buttrick, G. E., editor. *The Interpreters Dictionary of the Bible*, Volumes 1–4. New York: Abingdon Press, 1962–1976.

Cady, L. E., "Hermeneutics and Tradition," *HTR* 79 (1986): 439–63.

Carson, D. A., and Woodbridge, John D. eds., *Hermeneutics, Authority, and Canon*. Zondervan, 1986.

Chance, J. Bradley and Horne, Milton P., *Rereading the Bible: An*

Introduction to the Biblical Story, Upper Saddle River NJ: Prentice Hall, 2000.

Charles, R. H., ed. *The Apocrypha and Pseudepigrapha of the Old Testament in English*, Oxford: Clarendon Press, 1913.

Charlesworth, James H. and Weaver, Walter P., eds., *What Has Archaeology to Do With Faith?* Philadelphia: Trinity Press International, 1992.

Childs, Brevard S., "The Canonical Shape of the Prophetic Literature," *Int.* 32 (1978): 46–55.

Childs, Brevard S., *Introduction to the Old Testament as Scripture*, Philadelphia: Fortress Press, 1979.

Childs, Brevard S., *Myth and Reality in the Old Testament*, London: SCM Press, 1960.

Childs, Brevard S., *The New Testament as Canon: An Introduction*, Philadelphia: Fortress Press, 1984.

Chilton, Bruce, *Pure Kingdom: Jesus' Vision of God*, Studying the Historical Jesus, Grand Rapids: Eerdmans, 1996.

Cicero, *Rhetorica ad Herennium. LCL*, trans. Harry Caplan, Cambridge: Harvard University Press, 1954.

Clines, D. J. A., "Story and Poem." *Int.* 34 (1980): 115–27.

Collins, Adela Yarbro, ed., *Feminist Perspectives on Biblical Scholarship.* Chico, CA: Scholars Press, 1985.

Conn, Walter E., "Moral Development: Is Conversion Necessary?" in *Creativity and Method: Essays in Honor of Bernard Lonergan, S. J.* ed. Mathew L. Lamb, Milwaukee: Marquette University Press, 1981, pp. 307–24.

Coote, Robert B. and Coote, Mary P., *Power, Politics and the Making of the Bible: An Introduction*, Minneapolis: Fortress Press, 1990.

Court, John M., *Reading the New Testament*, London and New York: Routledge, 1997.

Craddock, Fred B., *Luke: Interpretation*, Louisville: John Knox Press, 1990.

Creamer, David G., *Guides for the Journey: John Macmurray, Bernard Lonergan, James Fowler*, Lanham: University Press of America, 1996.

Croatto, J. S., *Biblical Hermeneutics: Toward a Theory of Reading as the Production of Meaning*, trans. Barr, R. R., New York: Mary Knoll, 1987.

Crowe, Frederick E., *Lonergan*, Collegeville: Liturgical Press, 1992.

Culpepper, R. Alan, *Anatomy of the Fourth Gospel: A Study in Literary Design*, Philadelphia: Fortress Press, 1983.

Davies, W. D., "Reflections on the Mormon 'Canon'." *HTR* 79 (1986): 44–66.

Davis, Charles, "The Theological Career of Historical Criticism of the Bible." *Cross Currents* 32 (1982): 267–84.

De Margerie, Bernard, *And Introduction to the history of Exegesis: Volume III, Saint Augustine,* Petersham: Saint Bede's Publications, 1991.

Derrida, Jacques, *Apories.* Stanford: University Press, 1993.

Derrida, Jacques, *Of Grammatology,* Trans. Spivak, G. C. Baltimore: Johns Hopkins University Press, 1976.

DeVries, La Moine F., *Cities of the Biblical World,* Peabody: Hendrickson, 1997.

Dilthey, W., "The Rise of Hermeneutics." *NLH* 3 (1971–72): 229–44.

Diringer, David, *The Alphabet: A Key to the History of Mankind,* New York: Philosophical Library, 1948.

Diringer, David, *The Alphabet: A Key to the History of Mankind,* third edition. Volumes I and II. New York: Funk and Wagnalls, 1968.

Dodd, C. H., *The Interpretation of the Fourth Gospel,* Cambridge: University Press, 1953.

Dodd, C. H., *The Parables of the Kingdom,* New York: Charles Scribner's Sons, 1961.

Downing, F. Gerald, "Our Access to Other Cultures, Past and Present (or The Myth of the Culture Gap), *The Modern Churchman* 21 (1977–78): 28–42.

Duke, Paul D., *Irony in the Fourth Gospel,* Atlanta: John Knox Press, 1985.

Dunne, John S., "Insight and Waiting on God", in *Creativity and Method: Essays in Honor of Bernard Lonergan, S. J.* ed. Mathew L. Lamb. Milwaukee: Marquette University Press, 1981, pp. 3–9.

Efird, James M., *The Old Testament Writings: History, Literature, and Interpretation,* Atlanta: John Knox Press, 1982.

Eliade, Mercia, *The Myth of the Eternal Return or, Cosmos and History,* Princeton: University Press, 1954.

Elliott, Keith, and Ian Moir, *Manuscripts and the Text of the New Testament: An Introduction for English Readers,* Edinburgh: T & T Clark, 1995.

Elliott, Neil, *Liberating Paul: The Justice of God and the Politics of the Apostle,* Mary Knoll: Orbis Books, 1994.

Esler, Philip, *Galatians,* London: Routledge, 1998.

Eslinger, Lyle, "The Wooing of the Woman at the Well: Jesus the Reader and Reader-Response Criticism," *LT* 1 (1987): 167–83.

Eusebius Pamphilus, *The Ecclesiastical History of Eusebius*, Popular Edition, translated by C. F. Cruse, Grand Rapids: Baker Book House, 1955.

Ewert, David, *From Ancient Tablets to Modern Translations: A General Introduction to the Bible*, Grand Rapids: Zondervan Publishing House, 1983.

Exum, J. Cheryl, "Of Broken Pots, Fluttering Birds and Visions in the Night: Extended Simile and Poetic Technique in Isaiah." *"CBQ* 43 (1981): 331–52.

F. Brown, S. R. Driver, and C. A. Briggs, eds. *A Hebrew-English Lexicon of the Old Testament*, Oxford: Clarendon Press, 1907/1957.

Farmer, Ronald L., *Beyond the Impasse: The Promise of a Process Hermeneutic*, Macon, GA: Mercer University Press, 1997.

Farmer, William R., *The Synoptic Problem : A Critical Analysis*, Dillsboro, N.C. : Western North Carolina Press, 1976.

Fee, G. D., *New Testament Exegesis: A Handbook for Students and Pastors*, Philadelphia: Fortress Press, 1983.

Ferguson, David, "Meaning, Truth, and Reconciliation in Bultmann and Lindbeck," *RS* 26 (1990): 183–98.

Ferguson, David, *Biblical Hermeneutics: An Introduction*, London: SCM Press, 1986.

Ferré, Frederick, *Language, Logic and God*, New York: Harper & Row, 1961.

Fish, Stanley, *Is There a Text in This Class? The Authority of Interpretive Communities*, Cambridge: Harvard University Press, 1980.

Fitzmeyer, Joseph A., *Essays on the Semitic Background of the New Testament*, Grand Rapids: Eerdmans, 1997.

Ford, Richard Q., *The Parables of Jesus: Recovering the Art of Listening*, Minneapolis: Fortress Press, 1997.

Fowl, Stephen E., *Engaging Scripture: A Model for Theological Interpretation*, Oxford: Blackwell Publishers, 1998.

Fowler, James W. "Stages of Faith: Reflections on a Decade of Dialogue", *Christian Education Journal* 13.1 (1992): 1323.

Fowler, R. M., *Let the Reader Understand: Reader-Response Criticism and the Gospel of Mark*, Minneapolis: Fortress Press, 1991.

Frankfort, Henri *et al.*, *Before Philosophy: the Intellectual Adventure of Ancient Man*, Baltimore: Penguin Books, 1949.

Freedman, David Noel, ed., *The Anchor Bible Dictionary*, Volumes 1–6, New York: Doubleday, 1992.

Friedman, Richard Elliott, *Who Wrote the Bible?* San Francisco: HarperSanFrancisco, 1997.

Funk, Robert W., *Honest to Jesus: Jesus for a New Millennium,* San Francisco: HarperCollins, 1996.

Funk, Robert, *Language, Hermeneutic and Word of God: The Problem of Language in the New Testament and Contemporary Theology,* New York: Harper & Row, 1966.

Gadamer, Hans-Georg, *Truth and Method,* London: Sheed and Ward, 1979 (translated from *Wahrheit und Methode,* 1965, by William Glen-Doepel).

Gay, Craig M., *The Way of the (Modern) World: Or, Why It's Tempting to Live As If God Doesn't Exist,*. Grand Rapids: Eerdmans, 1998.

Gerhardsson, Birger, *The Shema' of the New Testament: Deut. 6:4–5 in Significant Passages,* Lund, Sweden: Nova Press, 1996.

Glassman, Eugene H., *The Translation Debate: What Makes a Bible Translation Good?* Downers Grove: Intervarsity Press, 1981.

Goldengay, J., "Models for Scripture," *SJT* 44 (1991): 19–37.

Goldengay, John, *Models for Interpretation of Scripture,* Grand Rapids: Eerdmans, 1995.

Goodspeed, Edgar J., *How Came the Bible?* New York: Abingdon Press, 1940.

Goppelt, Leonhard, *Typos: the Typological Interpretation of the Old Testament in the New,* trans. Donald H. Madvig, Grand Rapids: Eerdmans, 1982.

Gottwald, Norman K., *The Tribes of Yahweh : A Sociology of the Religion of Liberated Israel, 1250–1050 B.C.E.,* Maryknoll: Orbis, 1979.

Grant, Fredrick C., *Translating the Bible,* Greenwich: The Seabury Press, 1961.

Grant, Robert M., *An Historical Introduction to the New Testament,* New York: Harper & Row, 1963.

Greenlee, J. Harold, *Introduction to New Testament Textual Criticism,* Grand Rapids: Eerdmans, 1964.

Grenz, Stanley J., *A Primer on Postmodernism,* Grand Rapids: Eerdmans, 1996.

Gruenler, R. G., *Meaning and Understanding: The Philosophical Framework for Biblical Interpretation,* Grand Rapids: Zondervan, 1991.

Gudorf, Christine E., "Liberation Theology's Use of Scripture: A Response to First World Critics." *Int.* 41 (1987): 5–18.

Gunkel, Hermann, *Introduction to Psalms: The Genres of the Religious*

Lyric of Israel, Completed by Joachim Begrich, translated by James D. Nogalski, Macon: Mercer University Press, 1998.

Guroian, V., "Bible and Ethics: An Ecclesial and Liturgical Interpretation." *JRE* 18 (1990): 129–57.

Haller, Eduard, "On the Interpretive Task," trans. Ruth Grob. *Int.* 21 (1967): 158–66.

Hamilton, Kenneth, *Words and the Word,* Grand Rapids: Eerdmans, 1971.

Harris, Marvin. *Culture, People, Nature: An Introduction to General Anthropology,* New York: Thomas Y. Crowell Company, 1988.

Harrison, R. K., *Introduction to the Old Testament,* Grand Rapids: Eerdmans, 1969.

Harrisville, R. A., and Sundberg, W., *The Bible in Modern Culture. Theology and Historical Critical Method from Spinoza to Käsemann,* Grand Rapids: Eerdmans, 1995.

Hauer, Christian E. and Young, William A., *An Introduction to the Bible: A Journey into Three Worlds,* Fifth Edition. Upper Saddle River NJ: Prentice Hall, 2001.

Hauerwas, Stanley, "The Moral Authority of Scripture: The Politics and Ethics of Remembering." *Int.* 34 (1980): 356–70.

Haynes, Stephen R. and McKenzie, Steven L., eds., *To Each Its Own Meaning: An Introduction to Biblical Criticisms and Their Application,* Louisville: Westminster/John Knox Press, 1993.

Hays, Richard B., "Relations Natural and Unnatural. *JRE* 14 (1986): 184–215.

Hays, Richard B., *Echoes of Scripture in the Letters of Paul,* New Haven: Yale University Press, 1989.

Hays, Richard B., *The Moral Vision of the New Testament: A Contemporary Introduction to New Testament Ethics,* San Francisco: HarperCollins, 1996.

Hengel, Martin, *Between Jesus and Paul: Studies in the Earliest History of Christianity,* Philadelphia: Fortress Press, 1983.

Herzog, F., "Liberation Hermeneutic as Ideology Critique?" *Int.* 28 (1974): 387–403.

Herzog, William R. II, *Parables as Subversive Speech: Jesus as Pedagogue of the Oppressed,* Louisville: Westminster/John Knox Press, 1994.

Hilgard, Ernest R. and Atkinson, Richard C., *Introduction to Psychology,* Fourth Edition, New York: Harcourt, Brace and World, Inc., 1967.

Hilgard, Ernest R., Atkinson, Rita L. and Atkinson, Richard C., *Introduction to Psychology,* Seventh Edition, New York: Harcourt Brace Jovanovich, 1979.

Hinsley, F. H., ed., *The Cambridge Modern History,* Volume XI, Cambridge: University Press, 1962.

Hirsch, E. D. Jr., "The Politics of Theories of Interpretation." *Critical Inquiry* 9 (1982–83): 235–47.

Hirsch, E. D., *Validity in Interpretation,* New Haven: Yale University Press, 1967.

Horsley, Richard A., *Archaeology, History, and Society in Galilee: The Social Context of Jesus and the Rabbis,* Valley Forge: Trinity Press International, 1996.

Houlden, J. L., *The Interpretation of the Bible in the Church,* London: SCM Press, 1995.

Hunt, Allen R., *The Inspired Body: Paul, the Corinthians and the Inspiration,* Macon, GA: Mercer University Press, 1996.

Jacobus, Mary, "Is There a Woman in this Text?" *NLH* 14 (1982–83): 120–41.

Janzen, Waldemar, *Old Testament Ethics: A Paradigmatic Approach,* Louisville: Westminster/John Knox Press, 1994.

Janzen, Waldemar, *Still in the Image: Essays in Biblical Theology and Anthropology,* Winnipeg: Institute For Mennonite Studies, CMBC Publications, 1982.

Jeremias, Joachim, *New Testament Theology: Part One, The Proclamation of Jesus,* London: SCM Press, 1971.

Johnson, C. B., *The Psychology of Biblical Interpretation,* Grand Rapids: Zondervan, 1983.

Jonker, Louis C., *Exclusivity and Variety: Perspectives on Multidimentional Exegesis,* Kampen, The Netherlands: Kok Pharos, 1996.

Josephus, Flavius, *The Works of Flavius Josephus,* translated by William Whiston, Peabody: Hendrickson, 1987.

Kahle, Paul. *The Cairo Genizah,* Oxford: University Press, 1947

Kaiser, W. C. Jr. and Silva, M., *An Introduction to Biblical Hermeneutics: The Search for Meaning,* Grand Rapids: Zondervan, 1994.

Käsemann, E., "The Canon of the New Testament and the Unity of the Church," in *Essays on New Testament Themes,* London: SCM Press, 1964: 95–107.

Kee, Howard Clark, ed., *The Bible in the Twenty-first Century,* Philadelphia: Trinity Press International, 1993.

Keegan, T. J., "Biblical Criticism and the Challenge of Postmodernism," *BI* 3 (1995): 1–14.

Kenyon, Frederic G., *Handbook of the Textual Criticism of the New Testament*, Grand Rapids: Eerdmans, 1953.

Kenyon, Frederic, *The Story of the Bible*, London: John Murray, 1936.

Kenyon, Fredric G., *The Text of the Greek Bible: A Student's Handbook*, London: Gerald Duckworth & Co., 1949.

Kenyon, Fredric *Our Bible and the Ancient Manuscripts*, revised by A. W. Adams, New York: Harper & Row, 1958.

Kenyon, Kathleen M., *Archaeology in the Holy Land*, London: Ernest Benn Limited, 1970.

Kessler, M., "A Methodological Setting for Rhetorical Criticism," in Clines, D. J., Gunn, D. M., and Hauser, A., eds., *Art and Meaning: Rhetoric in Biblical Literature*, Sheffield: JSOT Press, 1982: 1–19.

Klein, Ralph W., *Textual Criticism of the Old Testament: The Septuagint After Qumran*, Philadelphia: Fortress Press, 1974.

Krentz, E., *The Historical Critical Method*, Philadelphia: Fortress Press, 1975.

Kümmel, Werner Georg, *Introduction to the New Testament*, Revised Edition trans. Howard Clark Kee, Nashville: Abingdon Press, 1975.

Ladd, George E., "The Search for Perspective," *Int.* 25 (1971): 41–62.

Lane, R. D., *Reading the Bible: Intention, Text, Interpretation*, Lanham: University Press of America, 1994.

Lawrence, Frederick, "Method and Theology as Hermeneutical", in *Creativity and Method: Essays in Honor of Bernard Lonergan, S. J.*, ed. Mathew L. Lamb, Milwaukee: Marquette University Press, 1981, pp. 79–104.

Lenski, Gerhard, *Power and Privilege: A Theory of Social Stratification*, New York: McGraw-Hill, 1966.

Lindbeck, George A., *The Nature of Doctrine: Religion and Theology in a Postliberal Age*, Philadelphia: the Westminster Press, 1984.

Lodge, John G., *Romans 9–11: A Reader Response Analyses*, International Studies in Formative Christianity and Judaism 6, Atlanta: Scholars Press, 1996.

Lonergan, Bernard J. F., *A Second Collection: Papers by Bernard J. F. Lonergan*, eds. William F. J. Ryan and Bernard J. Tyrrell, London: Darton, Longman & Todd, 1974.

Lonergan, Bernard J. F., *Method in Theology*, New York: Herder and Herder, 1972.

Lonergan, Bernard, *Collected Works of Bernard Lonergan: Understanding and Being* [The Halifax Lectures on *Insight*] eds. Elizabeth A. Morelli and Mark D. Morelli, with Frederick E. Crowe, Robert M. Doran, and Thomas V. Daly, Toronto: University Press, 1990.

Lotman, Y. M., "The Text and the Structure of its Audience," *NLH* 14 (1982)83): 81–7.

Louw, Johannes P. and Nida, Eugene A., *Greek-English Lexicon of the New Testament Based on Semantic Domains*, Second Edition, Vols. I and II, New York: United Bible Societies, 1989.

Maier, Gerhard, *Biblical Hermeneutics,* trans. Yarbrough, R. W., Wheaton: Crossway Books, 1994.

Malina, Bruce J. and Neyrey, Jerome H., *Portraits of Paul: An Archaeology of Ancient Personality*, Louisville: Westminster John Knox, 1996.

Malina, Bruce J. and Rohrbaugh, Richard L., *Social-Science Commentary on the Gospel of John*, Minneapolis: Fortress Press, 1998.

Malina, Bruce J. and Rohrbaugh, Richard L., *Social-Science Commentary on the Synoptic Gospels*, Minneapolis: Fortress Press, 1992.

Mark, J., "Relativism and Community," *Theology* 82 (1979): 161–3.

Marshall, I. Howard, ed., *New Testament Interpretation: Essays on Principles and Methods*, Grand Rapids: Eerdmans, 1977.

Marshall, I. Howard, *Luke: Historian and Theologian*, Grand Rapids: Zondervan, 1971.

Martin, Ralph P., A *Hymn to Christ: Phil. 2:5–11 in Recent Interpretation and in the Setting of Early Christian Worship*, Downers Grove: Intervarsity Press, 1997.

Mayor, Amihai, *Archaeology of the Land of the Bible: Anchor Bible Reference Library,* New York: Doubleday, 1990.

McEvenue, Seán, *Interpretation and Bible: Essays on Truth and Literature*, Collegeville: Liturgical Press, 1994.

McKim, D. K., ed., *The Authoritative Word: Essays on the Nature of Scripture*, Grand Rapids: Eerdmans, 1983.

McShane, Philip, "Features of Generalized Empirical Method and the Actual Context of Economics", in *Creativity and Method: Essays in Honor of Bernard Lonergan, S. J.,* ed. Mathew L. Lamb, Milwaukee: Marquette University Press, 1981, pp. 543–71.

Meeks, Wayne A., *The First Urban Christians: The Social World of the Apostle Paul*, New Haven: Yale University Press, 1983.

Metzger, Bruce M., "History of Editing the Greek New Testament," in *The Bible and the Church: Essays in Honour of Dr. David Ewert*, eds. A. J. Dueck, H. J. Giesbrecht and V. George Shillington, Winnipeg: Kindred Press, 1988.

Metzger, Bruce M., *The Text of the New Testament: Its Transmission, Corruption, and Restoration*, London: Oxford University Press, 1964.

Metzger, Bruce M., *A Textual Commentary on the Greek New Testament*, New York: United Bible Societies, 1975.

Metzger, Bruce M., *The Canon of the New Testament: Its Origin, Development, and Significance*, Oxford: Clarendon Press, 1987.

Metzger, Bruce M., *Reminiscences of an Octogenarian*, Hendrickson Publishers, 1997.

Meyer, Ben F., "The 'Inside' of the Jesus Event", in *Creativity and Method: Essays in Honor of Bernard Lonergan, S. J.* ed. Mathew L. Lamb, Milwaukee: Marquette University Press, 1981, pp. 197–210.

Meyer, Ben F., *Critical Realism and the New Testament*, Allison Park, PA: Pickwick Publications, 1989.

Meyer, Ben F., *Reality and Illusion in New Testament Scholarship: A Primer in Critical Realist Hermeneutics*, Collegeville: Liturgical Press, 1994.

Meyer, Ben F., *The Aims of Jesus*, London: SCM Press, 1979.

Meyer, Ben F., *The Early Christians: Their World Mission & Self-Discovery*, Wilmington: Michael Glazier Inc., 1986

Meynell, Hugo, "Lonergan, Wittgenstein, and Where Language Hooks Onto the World", in *Creativity and Method: Essays in Honor of Bernard Lonergan, S. J.* ed. Mathew L. Lamb, Milwaukee: Marquette University Press, 1981, pp. 369–81.

Millan, David L., ed., *Jung and the Interpretation of the Bible*, New York: Continuum, 1995.

Miller, Robert J., *The Complete Gospels: Annotated Scholars Version*, Sonoma CA: Polebridge Press, 1992.

Minor, Mark, *Literary Critical Approaches to the Bible: A Bibliographical Supplement*, West Cornwall: Locust Hill Press, 1996.

Montague, G. T., "Hermeneutics and the Teaching of Scripture, *CBQ* 41 (1979): 1–17.

Moore, Stephen D., *God's Gym: Divine Male Bodies of the Bible*, New York and London: Routledge, 1996.

Moore, Stephen D., *Literary Criticism and the Gospels: The Theoretical Challenge*, New Haven: Yale University Press, 1989.

Moore, Stephen D., *Post Structuralism and the New Testament: Derrida and Foucault at the Foot of the Cross*, Minneapolis: Fortress Press, 1994.

Morgan, Robert with Barton, John, *Biblical Interpretation*. Oxford: University Press, 1988.

Moulton, W. F. and Geden, A. J., *A Concordance to the Greek New Testament*, Edinburgh: T. & T. Clark, 1978.

Nestle, Eberhard, *Introduction to the Textual Criticism of the Greek New Testament*, London: Williams and Norgate, 1901.

Noll, Mark A., *Between Faith and Criticism: Evangelicals, Scholarship, and the Bible in America*, San Francisco: Harper & Row, 1986.

Olthuis, James H., *A Hermeneutics of Ultimacy: Peril or Promise?* Lanham: University Press of America, 1987.

O'Neill, J. C., *Who Did Jesus Think He Was?* Biblical Interpretation Series 11. Leiden/New York/Cologne: Brill, 1995.

Osborne, Grant, *The Hermeneutical Spiral: A Comprehensive Introduction to Biblical Interpretation*, Downers Grove: InterVarsity Press, 1991.

Patte, Daniel, *Ethics of Biblical Interpretation: A Reevaluation*, Louisville: Westminster John Knox Press, 1995.

Patzia, Arthur G., *The Making of the New Testament: Origin, Collection, Text & Canon*, Downers Grove: InterVarsity Press, 1995.

Petersen, Norman R., *Rediscovering Paul: Philemon and the Sociology of Paul's Narrative World*, Philadelphia: Fortress Press, 1985.

Petersen, Norman R., *The Gospel of John and the Sociology of Light: Language and Characterization in the Fourth Gospel*, Valley Forge: Trinity Press International, 1993.

Pfeiffer, Charles F., *Old Testament History*, Grand Rapids: Baker, 1973.

Polkinghorne, John, *Reason and Reality: The Relationship Between Science and Theology*, Valley Forge, PA: Trinity Press International, 1991.

Porter, Stanley E., "Reader Response Criticism and New Testament Study: A Response to A. C. Thiselton's *New Horizons in Hermeneutics, LT* 8 (1994): 94–102.

Porter, Stanley, "Why Hasn't Reader Response Criticism Caught on in New Testament Studies?" *LT* 43 (1990): 278–92.

Price, Ira Maurice, *The Ancestry of Our English Bible*, Third Revised

Edition by William A. Irwin and Allen P. Wikgren, New York: Harper & Brothers, 1956.

Quesnell, Quentin, "Beliefs and Authenticity", in *Creativity and Method: Essays in Honor of Bernard Lonergan, S. J.* ed. Mathew L. Lamb, Milwaukee: Marquette University Press, 1981, pp. 173–83.

Quintilian, M. F., *The Institutio Oratoria of Quiltilian. LCL*, Vol. I, translated by H. E. Butler, New York: G. P. Putnam's Son, 1920.

Rahner, Karl, *Theological Investigations II*, London: Darton, Longman and Todd, 1974.

Räisänen, Heikki, Schüssler Fiorenza, Elizabeth, Surirtharajah, R. S., Stendhal, Krister, and Barr, James, *Reading the Bible in the Global Village: Helsinki*, Atlanta: Society of Biblical Literature, 2000.

Ramm, Bernard, *Protestant Biblical Interpretation: A Textbook of Hermeneutics for Conservative Protestants*, Boston: W. A. Wilde Company, 1956.

Rang, Jack C., *How to Read the Bible Aloud: Oral Interpretation of Scripture*, New York: Paulist Press, 1994.

Reed, Walter L., "A Poetics of the Bible: Problems and Possibilities," *LT* 1 (1987): 154–166.

Reibel, David, ed., *Robert Lowth 1710–1787: The Major Works*, New York: Routledge, 1995.

Rendtorff, Rolf, *The Old Testament: An Introduction*, Philadelphia: Fortress, 1986.

Rensberger, David, *Johannine Faith and Liberating Community*, Philadelphia: The Westminster Press, 1988.

Ricoeur, Paul, "Biblical Hermeneutics: The Metaphorical Process", *Semeia* 4: 75–106.

Ricoeur, Paul, *Interpretation Theory: Discourse and the Surplus of Meaning*, Fortworth: Texas Christian University Press, 1978.

Ring, Nancy, "Alienation and Reconciliation: The Theological Methods of Paul Tillich and Bernard Lonergan", in *Creativity and Method: Essays in Honor of Bernard Lonergan, S. J.* ed. Mathew L. Lamb, Milwaukee: Marquette University Press, 1981, pp. 249–62.

Robbins, Vernon K., *Jesus the Teacher: A Socio-Rhetorical Interpretation of Mark*, Philadelphia: Fortress Press, 1984.

Robbins, Vernon K., *Exploring the Texture of Texts: A Guide to Socio-rhetorical Interpretation*, Valley Forge: Trinity Press International, 1996.

Robbins, Vernon K., *The Tapestry of Early Christian Discourse: Rhetoric, Society and Ideology*, London: Routledge, 1996.

Rogers, Jack, *Biblical Authority*, Waco: Word Books, 1977.

Rogerson, J. W., *Myth and the Old Testament*, New York: Walter de Gruyter, 1974.

Rohrbaugh, Richard L., *The Biblical Interpreter: An Agrarian Bible in an Industrial Age*, Philadelphia: Fortress Press, 1978.

Russell, Bertrand, *History of Western Philosophy and Its Connection with Political and social Circumstances from the Earliest Times to the Present Day*, London: George Allen & Unwin, 1961.

Sanders, James A., *Canon and Community: A Guide to Canonical Criticism*, Philadelphia: Fortress Press, 1984.

Sanders, James A., *Torah and Canon*, Philadelphia: Fortress Press, 1972.

Schneiders, S., "The Footwashing (John 13:1–20): An Experiment in Hermeneutics," *CBQ* 43 (1981): 76–92.

Schüssler Fiorenza, Elisabeth, *Rhetoric and Ethic: The Politics of Biblical Studies*, Minneapolis: Fortress Press, 1999.

Schüssler Fiorenza, Elizabeth, "The Ethics of Biblical Interpretation: Decentering Biblical Scholarship," *JBL* 107 (1988): 3–17.

Schüssler Fiorenza, Elizabeth, *In Memory of Her: A Feminist Theological Reconstruction of Christian Origins*, New York: Crossroad, 1983.

Seitz, C. R., *Word Without End: The Old Testament as Abiding Theological Witness*, Grand Rapids: Eerdmans, 1998.

Shillington, V. George, "Biblical Interpretation: the State of the Discipline" in *Direction* 24, 1 (1995): 3–13.

Shillington, V. George, "The Canonical Shape of 2 Corinthians" in *2 Corinthians BCBC*, Scottdale: Herald Press, 1998, 281–2.

Shillington, V. George, "Use of Scripture" in *2 Corinthians, BCBC*, Scottdale: Herald Press, 1998, 281–2.

Shillington, V. George, "Atonement Texture in 1 Corinthians 5:5" in *JSNT* 71 (1998): 29–50.

Shillington, V. George, *The Figure of Jesus in the Typological Thought of Paul*, Dissertation, Hamilton: McMaster University, 1985.

Shillington, V. George, ed., *Jesus and His Parables: Interpreting the Parables of Jesus Today*, Edinburgh: T & T Clark, 1998.

Shultz, Samuel J., *The Old Testament Speaks*, London: Harper and Row, 1960.

Sleeper, C. E., "Ethics as a Context for Biblical Interpretation," *Int.* 22 (1968): 443–60.

Spivey, R. A., "Structuralism and Biblical Studies," *Int.* 28 (1974): 133–45.

Stacey, W. D., *Groundwork of Biblical Studies*, Minneapolis: Augsburg, 1979.

Stout, J., "What is the Meaning of a Text?" *NLH* 14 (1982–83): 1–12.

Strong, James, *Strong's Exhaustive Concordance*, Nashville: Crusade Bible Publishing Inc., n.d.

Swartley, Willard M., *Slavery, Sabbath, War and Women*, Scottdale: Herald Press, 1983.

Taylor, Kenneth, *Words and the Word*, Grand Rapids: Eerdmans, 1971.

Torrance, T. F., *The Trinitarian Faith: The Evangelical Theology of the Ancient Catholic Church*, Edinburgh: T. & T. Clark, 1993.

Tracy, David, "Theologies of Praxis", in *Creativity and Method: Essays in Honor of Bernard Lonergan, S. J.*, ed. Mathew L. Lamb, Milwaukee: Marquette University Press, 1981, pp. 35–51.

Tracy, David, *The Achievement of Bernard Lonergan*, New York: Herder & Herder, 1970.

Tucker, Gene M., *Form Criticism in the Old Testament*, Philadelphia: Fortress Press, 1971.

Tyrrell, Bernard, "Passages and Conversions", in *Creativity and Method: Essays in Honor of Bernard Lonergan, S. J.* ed. Mathew L. Lamb, Milwaukee: Marquette University Press, 1981, pp. 11–33.

Vertin, Michael. "Maréchal, Lonergan, and the Phenomenology of Knowing", in *Creativity and Method: Essays in Honor of Bernard Lonergan, S. J.* ed. Mathew L. Lamb, Milwaukee: Marquette University Press, 1981, pp. 411–22.

Watson, Francis, *Text and Truth: Redefining Biblical Theology*, Grand Rapids: Eerdmans, 1997; Edinburgh: T&T Clark.

Weitzman, Steven, *Song and Story in Biblical Narrative: The History of a Literary Convention in Ancient Israel*, Bloomington: Indiana University Press, 1997.

Wellhausen, Julius, *Prolegomena to the History of Israel*, Atlanta: Scholars Press, 1994.

White, H., "Interpretation In History," *NLH* 4 (1972–73): 281–314.

White, J. B., *Taking the Bible Seriously: Honest Differences about Biblical Interpretation*, Louisville: Westminster John Knox Press, 1993.

Wilder, Amos N., *Early Christian Rhetoric: The Language of the Gospel*, London: SCM Press, 1964.

Wilder, Amos N., *Jesus' Parables and the War of Myths: Essays on Imagination in the Scripture*, Philadelphia: Fortress Press, 1982.

Wink, Water, *The Bible and Human Transformation: Toward a New Paradigm for Biblical Study*, Philadelphia: Fortress Press, 1973.

Wolff, Hans Walter, *The Old Testament: A Guide to Its Writings*, trans. Keith R. Crim, Philadelphia: Fortress Press, 1973.

Wright, G. Ernest, *Biblical Archaeology*, Philadelphia: The Westminster Press, 1962.

Wright, G. Ernest, *The Bible and the Ancient Near East: Essays in Honor of William Foxwell Albright*, Garden City NY: Doubleday & Co., 1961.

Würthwein, Ernst, *The Text of the Old Testament*, Translated by Erroll F. Rhodes. Grand Rapids: Eerdmans, 1979.

Young, E. J., *An Introduction to the Old Testament*, Grand Rapids: Eerdmans, 1964.

Young, Francis M., *Virtuoso Theology: The Bible and Interpretation*, Cleaveland: Pilgrim Press, 1993.

Scripture References

Author Indexes

In Discussion

Subject Index